A Dark California

A Dark California

*Essays on Dystopian
Depictions in Popular Culture*

Edited by Katarzyna Nowak-McNeice
and Agata Zarzycka

McFarland & Company, Inc., Publishers
Jefferson, North Carolina

"Freak," "Honeymoon," "God Knows I Tried" and "Swan Song": All songs: words and music by Elizabeth Grant and Rick Nowels; copyright © 2015 EMI Music Publishing Germany GMBH and R-Rated Music; All rights administered by Sony/ATV Music Publishing, LLC, 424 Church Street, Suite 1200, Nashville, TN 37219; International copyright secured, all rights reserved; *Reprinted by permission of Hal Leonard, LLC.*

LIBRARY OF CONGRESS CATALOGUING-IN-PUBLICATION DATA

Names: Nowak-McNeice, Katarzyna, 1977– editor. | Zarzycka, Agata, editor.
Title: A dark California : essays on dystopian depictions in popular culture / edited by Katarzyna Nowak-McNeice and Agata Zarzycka.
Description: Jefferson, North Carolina : McFarland & Company, Inc., Publishers, 2017. | Includes bibliographical references and index.
Identifiers: LCCN 2017036633 | ISBN 9781476667836 (softcover : acid free paper) ∞
Subjects: LCSH: California—In literature. | Dystopias in literature. | Popular culture—California. | Place (Philosophy) in literature. | Literature and society—California. | Mass media—California—Psychological aspects.
Classification: LCC PS283.C2 D37 2017 | DDC 810.9/9794—dc23
LC record available at https://lccn.loc.gov/2017036633

BRITISH LIBRARY CATALOGUING DATA ARE AVAILABLE

ISBN (print) 978-1-4766-6783-6
ISBN (ebook) 978-1-4766-2959-9

© 2017 Katarzyna Nowak-McNeice and Agata Zarzycka. All rights reserved

No part of this book may be reproduced or transmitted in any form or by any means, electronic or mechanical, including photocopying or recording, or by any information storage and retrieval system, without permission in writing from the publisher.

Front cover image © 2017 HeldaB/iStock

Printed in the United States of America

McFarland & Company, Inc., Publishers
  Box 611, Jefferson, North Carolina 28640
    www.mcfarlandpub.com

Table of Contents

Acknowledgments   vii

Introduction
    KATARZYNA NOWAK-MCNEICE *and* AGATA ZARZYCKA   1

Part I: California Under Construction

The Center Is Not Holding: Joan Didion and the California Dreamer   15
    KATHLEEN M. VANDENBERG *and* CHRISTOPHER K. COFFMAN

Desert Women: Constructions of Female Identity and Motherhood in Angela Carter and Claire Vaye Watkins's Feminist Dystopias   25
    DONNA MITCHELL

Playing Good Cop ... or Bad Cop? Exploring Hyperreal Urban Spaces in *L.A. Noire*   37
    MICHAEL FUCHS

"Feed the hole": Alienation, Neo-Marxism and the Real in Richard Kelly's *Southland Tales*   50
    ELIZABETH LOWRY

Tension of Exclusion: On Death Grips and the Californian Ideology   62
    BENJAMIN HALLIGAN

Part II: Californian Monsters

"Wolf howls and the roar of police sirens": Fractured Identities, Lycanthropy and the Streets of Los Angeles in Toby Barlow's *Sharp Teeth*   75
    CARYS CROSSEN

Stuck Here Forever: Los Angeles as Purgatory   88
in *American Horror Story*
ROSE BUTLER

Dreams Require Sacrifice: Fame, Fortune and Body-Horror   101
in *Starry Eyes*
CRAIG IAN MANN *and* LIAM HATHAWAY

Anywhere-Nowhere, California: The Real, the Imaginary   115
and the Lonely Vampire in the Golden State
SIMON BACON

True California: Vinci as Landscape of Terror   127
MARCIN CICHOCKI

Part III: Welcome to Dystopia

Thomas Pynchon's Hybrid California(s): In Search   139
of Spatial/Social Justice in *Inherent Vice*
DIANA BENEA

"Come to California": The Star as a Tragic Figure of American   153
Apocalypse in Lana Del Rey's *Honeymoon* (2015)
STEVE DRUM

Cop Shows, Sitcoms and Oral Histories in Thomas Pynchon's   162
Vineland
TOMAS POLLARD

These Kind of Dreams: Dystopian Depictions of California   174
in the Music Video "Californication"
DANIEL KLUG

Conclusion: Californias Everywhere   184
KATARZYNA NOWAK-MCNEICE *and* AGATA ZARZYCKA

About the Contributors   193

Index   195

Acknowledgments

Without assistance from individuals and institutions a long-term endeavor such as a book project would never come to fruition. At the end of this process, it is our pleasure to thank those who supported us throughout.

Katarzyna thanks the Universidad Carlos III de Madrid, Spain, and the Conex–Marie Curie Fellowship, which afforded her the necessary time and a creative environment to develop ideas that found a home in this collection. She especially thanks Prof. Julio Checa, who welcomed her in the Department of the Humanities, and the Conex team. Her alma mater, the University of Wrocław, Poland, graciously granted her a sabbatical which made work on the present volume possible. It also provided her with an inspiring scholarly community: special thanks to Prof. Dominika Ferens who has, throughout the years, acted as her kind and wise mentor and friend. In California, Prof. Mike C. Steiner offered immense intellectual generosity and encouragement that only confirms her intuition that whatever darkness might be found in California, it is dispelled by its people. Her husband, William McNeice, has been most supportive in every way, for which she is grateful. Without the enthusiasm, talent and intellectual rigor of her coeditor, Agata Zarzycka, this project would never have become more than a mere ghost of an idea.

Agata would like to thank the Institute of English Studies, University of Wrocław, Poland, for the years of academic guidance and for the sabbatical; her unimaginably patient and supportive family—especially Michał, Wojtek, and Saturnina; the infallible language expert William McNeice; and Katarzyna Nowak-McNeice—the super-resourceful coeditor, tireless collaborator, and awesome colleague.

We would like to thank our two anonymous readers for their

feedback and suggestions. We also wish to thank all of our contributors, whose creative powers, commitment and openness of mind have made this book possible.

Katarzyna Nowak-McNeice has received funding from the Universidad Carlos III de Madrid, the European Union's Seventh Framework Programme for research, technological development and demonstration under grant agreement nº 600371, el Ministerio de Economía y Competitividad (COFUND2013-40258), el Ministerio de Educación, Cultura y Deporte (CEI-15-17) and Banco Santander.

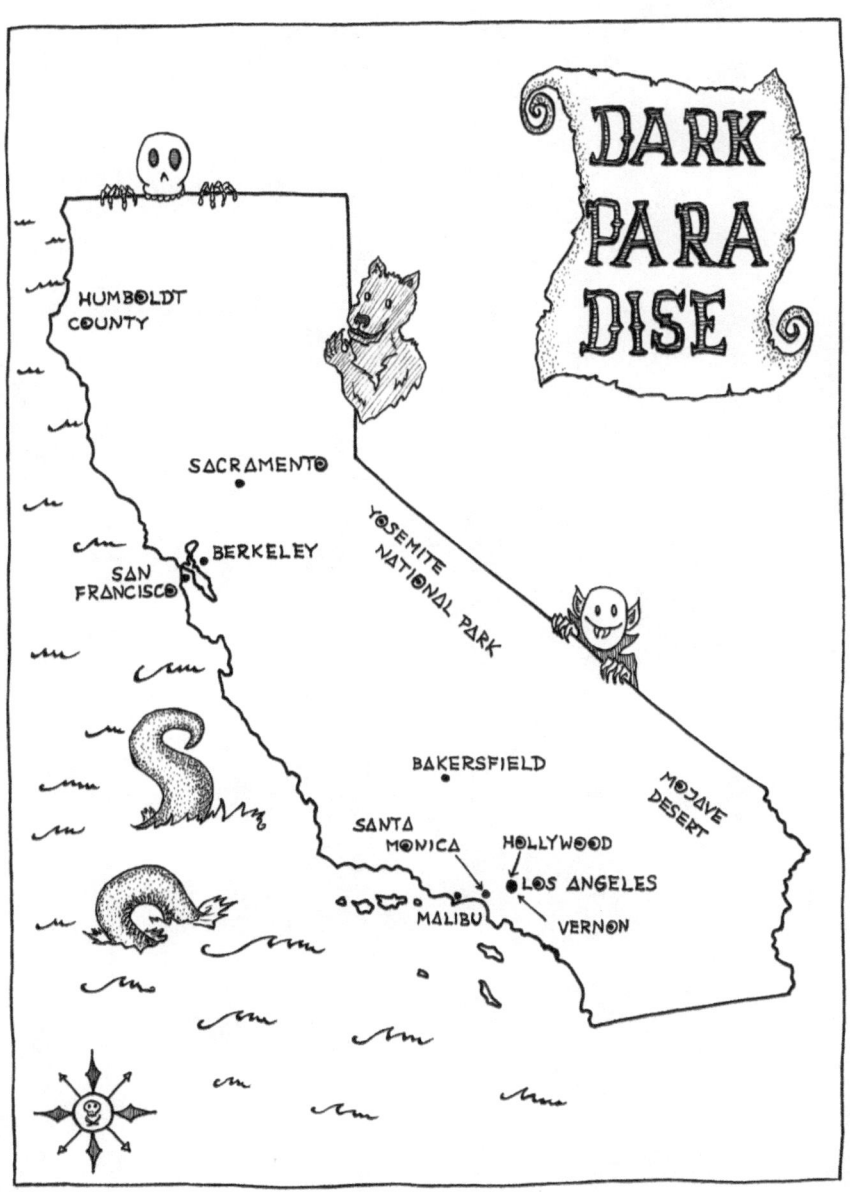

Drawing of the state of California by Agata Zarzycka.

Introduction

Katarzyna Nowak-McNeice
and Agata Zarzycka

> Nomadism, therefore, is not fluidity without borders but rather an acute awareness of the nonfixity of boundaries. It is the intense desire to go on trespassing, transgressing. As a figuration of contemporary subjectivity, therefore, the nomad is a postmetaphysical, intensive, multiple entity, functioning in a net of interconnections. S/he cannot be reduced to a linear, teleological form of subjectivity but is rather the site of multiple connections. S/he is embodied, and therefore cultural; as an artifact, s/he is a technological compound of human and post-human; s/he is complex, endowed with multiple capacities for interconnectedness in the impersonal mode. S/he is a cyborg, but equipped also with an unconscious.
> —Braidotti 36

Themes and Goals

Though officially named the Golden State, and less officially called the Land of Milk and Honey or El Dorado, California has a darker side to it, too. This collection results from our attempt to conceptualize the cultural significance of California as a nomadic phenomenon by scrutinizing its tendency to engage the dialectics of light and darkness, utopia and dystopia, happiness and tragedy, pleasure and fear in ways that destabilize their oppositional symmetries and transform them into a networked patchwork.

Whether it is about exploring the emergent, dark dimensions of the actual region's cultural identity, or reconsidering particular motifs in their implicit Californian context, the survey of cultural explorations offered by the authors contributing to this volume depicts Californian dystopia as the growingly influential part of its cultural representation, resonating with more general conventions of aesthetized darkness. Moreover, it urges a reflection upon relationships between the natural, historical, political, social and cultural multifacetedness of the Golden State, and the rhizomatic mode of absorbing the apparent binary oppositions, which often underpins the aesthetics of Californian themes; as Deleuze and Guattari assert, "the rhizome itself assumes very diverse forms.... The rhizome includes the best and the worst" (7).

Californian diversity has become a generator of icons and tropes that sometimes ascribe the Golden State with new symbolic, cultural, and discursive functions, and sometimes live their own semiotic lives in the global repository of cultural signs. As demonstrated by the scope of contributions to this book, the ways in which bits and pieces of California live on to transform culture and matter in it include inspirations for futuristic urban visions, settings reflecting post-apocalyptic wilderness, consumerist dystopias, transitory spaces between realities and supernatural dimensions, haunting residual presences, and many other manifestations of the modes of meaning.

Such multiplicity of aesthetic interpretations and their gravitation toward dark and disturbing themes can easily be traced back to California's conceptualization in the polyphony of America's self-narratives. When discussing the dichotomous scenarios played out in California and in the West, Michael C. Steiner describes the setting as "a land of last chances where the stakes are high because there's nowhere left to go, and a bi-polar dialectic of utopian dreams breeding dystopian despair runs rampant across the deserts, basins, mountains, and crowded coastlines" (184). Similarly, in *City of Quartz*, the classic study of Los Angeles, Mike Davis claims that "the ultimate world-historical significance—and oddity—of Los Angeles is that it has come to play the double role of utopia and dystopia for advanced capitalism" (18). Taking into consideration the whole spectrum of darkness presented by the texts of culture that particular authors have brought into this collection, one is tempted to stretch Davis's statement to include not only the City of Angels, but the whole of California. Therefore, in our volume we want to bring to light the tension between the two opposing meanings attributable to California that Steiner, Davis and other critics allude to: it is the dynamic interplay of oppositions that proves provocative and inspiring to many authors and provides a fertile ground for interpretation, signaling the necessity for the categories of otherness and alienation, which opens up many critical avenues to pursue in an effort to understand California. Jean Baudrillard hints at this possibility when he states, "The mythical power of California consists in this mixture of extreme disconnection and vertiginous mobility captured in the setting, the hyperreal scenario of deserts, freeways, ocean, and sun" (125–26). Such force that California possesses draws us to an attempt to resolve the state's perennial paradox, even as we remain aware of the impossibility of the endeavor.

Our collection, just like any project devoted to disentangling the many meanings of California and the discourses used to examine them, must come to terms with the fact that California studies are far from being a unified field. In popular parlance, it amounts to this: California does not make sense. It is the place of fads, diets, lifestyles, architecture, landscape, fashion, prosperity, and natural disasters that elsewhere would be deemed illogical, impossible, or simply crazy, but in California there is space for mutually exclusive ideas—Walt Whitman seems to prefigure California when he lets his lyrical I say, "Do I contradict myself? Very well then, I contradict myself, I am great, I contain multitudes" (977). Joan Didion recounts an anecdote in which this inapplicability of common sense becomes clear: she notes that after investing years into writing about California she realized that California history and its cultural memory often do not provide logical explanations of what the region is. She mentions "trying to find the 'point' of California, to locate some message in its history," but this project quickly exhausts itself as she comes to a dead point in her research: "I picked up a book of revisionist studies on the subject, but abandoned it on discovering that I was myself quoted, twice" (*Where I Was From* 17). An attempt to make sense of what California is becomes futile: it only points to itself. Didion's story also brings out a certain circularity that is the defining feature of California, and, by extension, California studies. California is its only valid point of reference, and while such a brand of exceptionalism might be wrong (if not dangerous) in other contexts, it should not be dismissed here, as it helps us understand that the state's uniqueness is suggested in and through its geological, geographical and environmental features. Carey McWilliams famously describes Southern California as "the island on the land"—a self-contained, self-referential entity, and there is much truth in that; McWilliams's formulation also employs a paradox, an apt figure of speech for describing California. The landscape diversity, the mind-boggling differences between cities and neighborhoods within them, the divisions between subregions in the region: all of these amount to an astounding variety which led Wallace Stegner to state famously that California is "just like the rest of the United States, only more so" (qtd. in Eymann and Wollenberg 13). This suggests a hyperbolic quality characteristic of California which means that one can only talk about California on California's terms.

The anecdote above also suggests that it is impossible to write about California's history and identity without referencing Joan Didion, just as it seems unlikely that any discussion of Los Angeles can be conducted without mentioning Edward Soja, about the desert without alluding to Mary Austin, or about California's forests without referring to Gary Snyder and John Muir.

Similarly, it is nearly impossible to find a study of California that does not delve into an examination of California's schizophrenic water politics (cf. Donald Worster); its self-indulgent and ultimately self-destructive car culture (cf. Reyner Banham); its extremely rich and at times explosive mix of ethnic groups—Chicano/a, Korean, Black, Chinese, Philipino/a—the list is far from exhaustive (cf. Mike Davis).... Without dismissing these issues, our aim is to go beyond the usual repertory of topics and preoccupations while discussing California and its place in popular imagination.

Nearly all these classics—including Stegner and McWilliams—talk about California without confidence, but rather from the point of view of a constant skeptic. Such skepticism derives from the impossibility to hold on to a single idea of California; as David Wyatt claims, "California has always been a place no sooner had than lost," and it is this persistent sense of a loss that pervades any theorizing about California (15).

All of the critics mentioned point in various ways to the ambiguity underlying any estimation of what California has been and may be in the future; in other words, they all suggest a certain dark lining to the golden cloud of California. Why, then, would we risk compiling a volume in which this darkness is taken to the foreground? Is it just another self-referencing, circular gesture? In our estimation, California's darkness has been variously suggested, yet what is needed is owning it, and through such admittance of the darkness as a constitutive element of California as a semiotic concept, and of California studies as a discipline, we would like to break the circle of repetitiveness and suggest another understanding: rhizomatic rather than linear or circular.

That California (not just SoCal, but the whole of it) prefers to see itself as an island rather than a part of a bigger entity is evidenced by its separationist tendencies: the idea of California separating from the United States returns with regularity (especially when the results of presidential elections in the state do not correspond to those of the nation). It is, after all, the sixth largest economy in the world. It is its own island, reference point—a construction, a hologram, a simulacrum.

Scope

As underlined by Zygmunt Bauman's concept of fluid modernity, eclecticism lies at the heart of contemporary postmodern cultural experience, and California, with its diversity of both landscape and cultures, changing political status, multilayered metaphorizations and Hollywood, is definitely high on the list of symbolic spaces responding to that phenomenon. Setting clear genre- or medium-based limits to the kinds of cultural practice adequate for a survey of Californian appearances in culture might, therefore, induce a risk of missing relevant case studies or, worse still, not giving a chance for a manifestation of such meanders of California's cultural identity that become visible only on the conceptual crossing points generated by resonance from the eclectic background.

Therefore, it seems more productive to approach the focal point of this book—namely, a dystopian, Gothicized or otherwise uncanny California as a point of reference in popular culture—in terms of its inclusiveness rather than exclusiveness. As already mentioned, the "darkness" signaled in the title is constituted by the interaction of various dystopian facets of California with aesthetic and narrative conventions specialized in addressing cultural anxieties. The scope of functions that conceptualizations of California may perform in such contexts is what hopefully emerges as a result of the glimpse into the rhizomatic spread that this collection offers. The term "popular culture," aimed to signal our predominant interest in the ways California interacts with aesthetic tropes and narrative formulas, tends to signify a prescriptive view on the discussed source texts. As argued by John Storey, "the idea of popular culture is always entangled with questions of social power" (xii), while Bauman, in his discussion of cultural eclecticism, does not so much erase the "high"–"low" polarity as rather sustain it, in order to illustrate the contrasts which such eclecticism reconciles (17–18).

Nevertheless, an aspect of popular culture that seems most useful for the sake of this project, and that perhaps justifies our employment of the discussed category in the first place, is not its capability of regulating the selection of primary sources or methodologies in the presented discussions, but its connection with conventions, genres and formulas, emphasized, among others, by John Cawelti in his seminal *Adventure, Mystery, and Romance: Formula Stories as Art and Popular Culture*. The sources of aesthetics especially visible in the corpus analyzed in this collection—horror, Gothic, disaster sci-fi, noir—are rich in dichotomies against which the rhizomatic spread of the Californian subject becomes all the more visible.

Still, embracing a formula-based approach to culture too tightly would bear the threat of reductionism or excessive universalization that might petrify the inherently dynamic character of our overall nomadic premise. In order to avoid that, we propose to combine Cawelti's perspective with the understanding of pop cultural conventions as "fuzzy sets"—an endeavor in which we follow in the steps of Brian Attebery, who applies the term in his theorization of fantasy literature. Leaning slightly on George Lakoff and Mark Johnson's employment of fuzziness (Lakoff and Johnson ix), Attebery reaches for that concept to deal with the problem of defining the fantasy genre, stuck between formulaic repetitiveness and "the potential anarchy of the fantastic" (9). His use of the "fuzzy set" implies a focus on the core of the explored convention, in which its characteristic features are most densely represented, and tracking down the process of their thinning or blurring that helps locate the viable reach of the core's impact (12–14). It is with a similar kind of logic that we approach the cultural impact of California in the hopes of capturing its many layers. The texts of culture explored in this collection share an overall investment in popular culture, whether it takes the shape of a single genre/formula that they embrace, an intertextual play with a number of such conventions, or more generalized reflections on mass media entertainment. Examples of such practices can be found in the TV shows *American Horror Story* by Ryan Murphy and Brad Falchuk and *True Detective* by Cary Futanaga and Justin Lin and in the *L.A. Noire* video game by Naresh Hirani and Josh Needleman. The verges of the pop cultural scope are, in turn, signaled, among others, by the deeply inquisitive confrontations of Joan Didion and William T. Vollman with nuances of California's historical and socio-cultural identity that give ground for further iconization of the place in more explicit pop cultural contexts or Thomas Pynchon's postmodern play with tropes and icons. The network of conventions, styles, aesthetics, narratives and intellectual solutions that emerges from the varying involvements of the source materials analyzed in this volume with popular culture constitutes a rich and flexible background against which California's cultural nomadism can be mapped.

Critical Context

Arguably, California has always existed in popular fiction—its name is first mentioned in the sixteenth century in *The Deeds of Esplandian*, a Spanish heroic romance that describes the land as situated in close proximity to paradise and inhabited by valiant and beautiful women warriors. Equally arguably, it has always produced popular fiction; the testimony is provided by romances such as Helen Hunt Jackson's *Ramona* (1884), or the numerous migrant letters and diaries written on the trail to California and there by the lucky ones who managed to survive the hardships of the journey. From the earliest representations of the land that was to become California, it provoked strong and contradictory responses from the narrators: it was portrayed as empty, yet with dangerous inhabitants lurking in the dark; a land of prosperity, yet also a land that guards its secrets, such as gold, and punishes those who are after them. As Stephen Fender notes in his study *Plotting the Golden West: American Literature and the Rhetoric of the California Trail*, the literary representations of the far frontier of the American West are ridden with paradoxes, often occupying a single text, and the perception of the seeming emptiness of the landscape combines with "obsessive overplotting" (2).

Such anxious responses to the land are not an exception even today, and they are a testament to the mythical grasp that California (and the West) has on artists and viewers, readers, and listeners alike. Joan Didion, for instance, one of the greatest "mythographers" of the state, reflects on the changes of the landscape in the span of several decades, and she comes to call it "a hologram that dematerializes as I drive through it" (*Where I Was From* 175). Didion documents the tendency of California (intimated by numerous other writers) to disappear like a mirage whenever a writer tries to grasp its essence; what we postulate in the present volume is that the very idea of essential character of California must be let go of.

Many writers have already commented on the impossibility of imagining California in terms other than hybrid; Richard Rodriguez, for instance, chooses the color brown to stand for the mixture of races, ethnicities, and other ways of identifications that California offers, and he equates brown with "impurity" to claim, "Brown confuses. Brown forms at the border of contradiction" (xi), qualifying it, to be sure, as positive. "I think brown marks a reunion of peoples, an end to ancient wanderings" (xiii), he states in a celebratory mode.

The multiethnic setup of California is in no way a new phenomenon, as even the plaques in El Pueblo de Los Angeles indicate when listing the names of the first inhabitants. Analyzing proliferation of the ideas about the American frontier in Europe, Ray Allen Billington concludes by saying that the contemporary vision of America that dominates in many parts of the world as a merciless exterminator of the native way of living, adverse to heterogeneousness and diversity, may be an heir to the similarly distorted vision of the western frontier in the nineteenth century as a lawless territory where only white, predatory brutes thrived, warning that if this is the case, then "the image-makers played a larger role in history than they anticipated, and must be recognized if we are to understand the world we live in" (*Land of Savagery, Land of Promise* 332). We propose that similar careful attention must be paid to the products of popular culture today, because they are the intimations as to what the future holds for us all. California has long been the place to look for signs of future developments in the arts and society alike.

William Everson's *Archetype West* is perhaps the first attempt to define the literary character of the Pacific West in terms of transmediality; writing in the 1970s, Everson muses upon the emergence of rock music to state that "the same eruption of dynamic creativity and spontaneous discovery" as the one he analyzed in literature "find[s] its inception in a new medium" (149); the necessity to find new modes of expression has haunted Californian authors for centuries now, and in the new millennium it includes many more artistic media than ever before. The new, convergent, intermedial modalities correspond to and grow out of the new modes of consciousness, yet they must necessarily work through the past—which produces the haunting quality characteristic of Californian modes of cultural production that we analyze in the present volume. Grounding her work in sociology, Avery F. Gordon claims forcibly that haunting is "a constituent feature of contemporary modern life" and stresses that recognizing the ghostly is imperative in our understanding of "the something more" (206); it is precisely this excess that manifests itself in a rhizomatic, unsystematized fashion.

The specters of California are many: as *A People's Guide to Los Angeles* declares: "Los Angeles is filled with ghosts—not only of people, but also of places and buildings and the ordinary and extraordinary moments and events that once filled them. There are many such places throughout the region; still others are being created while you read this" (4). The book, despite its title, is not simply a guidebook but rather, in the authors' clearly stated intentions, a "political intervention" (4), provocatively presenting the city as an outcome of creative energies of people of all races, classes and genders, and for that it provides an insight into what Los Angeles is but also what it might have been. This speculative element must be perceived as a characteristic feature of Californian culture, and it emerges as constitutive of the various narratives that make up the multifaceted, dynamic exchange that is constantly becoming California.

To understand California's culture and its tendency to evolve in rhizomatic, chaotic, unexpected ways, one may look at the society that sustains it. Commenting on the 2000 census which reveals California's multiethnic setup, Kevin Starr ascertains that "California has become a society in which minorities constitute the majority" which provokes him to ask, "Could not the Millennial Generation sustain its multiple identities within a context of interchange and common ground?" (319). For Starr, in the affirmative answer to the question lies the hope, the hope, we might add, whose meaning pivots on what is the core of American culture: renewability, sustainability, and reinvention which allow it to flourish rhizomatically, and in unexpected places.

Thus what we hope to portray in our collection is the brown, haunted, rhizomatic California, whose character is impossible to pin down or define with the use of rigid, linear, binary categories. Even though we stress darkness as one of the constitutive terms for our understanding of Californian cultural production, darkness is by no means devoid of hope; rather, it signals our attention to the complexity of California's popular culture that thrives against all odds and in the darkest places of the sunny Golden State.

All the diversified forms of interaction between culture and place are not without influence on the mutual positions of its human subject and the spatial tropes. In a rhizomatic network of cultural meanings the conventional position of the human agent exploring, taming, inhabiting, interacting with, reshaping, personalizing, objectifying or subjectifying, virtualizing and finally theorizing places stuck in passivity-laced narrative functions of settings, sceneries, backgrounds, contexts or local colors becomes susceptible to destabilization. The reversed influence of places upon the agent's identity, to some extent acknowledged already in the relationships listed above, may give a start to more complicated relations in which the cultural significance of the given locale becomes an end rather than a means in the process of its rhizomatic fusions with various fragmentary discourses that turn to it as a part of their own narratives. The Deleuzian nomadic subject—anchored more in geographic, linguistic and territorial terms by Rosi Braidotti—appears, therefore, to be constructed precisely around the affirmation of the relation of mutual exchange between an individual identity and the many metaphoric as well as literal places it comes in touch with. Its resultant deterritorialization—most frequently brought up in the context of political subversion—is also a discursive operation helpful in empowering the cultural identities of the territories it refuses to incorporate or hierarchize as fixed components. It is precisely such unpredictable dynamics that grant the trope of California an aura of rebelliousness interacting with the environment of popular culture, in which identities are perpetually negotiated between dominant narratives and hybrid, ephemeral fusions. Drawing comparisons between the nomad and Donna Haraway's "cyborg," and pointing to the nomadic consciousness's similarity to Foucault's "countermemory," Braidotti stresses: "Nomadic consciousness is a form of political resistance to hegemonic and exclusionary views of subjectivity" (23). She adds, "it is a form of resisting assimilation or homologation into dominant ways of representing the self" (23).

Thus, our project is motivated, among others, by an intention to see how far such an emancipation of a place in the polyphony of cultural negotiations can or should reasonably be taken. Does California—seen in a variety of theoretical, discursive, semiological and conceptual contexts—emerge from this book as a Deleuzian node? Or does it perhaps emerge as a posthuman nomadic subject in becoming, which communicates with its dialogical partners—texts of both practice and theory of culture which incorporate it, but by doing so, also invite it to trespass their own apparent territories and undermine their borders with its deterritorialized as well as deterritorializing specificity?

Organization

In a project dedicated to a place—even one loosely defined through nomadism—it would be difficult, and perhaps simply unwise, to avoid some kind of spatial navigation. However, in an attempt to mitigate the linearity and, therefore, progress-induced hierarchy that tends to accompany navigated movement, especially in the context of scholarly exploration, the scope of this collection has been structured around three axes. The shared undertaking of all texts they position within the network of Californian themes is the examination of darkness undercutting the California dream and its representations: darkness understood as a literary theme, a semantic trope, and a critical tool to understand California's complexities.

The development of the critical explorations in the present collection is by no means linear nor is it supposed to suggest a closed, definitive structure. Rather, it proposes a set of pillars that support the structure of the arguments, not unlike architectural poles supporting a nomad's temporary abode. With the move to the next location, the nomad takes the materials, but reproduces the structure in a slightly different way; our collection, too, could be organized around different axes. Each of these organizational principles is equally valid; they respond to differing needs of our projected nomadic reader.

In many senses of the word, California is itself a liminal phenomenon: after all, in Wallace Stegner's phrase, "the history of California is American history *in extremis*" (*Saturday Review* 1967). It comes as no surprise, then, that the cultural artifacts it produces are an expression of the liminal condition. That is why the first signpost for this collection is provided by the notion of liminality; the essays gathered in the opening part of our collection analyze various cultural formations and products that can be arranged along this axis. The notion of margin is defined in a nomadic fashion and suggests a dispersion of the clear-cut opposition between the center (metropolis, the city, high culture) and the periphery (empire, the suburbs, popular entertainment), a dispersion, we may add, animating the spirit of the whole collection.

The first part provides analyses of the arch stretching between Californian places which represent an escapist ideal of going against the establishment, through the dystopian Californian deserts where radical sociopolitical experiments are played out, leading us to experience the epicenter of hyperreality in Los Angeles, and then to see the city as the playground of apocalyptic forces, to finish at a California as a site of countercultural self-abnegation and demise. In "The Center Is Not Holding: Joan Didion and the California Dreamer," Kathleen M. Vandenberg and Christopher K. Coffman explore the palimpsestic nature of California, placing emphasis on the rhetoric in which California is textually constructed as the place where we are supposed to be able to go off the grid.

The second essay, while continuing the discussion on spatial metaphors, provides a counterpoint to Didion and Vollmann's visions of California in its being a darker, dystopian version of the land's portrayal: in "Desert Women: Constructions of Female Identity and Motherhood in Angela Carter and Claire Vaye Watkins's Feminist Dystopias," Donna Mitchell focuses on the

Californian desert as an arena for the interplay of gender subversion and illustrates the issue comparing two texts, Angela Carter's *The Passion of New Eve* and Claire Vaye Watkins's *Gold Fame Citrus*.

Michael Fuchs, in "Playing Good Cop … or Bad Cop? Exploring Hyperreal Urban Spaces in *L.A. Noire*," undertakes the task of analyzing the genre of video games, stressing the constructedness of the experience of Los Angeles's hyperreal spaces: Fuchs thus proposes to analyze the question of "authenticity" and the city's virtualization.

Drawing on Lacanian psychoanalysis, in "'Feed the hole': Alienation, Neo-Marxism and the Real in Richard Kelly's *Southland Tales*," Elizabeth Lowry examines the rhetoric of the "hole" in Neo-Marxist discourses. Just as the eponymous void repels and attracts in an ambiguous double play, this essay presents a similarly equivocal portrayal of California, suggesting a diagnosis of the neoliberal/consumerist culture whose symptom is the lack.

Continuing with a critique of neoliberal misuse of counterculture, Benjamin Halligan's "Tension of Exclusion: On Death Grips and the Californian Ideology" explores the liminal spaces in music, considering the intersections between bodily manifestations of angst and metaconscious expressions of powerlessness of various modes of cultural appropriation.

The liminality of the tropes represented in this part accounts for the in-depth examination of the social aspect of Californian life exposed in the products of culture discussed, while also allowing us to keep in mind their nomadic character, as it exposes the paradox of "movement toward" as being always already "movement back" inherent in the very concept of the limit. As much as the first part is an exposition of the radical angst permeating and undercutting cultural products and the circumstances of their production, the second part suggests that there might be a way out, even if, in a Gothic fashion, it entails death and demise.

Thus the second part focuses on Gothic tropes in the Californian contexts, considering the peculiar paradoxical nature of the Californian gothic. It starts with Carys Crossen's "'Wolf howls and the roar of police sirens': Fractured Identities, Lycanthropy and the Streets of Los Angeles in Toby Barlow's *Sharp Teeth*." In this analysis, the werewolf is the liminal, Gothic figure, exposing the conflicting natures of California, while at the same time suggesting, contrary to the apathy examined in the previous section, the transformative power of the embodied revolt against the grid.

The preoccupation with the Gothic, focusing on the undead, is continued in in Rose Butler's "Stuck Here Forever: Los Angeles as Purgatory in *American Horror Story*." California is a space of cruel, horrifying entrapments and illusions: a truly Gothic landscape. Butler's essay focuses on Los Angeles as a warped and hopeless purgatory-like place of suspension, denying gratification or a possibility of exit to those who go there.

In "Dreams Require Sacrifice: Fame, Fortune and Body-Horror in *Starry Eyes*," Craig Ian Mann and Liam Hathaway turn their attention to Los Angeles's celebrity culture and undertake the discussion of the politics of gender in an analysis of body-horror films which focus on Hollywood as a space of deadly alienation and self-destruction.

California is presented as a similarly unreal space in Simon Bacon's essay "Anywhere-Nowhere, California: The Real, the Imaginary and the Lonely Vampire in the Golden State." California is the filming location, but it also becomes a point of reference without anchoring in any external reality; thus the essay situates California within the realm of Baudrillard's hyperreality.

Marcin Cichocki's "True California: Vinci as Landscape of Terror," which closes the second part of the collection, combines the excessive aesthetics of the Gothic and neo-noir to depict the Californian setting as claustrophobic and dominant over human subjects. The Gothic pole supporting the discussion in this part serves to illustrate the nomadic impossibility—and distrust—of any clear-cut distinctions and definite delineations, simultaneously suggesting optimism inherent in the reading of Californian landscape as (post–)Gothic which can be located in its providing a response to the inescapability of countercultural recycling and appropriation.

However feeble such hope might be, the narratives displaying it always return to the point of departure: utopian dreams in which California plays the role of the ultimate space of fulfillment of countercultural scenarios. Thus, the pillar of the third part of the book is a dystopian one, with the essays focusing on the facets of spatial organization reflecting the utopian ideals, discussing the dystopian angle of celebrity culture and its propensity of recycling. While they suggest some hope in either oral history in contrast to medialized hyperreality of capitalist indoctrination or in particular exemplification of counterpoint to the Californian myth, they do so only to withdraw the cautious optimism and show how neoliberal myths are perpetuated in the hyperreal bubble. Starting with the very first textual references to California, till those operating today, the trend to situate the place in the fictional territory that either answers to or corrupts one's dreams of perfect existence has deemed it a utopia (a good place, but also ou-topia, no place), quickly degenerating to dystopia, not-a-good-place.

Drawing on Edward Soja's concept of spatial justice, Diana Benea in "Thomas Pynchon's Hybrid California(s): In Search of Spatial/Social Justice in *Inherent Vice*" analyzes Pynchon's novel, which allows her to muse upon the societal and environmental consequences of urban organization.

Steve Drum, in "'Come to California': The Star as a Tragic Figure of American Apocalypse in Lana Del Rey's *Honeymoon* (2015)," analyzes a music album which exemplifies the complex myth of American individualism in the celebrity culture of Hollywood and yet again testifies to the destructive side of the mythical Californian place.

Tomas Pollard continues with the issues of political struggle against media-controlled paradigms of identity: in "Cop Shows, Sitcoms and Oral Histories in Thomas Pynchon's *Vineland*," Pollard investigates the interplay between popular culture and state politics as represented in Pynchon's novel.

Similarly attuned to the paradoxical nature of California's attraction, Daniel Klug in "These Kind of Dreams: Dystopian Depictions of California in the Music Video 'Californication'" focuses on the textual, verbal and visual aspects of one particular example of a dystopian vision set in California in order to provide a critical presentation of California's social and cultural crises.

Thus the whole part presents an axis of dystopian explorations of space, with its implications for gender and class politics, providing analyses of various media, with the classical rendition of California as a good or no place: the ideas explored in the essays are nomadic ideas, unsettling and disrupting any attempt at pinning down the intrinsic nature of Californian culture, or, for that matter, undermining the very idea that such a unified entity exists.

As emphasized at the beginning, the tripartite arrangement of the essays included in this book is meant as our response to the rhizomatic diversity of the Californian subject rather than an attempt at taming it—and its individual explorations—in a fixed analytical structure. The proposed conceptual categories: Gothic aesthetics, dystopian discourses, marginality and liminality are by no means mutually exclusive and frequently collaborate with one another in the source materials as well as analytical undertakings collected in this volume.

In the spirit of nomadism, the conclusion is prompted by the question of Golden State's globalized visibility as a cultural subject. Moving from a consideration of the Californian position within pop cultural cosmopolitanism through a more detailed look at the state's relevance for European culture to an exploration of the ways Californian referents inform identity narratives in highly local Polish contexts, we hope to offer a finishing peek into the spread of California's rhizome across culture.

Works Cited

Attebery, Brian. *Strategies of Fantasy*. Bloomington: Indiana University Press, 1992.
Austin, Mary. *The Land of Little Rain*. London: Penguin, 1997 [1903].
Banham, Reyner. *Los Angeles: The Architecture of Four Ecologies*. Berkeley: University of California Press, 1971.
Baudrillard, Jean. *America*. Trans. Chris Turner. London: Verso, 1988.
Bauman, Zygmunt. *Liquid Modernity*. London: Polity, 2000.
Billington, Ray Allen. *Land of Savagery, Land of Promise: The European Image of the American Frontier*. New York: Norton, 1981.

Braidotti, Rosi. *Nomadic Subjects: Embodiment and Sexual Difference in Contemporary Feminist Theory.* New York: Columbia University Press, 1994.
Cawelti, John G. *Adventure, Mystery, and Romance: Formula Stories as Art and Popular Culture.* Chicago: University of Chicago Press, 1976.
Davis, Mike. *City of Quartz: Excavating the Future in Los Angeles.* London: Verso, 2006 [1990].
Deleuze, Gilles, and Félix Guattari. *A Thousand Plateaus.* Trans. Brian Massumi. Minneapolis: University of Minnesota Press, 1987.
Didion, Joan. *Where I Was From.* London: Harper Perennial, 2003.
Everson, William. *Archetype West: The Pacific Coast as a Literary Region.* Berkeley: Oyez, 1976.
Eymann, Marcia, and Charles M. Wollenberg, eds. *What's Going On? California and the Vietnam Era.* Berkeley: University of California Press, 2004.
Fender, Stephen. *Plotting the Golden West: American Literature and the Rhetoric of the California Trail.* Cambridge: Cambridge University Press, 1981.
Gordon, Avery F. *Ghostly Matters: Haunting and the Sociological Imagination.* Minneapolis: Minnesota University Press, 2008 [1997].
Haslam, Gerald. *Many Californias: Literature from the Golden State.* Reno: University of Nevada Press, 1992.
Lakoff, George, and Mark Johnson. *Metaphors We Live By.* Chicago: University of Chicago Press, 1980.
McWilliams, Carey. *Southern California: An Island on the Land.* Salt Lake City: Peregrine Smith, 1980 [1946].
Muir, John. *Nature Writings.* New York: The Library of America, 1997.
Pulido, Laura, Laura Barraclough, and Wendy Cheng. *A People's Guide to Los Angeles.* Berkeley: University of California Press, 2012.
Rodriguez, Richard. *Brown: The Last Discovery of America.* New York: Viking, 2002.
Snyder, Gary. *The Practice of the Wild.* Berkeley: Counterpoint, 1990.
Starr, Kevin. *California: A History.* New York: The Modern Library, 2005.
Soja, Edward. *Thirdspace: Journeys to Los Angeles and Other Real-and-Imagined Places.* Malden: Blackwell, 1996.
Stegner, Wallace. "California: the Experimental Society." Editorial. *The Saturday Review.* September 23, 1967. http://www.unz.org/Pub/SaturdayRev-1967sep23-00028.
Steiner, Michael C. "Utopias West: Or the Trouble with Perfection." *American Studies* 53:1 (2014): 183–93.
Storey, John. *Inventing Popular Culture.* Malden: Blackwell, 2003.
Whitman, Walt. "Song of Myself." In *The Norton Anthology of American Literature.* Ed. Nina Baym, Wayne Franklin, et al. New York: Norton, 1995. 936–978.
Worster, Donald. *Under Western Skies: Nature and History in the American West.* Oxford: Oxford University Press, 1992.
Wyatt, David. *The Fall into Eden: Landscape and Imagination in California.* Cambridge: Cambridge University Press, 1986.

PART I: CALIFORNIA UNDER CONSTRUCTION

The Center Is Not Holding
Joan Didion and the California Dreamer

KATHLEEN M. VANDENBERG and
CHRISTOPHER K. COFFMAN

Few serious literary figures have such a famously complex standing in relation to popular culture—and to California's culture—as does Joan Didion. She is undoubtedly a fixed star in the sphere of our cultural imagination, as evinced not only by the continued, and even increased, popularity of her books, but also by a persistent interest in her image. Indeed, the photographs of her by Juergen Teller would seem to have become iconic: Chelsea's Danziger Gallery has recently offered an exhibition of these pictures, including his famed shots with her white Corvette Stingray of almost five decades ago, as well as many of those that came later. Too, his work includes the session with Didion on which French luxe fashion flavor du jour, Céline, drew for a 2015 advertisement. Among the items in that house's recent collections: a $1200 leather jacket featuring Didion's portrait on its back. Also notable in terms of her popular-cultural profile is Didion as a Hollywood personality: she served for nearly three decades as an erstwhile writer of screenplays, contributing material to such films as the Barbra Streisand vehicle *A Star Is Born*. Didion is, in short, a presence in the American pop-culture imaginary.

At the same time, she intentionally stands apart from this world of popular culture in which she seems so thoroughly present, serving out an indefinite term of self-imposed exile as one of our most incisive (some might say vitriolic) cultural critics. From the first pieces she penned, an array of widely held but finally delusory assumptions, and the (ab)uses of language that promulgate them, have been squarely in her line of fire. Even casual readers will likely be aware that while Didion sometimes roams quite far from Sacramento or Malibu (Miami, El Salvador, Central Park, Washington) on her quest to find targets, she also returns with some frequency to her home state for material.

Beginning with her earliest essays, and continuing through her first book—1963's *Run River*—and then through all that has followed, California has served Didion as a window on the self and on the nation; its hypocrisies and the self-mythologizing discourses that undergird them offer her rich material with regard to which she can unfold her defenses of clarity, precision, and honesty. In many senses, the early books on which we particularly focus in this essay—*Slouching Towards Bethlehem* and *The White Album*—cannot be conceived separately from critiques of an American ethos she suggests one may find manifest most forcefully in California. These writings explore California's darkness, its regional imagination, and its millenarian anxieties from countless angles, all of which bear the stamp of Didion's remarkable perceptions and preoccupations. The promise of an elaborate engagement with California contained in these early texts has since been most fully realized in 2003's *Where I Was From*, to which we also devote significant attention. (Although California retains something of a presence in her most recent works—*The Year of Magical Thinking* and *Blue Nights*—their focus is more directly on the unfolding of personal crisis, and as such they speak less to darkness of California and more to her own tragedies.) In every case, Didion reminds us that the generations-old sentimental vision of the state as a space in which fierce independence and hard work guarantee liberty and wealth cannot be reconciled with the reality of government subsidies, a laboring underclass, and unjust discriminations. Too, she repeatedly demonstrates that an equivalent to this political myth is manifest in the register of popular culture, particularly insofar as the Californian pop world of the 1960s appeared to her as ahistorical and detached from reality as does the state's socio-economic self-understanding.

In this essay, we read Didion's arguments regarding California through the lens of some of William T. Vollmann's remarks about "going off the grid," the effort to establish a self-sufficient life that allows one to enjoy the liberty that comes with thorough independence. From Didion's perspective, as from Vollmann's, such independence is nigh impossible, and any claims to the self-sufficiency it requires highly suspect. Yet, an acceptance of the notion that such liberty from the weight of the past is real, in the face of all evidence to the contrary, has come to define not only the popular notion of California, but also many of the visions California's powerful popular-culture industries have sold to audiences both far and near.

All place is palimpsest—geographical space is shot through with traces of the lives lived upon it and visible only through the histories layered over it. Perhaps nowhere is this more true than in California—a place often romanticized, mythologized, and idealized. "Going off the grid has always been an

American aspiration," writes Sacramento resident William T. Vollmann. He continues: "[f]rom the Quakers who fled English persecution, to David Koresh ... our people have set their faces hard away from the order and authority of others" (20). In the essay from which these remarks are drawn, "Let's Get Lost," Vollmann contends that almost every fictionalized westward flight—from that of the "gentle hedonists" who flee the Puritans in Nathaniel Hawthorne, through those wilderness wanderings of Natty Bumppo in James Fenimore Cooper, to the hardscrabble travel to California of John Steinbeck's Joads—has expressed a quintessentially American drive toward the pursuit of liberty, the pursuit of freedom from the restrictions of the "grid," "the authoritarian constraints of present necessity" (20). As the Steinbeck example makes evident, this tendency to seek freedom only to be brought up short by "the grid" is not only a definitively American trait, it is one that accepts California—the continent's most distant frontier—as emblematic of the national imaginary. While the ideals of liberty and happiness that California may be said to represent are in Vollmann's eyes not to be found via simple geographic repositioning, they are not for that reason any less seductive.

In its early days, when California's siren call first reached the ears of Americans, many died in their attempts to reach it or struggled mightily once established upon its often unforgiving (though no less beautiful for being so) lands. Paradoxically, Vollmann notes, movement westward, away from the center of power, often results not in escape from the grid, but in the extension of its reach. In this way, one's journey to the frontier adds to the grid's power, and inevitably involves the destruction and/or marginalization of the Other who inhabited the space constructed as "empty" by the discourse of the grid. And those who seemed to escape the grid successfully faced another peril: their imbrication within a new grid that was not significantly different from that which they left behind in its circumscription of freedom and frustration of happiness.

At various points throughout her career, which has spanned the last sixty-odd years, Sacramento native Joan Didion has explored the rhetoric of California, tracing the impulses of those drawn to it, mapping the mythological territory in which their dreams encounter their destinies, delineating the ways they fail, and diagnosing the ways California fails them. Vollmann's contention that the quintessentially American compulsion to "get lost" is inevitably frustrated by the impossibility of escaping geographical and cultural baggage is made manifest in her essays across the last decades of the twentieth century, filled as they are with the deluded dreams of those who find only darkness under California's large skies.

For Didion, the "California Conundrum" is that it is a land of travelers, dreamers, survivors, and pioneers, yet, "[s]caled against Yosemite, or against the view through the Gate of the Pacific trembling on its tectonic plates, the slightest shift of which could and with some regularity did destroy the works of man in a millisecond, all human beings were ... as worms, their 'heroic imperatives' finally futile, their philosophical inquiries vain" (994). In her writings, she composes an image of California that frames it as a paradoxical place, a landscape both natural and urban that has spoken to and continues to speak to those pulled toward its borders or the spectacle of the lives lived within them. Her writings work as a sort of Claude glass, rhetorically framing California in ways that suggest both its beauty and its darkness. It appears a land of excess and unrestraint, a stage set for dreams both visionary and dark, a space that encourages both adventure and tragedy, "a place in which ... the mind is troubled by some buried but ineradicable suspicion that things better work here, because here, beneath the immense bleached sky, is where we run out of continent" (131).

Didion's upbringing in the Sacramento Valley as a fifth-generation Californian played a large part in her initial interest in the gaps between reality and mythology. Hers was a childhood spent as a descendent of "a congeries of families ... that has always been in the Sacramento Valley" (131). These families passed down not only quilts, photographs, and flatware, but also stories, narratives about "crossings," abandonment, survival, resilience, and the frontier mentality. For Didion, the portion of this legacy that has remained, and indeed grown stronger across the years, cannot be apprehended as a catalogue of physical objects or their sentimental meanings. Instead, her primary inheritance is a distrust of mythologies generated by those invested—historically, personally, financially, and politically—in a certain idea of California as a western Eden. Fairly early in her career she remarks on her doubts regarding this vision, reflecting as a thirty-one-year-old that "[i]t is hard to find California now, unsettling to wonder how much of it was merely imagined or improvised; melancholy to realize how much of anyone's memory is no true memory at all but only the traces of someone else's memory, stories handed down" (135). This distrust of memory and mythology, especially insofar as it related to her own understanding of the land of her childhood, only grows as she gets older and is able to see that land from literal and figurative distances.

Born in a "golden land," a land settled and sought throughout American history by dreamers, opportunists, and transplants aspiring to fame and fortune, Didion is not immune to the appeal of California's apparent ungriddedness. Writing of her childhood in Sacramento, she notes that its ambiance was not one

> that tended toward a view of life as defined or limited or controlled, or even in any way affected, by the social and economic structures of the larger world. To be a Californian was to see oneself ... as affected only by "nature," which in turn was seen to exist simultaneously as a source of inspiration or renewal ... and as the ultimate

brute reckoning, the force that by guaranteeing destruction gave the place its perilous beauty [993].

A conflicted daughter of this place, she returns repeatedly to its borders, writing, across several works, to probe the tensions at work between its history and its representation, writing, as she says "to find the 'point' of California" (962).

Despite the apparent freedom it offered, she rejected, early on, the rhetoric of California in favor of reality, and turns, in much of her work, a critical eye on those California inhabitants—both established and new—who buy into its illusions. For instance, she writes condescendingly of the San Bernardino Valley in the 1960s, describing it as a country "in which a belief in the literal interpretation of Genesis has slipped imperceptibly into a belief in the literal interpretation of *Double Indemnity*, the country of ... girls for whom all life's promise comes down to a waltz-length white wedding dress and the birth of a Kimberly or a Sherry or a Debi and a Tijuana divorce and a return to hairdressers' school" (13). Thirty years later, she points to the artificiality of Los Angeles, describing it as "the most idealized of American cities, and the least accidental" (680).

Even as it is a place about which she writes with an unflinching eye, it remains an object of frequent recollections and affections. Her ability to balance these positive feelings with harder truths offers her work its singular flavor. Her ambivalence and anxiety regarding its influence remains apparent across the decades. Years after she has decamped for the East Coast, she reflects on her place of origin with uncertainty. "I was born in Sacramento," Didion writes in 2003, "and lived in California most of my life. Yet California has remained in some ways impenetrable to me, a wearying enigma, as it has to many of us who are from there. We worry it, correct and revise it, try and fail to define our relationship to it and its relationship to the rest of the country" (975). She lays bare, in many of her essays, the disconnect between utopian visions of California as a land of opportunity, rugged individualism, and freedom and the harsh realities of life lived in a place where the water supply is carefully monitored, maintained, and controlled, large portions of the population are reliant on government assistance, and starkly beautiful mountains and shores can become the sites of disruptive and dangerous winds, mudslides, and fires. She writes nostalgically of how the Sacramento Valley would—after the rains ended and spring began—"dissolve into a brilliant ephemeral green" but also recollects standing, in the fall of 1978, at an upstairs window of her house in Brentwood, watching as two fires burn toward each other, wiping out "large parts of Malibu and Pacific Palisades," and seeing a house on a hill above Sunset implode, "its oxygen sucked out by the force of the fire" (122, 656).

In *Where I Was From*, her collection of essays on her childhood and California, she reflects on a speech (entitled "Our California Heritage") she delivered at her eighth-grade graduation, noting that "[s]uch was the blinkering effect of the local dreamtime that it would be some years before I recognized that certain aspects of 'Our California Heritage' did not add up.... It was after this realization that I began trying to find the 'point' of California, to locate some message in its history" (962). Her effort to uncover the point of California became a career-long study in change, loss, and disillusionment: themes to which she returns repeatedly.

Again, some of Didion's most powerful and enduring writing on California emerged in the 1960s and the 1970s, a time when her life and work ensured her a unique position in time, place, and society. With the dawning of the 1960s, her presence at the periphery and the center of celebrity culture became pronounced. Having established a literary reputation in her early twenties and married the screenwriter John Gregory Dunne, she enjoyed an entrée into elite political and cultural circles. She shared a godchild with Roman Polanski, sat with Joan Baez as she ate cold potato salad with her fingers, drank Pouilly-Fuissé with John Wayne in Mexico, stood in a room where Paul Newman and Jack Lemmon debated the state of the university in America, chatted with Jerry Garcia while he took a break from rehearsing, befriended Linda Kasabian, waited with members of The Doors for Jim Morrison to come to a studio session, and hosted Janis Joplin at a house party (51, 39, 63, 171, 192–96).

At the elbow of some of the most famous (and infamous) figures of the time, she remained apart from them enough to retain her critical eye and to write some of the most seminal journalistic pieces of the decade, pieces that married the personal with the cultural and the political. A prominent and persistent cultural and political critic of late twentieth-century California culture, she was an influential voice drawing attention to the dark currents at work beneath its apparently sunny and limitless skies. Her famously long and incantatory sentences link seemingly disparate events with studied understatement. She writes of buying, for instance, on the morning of JFK's death, a short silk dress for her wedding, and in the next lines notes that "[a] few years later this dress of mine was ruined when.... Polanski accidentally spilled a glass of red wine on it. Sharon Tate was also a guest at this party... . On July 27, 1970, I went to the Magnin-Hi Shop ... and picked out, at Linda Kasabian's request, the dress in which she began her testimony about the murders at Sharon Tate Polanski's house" (210). This casual juxtaposition of the banal—two different shopping trips for dresses, spilled wine at a party— and the profound (Sharon Tate was of course murdered by Linda Kasabian's fellow Manson followers as Kasabian watched), this linking together of disparate tragedies to which she has only a tenuous connection, is vividly evocative of the tangle of forces at work in the grid of California celebrity culture. It is a culture she was embedded in long before O.J. Simpson drove his white Bronco down a California freeway and became the subject of (her brother-in-law) Gregory Dunne's writings for *Vanity Fair*, decades before the ubiquity of the Kardashians (also connected to O.J. Simpson) ensured that California celebrity culture became daily news.

Her reflections on this culture first appeared in her 1968 volume of essays, *Slouching Towards Bethlehem*, whose publication predated the Manson murders by a year. In it, she warned, presciently, that "[t]he center was not holding" (67). This claim, and the very title of collection, borrowed as they are from Yeats's "The Second Coming," immediately evoked his apocalyptic vision of post-war Europe, his claim that "anarchy is loosed upon the world," and his contention that "the best lack all conviction, while the worst/Are full of passionate intensity" (4, 7–8). It does not seem impossible to imagine, when one reads Didion, how such anarchy might come to be in a land where massive fires might ignite at any time and epically hot winds might blow down from the northeast and kick up sandstorms. "The Pacific turned ominously glossy during a Santa Ana period," she writes in "Los Angeles Notebook," "and one woke in the night troubled not only by the peacocks screaming in the olive trees but by the eerie absence of surf. ... My only neighbor would not come out of her house for days, ... and her husband roamed the place with a machete" (162).

It is within this landscape that she situates *Slouching Towards Bethlehem*; the collection begins with the essay "Some Dreamers of the Golden Dream," which works to reveal the profound disconnection between reality and rhetoric at work among the residents of the San Bernardino Valley, a place founded by Mormons but now inhabited by those whose first devotion is to self as understood through reference to popular and celebrity culture. In lieu of roots, tradition, and reality, residents of the valley, drawn to the place as a kind of last stop on journeys from their pasts, try, according to Didion, to make sense of life by means of the only coordinates that they register, "the movies and the newspapers" (14). The focus of the essay—the case of Lucille Marie Maxwell Miller—Didion writes, serves as "tabloid monument to that new life style" (14).

An emblem for the "California Dreamer," Lucille is accused of wanting "too much," of wanting more—more money, more love, more material goods. Not a native Californian, she had come to the state seeking something that the popular media promised. She ends up being found guilty of drugging her husband and burning him alive in the couple's Volkswagen early one dark October night in 1964. Prosecutors worked to prove that she was motivated by her desire for her lover and a hope of collecting on her husband's life insurance policy. Her trial spanned three months, and enthralled onlookers with its sensationalistic details: her pregnant figure handcuffed in the court room, a body so charred there was little left for their three children to see, a lover who was the married father of her young daughter's friend and a well-known attorney in the area. By the essay's end, she has been sentenced to life in prison and her lover has remarried, this time to "his children's ... governess," whom Didion describes as wearing "[a] coronet of seed pearls" that "held her illusion veil" (29).

This image of willful self-deception works emblematically—as most Didion details do—to suggest the paradoxical nature of the California dreamer, the person determined to escape and thus to arrive, to find herself by getting lost. Such a person embodies, in Vollmann's words, a tension between a hope for "perfect freedom and happiness" and "history" (20). While Vollmann finally accedes the geographic inescapability of the grid, he offers (via Whitman) a declaration of a private liberation: people can escape when they decline the terms of the grid's power, when they decline to submit to other people's power or to exercise power over others (21). When people step out of the circulation of power in this way, they are liberated as individuals and collectively, free to seek their happiness (21). But, for Didion, escape from the geopolitical grid to some California of unmitigated liberty and nearly-unlimited potential for happiness is not just elusive but illusory.

She sees these illusions played out most palpably in the 1960s on the streets of San Francisco's Haight-Ashbury, epicenter of pop culture dreams of freedom from constraint and authority, the ultimate "ungridded" space. In the title essay, Didion examines the counter-culture alive in its streets in 1967, a time when "it might have been a spring of brave hopes and national promise, but ... was not" (67). She immerses herself in the scene, profiling young runaways who spend their days dropping acid, smoking pot, and looking for food and housing. What she sees is "the desperate attempt of a handful of pathetically unequipped children to create a community in a social vacuum." This population, she writes, "grew up cut loose from the web ... [that] had traditionally suggested and enforced the society's values. They are children who have moved around a lot, *San Jose, Chula Vista, here*" (93). Even, however, as they roam free from the traditional "grids" of family and community and authority, they carry with them the weight of expectations and dreams, a desire to be somewhere.

She talks with twenty-three year-old Steve, waiting as he moves "nervously around the room," and realizing that the conversation is going nowhere. "We do not," she writes, "seem to be getting to the point." As he paces and lights a cigarette with shaking hands, Steve talks: "This chick tells me there's no meaning to life but it doesn't matter, we'll just flow right out. There've been times I felt like packing up and taking off for the East Coast again, at least there I had a *target*. At least there you expect that it's going to *happen*...."

Here you know it's not going to" (76). Didion asks him what is supposed to happen. "'I don't know,' he says. 'Something. Anything'" (77). Confronting the boundaries, both geographical and ideological, of his California dreamscape, Steve knows nothing else but to attempt another escape.

Didion refuses to idealize or to romanticize a scene so many at the time and so many since have embraced as mythic in its freedom from constraint and authority, seeing it as composed of "children" who are "less in rebellion against the society than ignorant of it, able only to feed back certain of its most publicized self-doubts, *Vietnam, Saran-Wrap, diet pills, the Bomb*." These children are avidly anti-intellectual, she says, "their only proficient vocabulary is in the society's platitudes," and this disturbs her, committed as she is "to the idea that the ability to think for one's self depends upon one's mastery of the language" (36). Pop culture images of beaded vests, flower power, and idyllic, long-haired, and barefoot hippies are replaced, in Didion's text, by the brutal realities of life for the smallest inhabitants of this grid. The essay ends with talk of five-year-olds on acid—self-proclaimed attendees of "High Kindergarten"—and a description of a three-year-old being screamed at by his hippie mother for chewing on an electrical cord. His scolding goes seemingly unnoticed by the trio of adults in the kitchen, who are "trying to retrieve some very good Moroccan hash which had dropped down through a floorboard" (97).

"When Americans go off the grid," Vollmann writes, "they ... like to take possession" (20). A certain logic prevails in America, Vollmann argues, one that begins with the assumption that impoverishment is due to lack of ownership, and that potency will be realized or renewed when one gains control of space off the grid. So it is that generations of Americans have fled west, taking up residence in California's bountiful lands, despite droughts, fires, landslides, and earthquakes, hoping to escape to a place "ungridded by memory, commerce, necessity, and atrocity" (Vollmann 20). "In California," Didion writes, "we did not believe that history could bloody the land, or even touch it" (996). But, as her essays demonstrate time and again, there is no "ungridded place" where someone like Linda Kasabian, or Lucille Marie Maxwell Miller, or even Joan Baez or Patty Hearst can shrug off her personal history and cultural baggage and travel uninhibited and unwatched, no matter the scale of the Californian landscape or the attempts at reinvention that have infused its history with so much pathos and spectacle.

John Leonard, who frequently reviewed Didion's work and provided the introduction for the 2006 Everyman Collection *We Tell Ourselves Stories in Order to Live*, observes of Didion that, over the years, "[s]he seemed sometimes so sensitive that whole decades hurt her feelings, and the prose on the page suggested Valéry's 'shiverings of an effaced leaf,' as if her next trick might be evaporation." In assessing health problems at the end of the 1960s, Didion notes that she will "offer only that an attack of vertigo and nausea does not now seem to me an inappropriate response to the summer of 1968" (188). Finely attuned to the dark currents passing through the turbulent air of the decade, Didion glimpsed a dystopic California, one where a glamorous movie star could be fatally stabbed while eight months pregnant and begging for her life and a blonde heiress to a legendary California fortune could take up a machine gun and rob a bank.

The California imagination, Didion concludes, derives from the claiming of the landscape and "the romance of emigration, the radical abandonment of established attachments," and it remains insistently invested in the symbolic to the exclusion of the merely literal (584). It is a dream predicated on escaping the grid while remaining blind to one's own oppressive extending of it. In this sense, she shares with Vollmann a recognition of the dark side of the dynamic that motivates the "California dreamer"—the people oppressed, lands stolen, and lives destroyed. American utopian visions, as he argues, from the City on the Hill to the Last Good Place, are always "costly" and "obtained at the expense of other people" (20). Few writers tally these costs as consistently and evocatively as Joan Didion.

Works Cited

Didion, Joan. *We Tell Ourselves Stories in Order to Live: Collected Nonfiction*. New York: Everyman's Library-Knopf, 2006. Print.
Leonard, John. "Books of the Times; Dread in the Sunlight Vietnam Unmentioned." *New York Times* 5 June 1979: C11. Print.
Vollmann, William T. "Let's Get Lost." *Bookforum* June–Aug. 2013: 20–21. Print.
Yeats, W.B. *The Collected Works of W.B. Yeats*. Vol. 1. New York: Scribner-Simon, 1997. Print.

Desert Women
Constructions of Female Identity and Motherhood in Angela Carter and Claire Vaye Watkins's Feminist Dystopias

DONNA MITCHELL

In 2011, Margaret Atwood coined the term "ustopia" to describe the correlation between utopian and dystopian narratives, as she believes that one can find "within each utopia, a concealed dystopia; [and] within each dystopia, a hidden utopia, if only in the form of the world as it existed before-[hand]" (85). While her definition of such texts is still relatively new, the genre itself is not; according to one of the most influential critics of ustopian fictions, Fredric Jameson, it is believed to have originated "either with Wells's *The Time Machine* (1895) or [even] earlier with Shelley's *Frankenstein* (1818)" (Wilson 1). Sharon Rose Wilson breaks down and clarifies the defining elements of each category in her assertion that "[t]o think about utopia ... one must think about the ideal or perfect. Dystopia involves utopia's opposite: a nightmare ... or a society worse than the existing one" (9). Furthermore, she notes that dystopias often function as warnings "against the repercussions of current social and political trends and [reveal] their anxiety over the female body" (3). As a popular subcategory of ustopian fiction, feminist dystopias therefore offer a narrative that considers the problematic relationship between patriarchal society and womankind. Atwood's *The Handmaid's Tale* (1985) is one of the most famous feminist dystopias to highlight the genre's ability to provide a platform for the discussion of social and political issues belonging to the real world as, in Atwood's own words, it "contains incidents that have already happened in real life" (Atwood, cited in Wilson 2). While a vast period separates the publication of the feminist dystopias that I discuss in this essay—namely Angela Carter's *The Passion of New Eve* (1977) and Claire Vaye

Watkins's *Gold Fame Citrus* (2016)—the representation of womanhood in both is dictated by a cultural hegemony that perpetuates female oppression. Both texts demonstrate the importance of the feminist dystopia as a narrative that challenges the fixed ideology of womanhood by exposing the unnatural state of the female condition in relation to the social maintenance of its identity.

Freud's contemptuous definition of female sexuality as a "Dark Continent" that could never be understood or conquered ensured that, from a theoretical perspective, darkness has long been equated with womanhood (212). His classification not only reflects patriarchal notions toward women but also perpetuates the idea of essentialism by rigidly defining sexuality as a binary opposition composed of the familiar masculine and the unfamiliar feminine. As one of the most liberal states in America, California is widely recognized and celebrated for its acceptance and legal protection of its LGBTQIA community. This progressive attitude establishes California as a location where classifications of gender and sexual identity are less rigid and therefore open to reinterpretation. This highlights the significance of location within these texts as events tend to unfold and culminate at peripheral sites that are separate from the central catchment area of civilization with desert California acting as the setting for both novels. While the exact site of Carter's tale is not specified, it appears to be somewhere in the central desert region of California while Watkins bases her story more specifically in the Mojave Desert. The extreme environment within these desert settings appropriates the formula of the dystopian narrative, which often contains self-governed regions of great disparity with much discrimination among their inhabitants. Life in this environment often becomes an exercise in survival as, within the context of American fiction, the desert is often associated with death, according to historian Patricia Limerick. Her analysis of desert life in Edward Abbey's classic *Desert Solitaire*, focuses on his portrayal of the traveler's experience of "thirst, heat, hardship, risk, and human insignificance" (156) within such terrain. Limerick categorizes the American attitude toward the desert as evidenced in literature into three major phases, which she claims "overlap and continue into the present" (7). She identifies the first phase as the 1820s, when the desert was regarded "simply a threat to life [or] an ordeal to be endured" (6), the second as 1859 onward, when it was considered to be a "valuable ... wasteland capable of becoming irrigated farmland" (7), and locates the third at the turn of the century, when it "began to qualify in some circles as beautiful and suitable for appreciation" (7). Additionally, Limerick's assertion that the desert is "an environment with a great power to change the form and behavior of organisms" (5) is most important for this essay as it is concerned with the creation and evolution of the female figure. I will examine this issue by using characters from the aforementioned novels to consider how womanhood is constructed and represented within sites of conflict and struggle in feminist dystopias that are based in a desert California setting.

The Construction of Womanhood

Carter's tale is initially set in a ravaged, war-torn version of New York which has been overtaken by various factions of warring rebels, and it is here that the construction of womanhood begins in relation to the male protagonist, Evelyn, and his careful observation of his lover, Leilah. Female identity within the city is constructed along the lines of male desire as demonstrated by Evelyn's surveillance of Leilah's daily beauty ritual which creates a more sexualized version of herself. Their gendered behavior during this practice exemplifies aspects of the social demands on women's appearance and the female experience of "the male gaze" that Evelyn will later experience as a transsexual woman. According to feminist film critic Laura Mulvey, the concept of "the male gaze" stems from the "sexual imbalance" of a "split between [an] active/male [onlooker] and [a] passive/female [recipient]" (19). The function of this gaze is to project man's "fantasy onto the female figure, which is [then] styled accordingly" and "coded for strong visual and erotic impact," so that she can "play to and signify male desire" (19) by being "on display [and] sexualised" (21). Mulvey expands upon this theory in her essay, "Afterthoughts on Visual Pleasure and Narrative Cinema." Her most significant revision, in terms of this essay, relates to what she identifies as "the melodrama issue" (31) concerning the position of the female figure within the narrative frame. This issue considers "how the text and its attendant identifications are affected by a *female* character occupying the centre of the narrative arena" (31, original italics) and focuses specifically on "a woman central protagonist [who] is shown to be unable to achieve a stable sexual identity" (32) as she exists somewhere between a "passive femininity and ... regressive masculinity" (32). She examines the effect that the "interior drama of a girl caught up between two conflicting desires" has on a story and concludes that "the female presence as centre allows the story to be actually, *overtly*, about sexuality [as] it becomes a melodrama [that asks w]hat does *she* want?" (37, original italics).

The ambiguity surrounding the feminization and sexualization of Mulvey's female character here ties in with Simone de Beauvoir's assertion that women play up to the version of themselves that will be objectified by the male onlooker as de Beauvoir believes that "when [the young girl] admires herself in the mirror, she is still only dreaming of herself as seen through masculine eyes" (402). In other words, she uses the mirror as a reflection of combined masculine and feminine inclination and subsequently defines her beauty and sexuality solely in terms of male desire and the masculine concept of feminine beauty. This common practice also perpetuates the notion of essentialism and endorses the polarizing characteristics of masculine and feminine sexuality that are described in Naomi Wolf's notion of "the beauty myth [which] keeps a gap of fantasy between men and women. That gap is made with mirrors; no law of nature supports it" (144). Therefore, in relation to Carter's text, the mirror is the focal point of the male gaze and Leilah's creation of a false public face. This action personifies the female manufacture of a "not-self [that] is specifically designed to suit masculine taste [because Leilah carefully] constructs herself as a reflection of a masculine view of what makes her erotically desirable" (Day 10). This is a common aspect of womanhood which represents the fabrication of a false identity that is dictated by the exact preferences of patriarchal society. The imbalance of power in relation to sex and gender in this theory highlights how women are trained to rely on men for the validation of their sexual identity while simultaneously recognizing their role as a passive recipient and sexual object of the male subject. Man's requirement of a female stimulant for his sexual pleasure is overlooked in an effort to portray women as being more dependent on men, which in turn perpetuates essentialist notions. Therefore, Evelyn's role in the creation of Leilah's false self can be read as a patriarchal management of the female figure, which he will later experience firsthand in California.

Womanhood in the desert wasteland of Watkins's novel is equally performative in relation to the male gaze in both Mulvey and de Beauvoir's theories and is represented by Luz, who initially appears to be superficial, unstable, and carefully managed by her boyfriend, Ray. Living in an unknown starlet's deserted mansion, her main concern, similar to Leilah, is to perform to the male gaze by adorning herself in various riches and garments from the master closet: "Luz ... wiggled into a clinging cobalt mermaid gown dense with beads. It was gorgeous and she was gorgeous in it, even with her filthy hair and bulgy eyes and bushy brows.... She looked liquid and wanted to show Ray" (4–5). By reducing her face's reflection to a series of dissected features (hair, eyes, brows), Luz exemplifies one of the other main aspects in Wolf's "beauty myth" theory, which specifically relates to the daily "torrent of media images that show the female face and body split into pieces. [This] is how the beauty myth asks a woman to think of her own body parts" (230). Additionally, her wish to provoke a positive reaction from Ray suggests a need to both incite his desire and gain his approval. These objectives can be understood through Wolf's hypothesis that what "girls learn is not the desire for the other, but the desire to be desired" (157). This is an exclusively female practice that reverts the girl's attention back to her own body, thereby causing her to obsessively monitor any personal physical changes and engage in the objectification of her own physicality while also comparing herself to her female peers.

Although the previous occupant has abandoned the mansion, many of her possessions have been left behind, causing Luz to see herself in terms of the starlet's absence as she defines her present identity as being that of "another woman's ghost" (6). When reminiscing on her past selves, she reveals that performance has always been a part of her life as she was the public face of the California Conservation administration, which was a political lobby group that promised (but failed) to expand the California Aqueduct in order to protect the water supply for future generations: "She wept ... for all her selves in reverse. First for Luz Dunn, whose finest lover and best friend was a murderer ... then for Luz Cortez, mid-tier model spoiled then discarded.... Then ... for Baby Dunn.... Born with a gold shovel in her hand, adopted and co-opted by Conservation ... her life literal and symbolic the stuff of headlines" (10–11). It can be read from this revelation that her performance will continue as, in her current situation, she appears to be completely reliant on Ray and basks in his infantilization of her. Her childlike status at this point is a vast contrast to her later adoption of a maternal role, which is a development that occurs during a trip into the Valley wasteland. Her transformation into a mother figure demonstrates Limerick's statement regarding the desert's metamorphosing power as illustrated by how a journey into desert California can signify substantial changes in the female figure of the feminist dystopia.

Motherhood in the Feminist Dystopia

After a brief, sadomasochistic love affair with Leilah, Evelyn finds himself stranded within a desolate desert terrain where he is captured by a group of female rebels. These women take him to their laboratory and force him to undergo a sex-change operation that will destroy his male physicality and force him to experience the remainder of his life as a woman. Evelyn reveals the significance of the desert compound in relation to the creation of his new identity as a transsexual woman by describing it as "the place where I was born" (Carter 43). His rebirth is instigated by the cult's deity and figurehead known simply as Mother, whose very physicality is a literal personification of the female body as a constructed patchwork of gendered subjects. She represents the maternal aspect of Carter's presentation of womanhood within a dystopian setting and is depicted as a scientist/surgeon who has "made herself ... reconstructed her flesh painfully, with knives and with needles, into a transcendental form as an emblem" (57). Her self-assembled physicality represents the collective principles of the cult which seeks to create a female utopia where the mother figure is recognized and revered for her role as a creator rather than as a creation: "Mother ... has undergone a painful metamorphosis of the entire body.... She is also a great scientist who makes extraordinary experiments and I was destined to become the subject of one of them ... she had been human, once; and now ... she is the hand-carved figurehead of her own, self-constructed theology" (46–55). Evelyn, horrified by Mother's patchwork anatomy, likens her to "a sacred monster" (56). But when considered in feminist terms, her self-created physicality signifies her revolt against the patriarchal definition of woman as a masculine reflection of desirability. Mother's location within the California compound is therefore crucial, as it provides a safe environment for both her feminist expression and utopian vision. Furthermore, it gives her power to subvert patriarchal maintenance of womanhood by forcing Evelyn to experience the disjointed paradigm of female identity as well as the demands that come with it.

While staying in the desert compound, Evelyn learns that he will be the first of Mother's new race of (wo)manmade women. He undergoes a psychosexual re-education that forces him "to view socially constructed images of the feminine as well as atrocities committed on women by men throughout time" (Rubenstein 110). These lessons are a radical introduction to his new female status which both depict the inspiration behind Mother's reason for creating a new race and reinforce her belief in the faculty of womanhood. She wants to construct a female utopia where the male hegemonic position has been demoted and deconstructed to a point where only women have power. Evelyn is told, in very precise terms, that his male reproductive organs will be replaced with a "fructifying feminine space [that will] make [him] a perfect specimen of womanhood. Then, as soon as [he is] ready, [Mother will] impregnate [him] with [his] own sperm" (65). This process would make him the "first of all beings in the world [to] seed [him]self *and* fruit [him]self ... [to be] entirely self-sufficient" (73, original italics). Despite its focus on his physical form, which will be made as a reflection of Mother, this operation ensures a change in his entire identity as henceforth he will be expected to fulfill the cultural demands of objectified womanhood as discussed by Mulvey, de Beauvoir, and Wolf.

Immediately after the procedure, Evelyn is referenced in female terms as Eve. Eve recognizes the complexity of her new identity by noting a disconnection between her (wo)manmade female form and the male psyche she previously inhabited, which suggests a residual presence of both sexes within her. The struggles that she will soon encounter as a woman illustrate de Beauvoir's concept of how femininity is a social construction rather than a biological state of womanhood: "One is not born, but rather becomes, a woman. No biological, psychological, or economic fate determines the figure that the human female presents in society; *it is civilization as a whole that produces this creature*, intermediate between male and eunuch, which is described as feminine" (295, my italics). De Beauvoir's notion of womanhood as a social construct is exemplified through Eve's inability to see herself as female despite her new physicality. In other words, she does not feel like a proper woman because she still lacks the training to perform in a correlating feminine manner. The central aspect of this philosophy is captured in the first moment that Eve sees her new form, and with it, her new identity "as a variation upon what Leilah had been, an incarnation of male sexual fantasy, a not-self" (Day 116): "When I looked in the mirror, I saw Eve; I did not see myself. I saw a young woman who, though she was I, I could in no way acknowledge as myself, for this one was only a lyrical abstraction of femininity to me, a tinted arrangement of curved lines.... I was a woman, young and desirable" (Carter 71). This can be read as a male response to a female reflection which depicts her awareness of the existential disharmony between her new and old selves. Furthermore, it epitomizes, in a very literal sense, the main factors in art critic John Berger's concept of men's influence on women's perception of their identity, which links back to Mulvey's theory. Berger breaks down the correlation between women and the male gaze in his analysis of the surveyed female figure in art: "[A] woman's self being [is] split in two. A woman must continually watch herself.... Men look at women. Women watch themselves being looked at. This determines not only most relations between men and women but also the relation of women to themselves. The surveyor of woman in herself is male: the surveyed female. Thus she turns herself into an object—and most particularly an object of vision—a sight" (Berger, cited in Day 111). Eve's inner monologue further confirms this paradoxical state and demonstrates her awareness that, she has "not yet become a woman," despite having "a woman's shape" (79). She labels herself as an artificial or "monstrous" (79) being "like Mother" (79) as a reaction to the foreign components that make up her post-operative anatomy. Her identification with Mother is particularly significant when considered from the perspective that she has deliberately constructed Eve to be a future mother as well as an ironic "reflection of masculine images of the female [and] according to a masculine view of what the perfect woman should look like" (Day 116). Furthermore, Eve's preoccupation with her new form suggests a corresponding awareness that, henceforth, her worth will be governed by her physical beauty, as she now experiences the female perspective of "a culture in which it is taken for granted that women will be valued primarily for their sexual attractiveness" (Walter 61).

Motherhood is also a complex issue in Watkins's novel and arises during Luz's journey into the Mojave Desert, which changes her life drastically on two occasions; the first incident occurs when she travels into the wasteland with Ray and finds an abandoned child in need of their protection. Luz recounts how the young girl, who appears to be about two years old, immediately treats her like a mother by attaching herself to her and seeking comfort, causing her to feel "uncannily at ease" (31) despite their unfamiliarity with each other. After a failed attempt to reconcile the child with her family, she fears that the girl is in danger and decides to help her. In doing so, she epitomizes de Beauvoir's hypothesis of motherhood, which argues strongly against the inherent existence of a maternal "instinct" in all women. De Beauvoir discusses how common it is for a young mother to feel overwhelmed and even threatened by her baby, and notes that it is her "attitude ... and reaction to [her new situation]" (526) that ultimately decides whether she will accept or reject the child. When considered through the lens of this claim, Luz's progression toward a maternal role can be read as a reaction whereby she decides to save the girl from fatal danger in the Valley. She recounts the dejected fate of children who had been abandoned by their parents after the Conservation movement failed and extreme drought destroyed the land, as traffickers exploiting the situation charged "quadruple for children" (38) and as "many hosts refused to take them ... toddlers were left to cook in cars, older kids locked in the apartments parents fled ... [soon] children became the currency" (38). Luz's certainty of the child's terrible fate convinces her to become a substitute mother. She learns that the child calls herself Ig and gains firsthand experience of caring for an infant as she feeds, cleans, and cares for her. Fearing both human and environmental dangers within the canyon, the family decides to leave their villa and brave the Mojave Desert once again in the hope of finding a better life for Ig. This marks the second desert journey that has a repercussive and irreversible effect on Luz's life. As they begin to drive, Luz considers Ig's future in relation to her status as part of the last generation born before the drought; she notes the uncertainty of their ability to survive in the desert and tries to imagine "where Ig would grow up, saying, *I was born in California*, maybe one of the last, onward into the fine future ... which would lead them to ...what?" (92, original italics). Her reservations are quickly justified as their car breaks down and Ray leaves them in an attempt to find help. Luz tries to survive on their limited supplies all the while maintaining her maternal role by giving the majority of food and water to the child, but despite her efforts, they cannot survive the desert heat and begin to die from sunstroke.

 She later awakens to find herself part of a desert compound where her maternal role is threatened by another woman's ability to nurse the infant. The arrival of Dallas undermines Luz's already vulnerable claim to Ig and her fear is signified by her first impression, which merges the woman's identity with Ig through the maternal representation of her nursing breast: "The woman stood. She was massive, her head threatening the ceiling of the bus.... [A] filthy bandana ... was cinched around her neck. [She] came toward Luz. Her gait was tender, but not tentative. From the bundle hung a pale spindle leg. Long toes ... there, in the wad of cloth was Ig, suckling the giantess's left breast" (129–130). Dallas's ability to produce milk during the drought ensures that she is defined in terms of her maternal physicality and so she is portrayed as a voluptuous woman who personifies the traditional depiction of motherhood. She also nurses Luz by bringing her back to her full health with medicine and water, and in doing so, fulfills a maternal role to her as well. This suggests that she can be a read as a universal mother figure to all within the desert compound, similar to Mother in Carter's text. Dallas's efforts to nurture Luz are detailed in a hazy third-person narrative which suggests that Luz represses the memory in order to protect her own maternal identity and not attach similar terms to her new rival: "She would not remember the plates of food Dallas brought.... Dallas nursing Ig until she fell asleep.... Dallas telling her to spray herself down.... Dallas misting up her left leg and down her right leg.... Dallas spritzing the blankets or soaking torn segments of cloth in water and instructing [her] to lay these where the blood was closest [to the surface of the skin]" (135). Despite this, Dallas takes on the responsibility of Ig when Luz is too overcome with grief for Ray to continue caring for her. As a result, when the child learns how to talk, she quickly associates the words "milk" and "Mama" with Dallas, thus strengthening their bond. When Ray eventually reappears and is given the option to leave the compound alive and with Luz on the condition that Ig remains, Luz tells Dallas the child's real name, or rather, the secret name they gave to her. This information, as well as the child's calm reaction to their departure while remaining within the desert with Dallas, confirms that by the end of the text, Luz is no longer her mother. Despite this conclusion, her experience of motherhood remains a hugely significant factor in the transformation of her identity. While the Mother icon of Carter's tale is very much enforced on Evelyn from the outside in order to achieve her radically feminist vision, it arises in Watkins's novel through Luz's adoption of a maternal role which she molds according to her own design. It is not until she is confronted with the traditional and predefined icon of motherhood in the form of Dallas, that she succumbs to her fear of failing Ig and abandons this aspect of her identity altogether.

Harem Life in the Dystopian Desert

Eve manages to escape the desert compound before she is impregnated to become a mother herself. Her freedom, however, is short-lived, as she is immediately captured by a poet and villain called Zero, a "stereotyped, phallic figure ... of wicked, irredeemable misogyny" (Rubenstein 107), who forces her to become a part of his harem of wives. Her new circumstances ensure daily interaction with people who have no knowledge of her previous masculinity and so it demands a very compelling act of femininity on her part. In order to present a convincing masquerade of womanliness, she resorts to her earlier (male) practice of careful observation and then mimics the feminine behavior of Zero's other wives. This exercise can also be read as an internalization of the male gaze as she watches herself gradually become a woman: "I kept as silent as I could and tried to imitate the way they moved and the way they spoke for I knew that.... I would often make a gesture with my hands that was out of Eve's character or exclaim with a subtly male inflection that made them raise their eyebrows. This intensive study of feminine manners, as well as my everyday work about the homestead, kept me in a permanent state of exhaustion" (97). Her performance can be further understood in relation to Luce Irigaray's claim that "femininity" is not a natural part of the female anatomy, but rather it is "a role, an image, a value, imposed upon women by male systems of representation" (84). As Eve escapes the desert compound before Mother can educate her on the additional demands of her new female form, she must rely solely on her ability to imitate these gender components in order to effectively partake in the female masquerade. Her eventual ability to do so confirms her possession of a feminine thought-process that is reflected in her behavior.

Zero secures his status within the hierarchy of his household by inflicting physical, mental, and sexual abuse upon his wives on a daily basis, which in turn allows Eve to experience the powerlessness of a woman who is subject to the perverted desires of a misogynistic man. His actions also subvert Eve's earlier mistreatment of Leilah by enforcing her to experience the other/female perspective of sexual violation: "Because of his suspicion that I might be too much of a woman for him, he took great fancy to me and our marital encounters, therefore, took place at a pitch of intensity that filled me with terror.... [A]nd the experience ... [a]lways brought with it a shock of introspection [that] forced me to know myself as a former violator at the moment of my own violation" (98). Eve likens the traumatic effects of his actions to a horrific type of initiation into womanhood; she even considers it to be a fitting punishment for her previous crimes against women as it is Zero's daily abuse and repeated rapes "that succeed in finally fitting [her] mind to her body" (Day 117), thus completing her transformation: "I had spent three months as a wife of Zero. It was as savage apprenticeship in womanhood as could have been devised for me and, if Mother had selected me, however arbitrarily, to atone for the sins of my first sex vis-à-vis my second sex via my sex itself, I would say that.... I had become the thing I almost was. The mediation of Zero turned me into a woman" (Carter 104).

Harem life is also a part of the female experience in Watkins's novel and is similarly led by a patriarchal figurehead in the form of Levi, a self-proclaimed prophet and gifted dowser whose true identity is that of a violent and manipulative drug lord. His influence on the residents and their dependency on him ensure his role as deity of the desert compound. Luz notes that his followers dress and perform according to his every instruction as she surveys the many figures dressed "all in white" (162) that fulfill his every command. Levi ensures Luz's submission by getting her addicted to the drug which keeps her in a continuous state of fatigue. Aware of her previous image as Baby Dunn, the poster child of the California Conservation administration, he takes a great interest in her and a relationship develops between them. Both Luz's addiction and loneliness make her completely dependent on him and she becomes one of his many concubines. His objective, however, is in relation to her maternal role as well as her ability to perform to the public, as he voices his intent for Luz and Ig to be presented publicly as a "Madonna and child" (229) in an effort to further expand his position of power. The specific setting of the Mojave Desert is a significant component of his plan as it represents the locus of new life after the terrible drought: "Baby Dunn's *baby....* People remember Baby Dunn.... We'll take them right back.... You of all people were brought here. No one survives out there, but *you* did. Ig did. This is Zion, Deseret, the New World's Holy Land.... Ig is our baby Moses" (229, original italics). His intention confirms that Luz's value to him lies within her relation to Ig. When Ray uncovers Levi's true identity as a criminal and a fraud, and in return is told to leave the compound, Levi gains support for his wish to keep Ig by declaring that "she is a child of the dune sea" (320) who must remain in the Mojave desert with his people. He proclaims her "atypical. An anomaly [whose] moaning is of the same frequency as the dune's song" (334), thus implying that she may also possess the power to become a dowser. This development also suggests that her future will remain a part of the desert harem and continue to be dominated by performance and fraud.

The hopelessness of Ig's future at the end of Watkins's novel signifies the bleak state of womanhood that exists at the conclusion of many feminist dystopias. It suggests that womanhood will continue to be a false construction that remains governed solely by its appeal to man and its ability to procreate. Even Mother's attempts to create an ironic version of woman based on a male subject are reduced to female suffering, as Eve is subject to the same hardships of performance and sexual violation as her female counterparts. As explored in this essay, gender inequality is the underlying medium of discrimination in these texts. Feminist dystopias present these versions of womanhood in relation to gender construction and reproductive ability in an attempt to expose the root of the problem and instigate a dialogue through literary means that might, in some way, contribute to a more equal future for women. Both Carter and Watkins's decision to use the California desert as the core setting of their narratives highlights its significance as both an area that challenges patriarchal notions of gender and sexuality and offers itself as a platform for the discussion of social and political factors regarding these issues.

Works Cited

Abbey, Edward. *Desert Solitaire: A Season in the Wilderness*. New York: Random House, 1968. Print.

Atwood, Margaret. *In Other Worlds: SF and the Human Imagination*. New York: Anchor Books, 2011. Print.

Carter, Angela. *The Passion of New Eve*. London: Virago Press, 1992. Print.

Day, Aidan. *Angela Carter: The Rational Glass*. Manchester: Manchester University Press, 1998. Print.

De Beauvoir, Simone. *The Second Sex*. London: Vintage, 1997. Print.

Freud, Sigmund. "Inhibitions, Symptoms and Anxiety" [1926], *Standard Edition*, vol. 20. London: The Hogarth Press, 1956–1974. 77–174.

Gamble, Sarah. *The Fiction of Angela Carter: A Reader's Guide to Essential Criticism*. Hampshire: Palgrave Macmillan, 2001. Print.

Germanà, Monica. *Scottish Women's Gothic and Fantastic Writing: Fiction Since 1978*. Edinburgh: Edinburgh University Press, 2013. Print.

Irigaray, Luce. *This Sex Which Is Not One*. Ithaca: Cornell University Press, 1985. Print.

Limerick, Patricia Nelson. *Desert Passages: Encounters with American Deserts*. Albuquerque: University of New Mexico Press, 2001. Print.

Mulvey, Laura. *Visual and Other Pleasures*. Basingstoke: Palgrave Macmillan, 2009. Print.

Rubenstein, Roberta. "Intersexions: Gender Metamorphosis in Angela Carter's *The Passion of New Eve* and Lois Gould's *Sea-Change*." *Tulsa Studies in Women's Literature* 12 (1993): 103–18. JSTOR. Web. 7 Feb. 2014.

Vaye Watkins, Claire. *Gold Fame Citrus*. London: Quercus Publishing, 2016. Print.

Walters, Natasha. *Living Dolls: The Return of Sexism*. London: Virago Press, 2010. Print.

Wilson, Sharon Rose. *Women's Utopian and Dystopian Fiction*. Newcastle upon Tyne: Cambridge Scholars, 2013. EBook.

Wolf, Naomi. *The Beauty Myth: How Images of Beauty Are Used Against Women*. New York: Harper Perennial, 2002. Print.

Playing Good Cop ... or Bad Cop?
Exploring Hyperreal Urban Spaces in L.A. Noire

Michael Fuchs

"A city of undercurrents, where not everything is as it seems": this poignant line introduces Los Angeles in the film-noir-inspired video game *L.A. Noire*. The emphasis on the city's defining dualisms echoes urban historian Mike Davis, who has stressed that the City of Angels plays a dual function in the American imagination: on the one hand, it represents the "Land of Endless Summer" and a "lifestyle against which other Americans measured the modernity of their towns and regions" (*Ecology* 349, 377). On the other hand, Los Angeles has become "a dystopian symbol of Dickensian inequalities and intractable racial contradictions"; due to the racial tensions the city has become known for and its role as "the First World capital of homelessness, with an estimated 100,000 homeless people" (*Ecology* 377; *Planet* 36). Whereas Tinseltown was the shiny harbinger of modernity, the city has come to embody "the collapse of [the] American belief in a utopian national destiny" (*Ecology* 377). Significantly, Davis has focused on how La-La Land functions "as the icon of a really bad future" (295). While media texts have repeatedly imagined the city's future to diagnose problems in the present moment, *L.A. Noire* directs its attention to the past, the years after World War II in particular. In so doing, the game not only suggests a continuity between the past and the present, but it also highlights the fact that the idea of Los Angeles feeds into its worldly materiality and vice-versa.

Indeed, when *L.A. Noire* was released in the spring of 2011, critics primarily highlighted two features: its MotionScan technology, which is central to the game's interrogation mechanic, and the great efforts the Australian developers took upon themselves in order to faithfully re-create post–World War II Los Angeles, as they spent weeks at various libraries in California, studying numerous maps and hundreds of photographs of the era. Reviewers hailed MotionScan as "little short of groundbreaking" (N. Kelly), for it "reach[es] a level of richness that is simply mind-boggling" (Hurel; my translation). The game's representation of Los Angeles, on the other hand, was praised for its inclusion of "innumerable authentic details" (Videogames Zone; my translation), which is why the city's virtual double "looks exactly the way you imagine it" (Videogames Zone; my translation).[1]

While the game's technology and the development team's attention to detail were often singled out, the gameplay mechanics also add to the game's realism: collecting evidence, examining corpses, chasing suspects on foot or in a car, and interviewing witnesses and suspects simply feels like "doing the job" of a police officer (N. Kelly; original in italics), critics suggested. In combination, the MotionScan technology, the painstaking recreation of post–World War II Los Angeles, and the gameplay mechanics made some critics proclaim that *L.A. Noire* "represent[ed] a new benchmark ... for realism in the medium" (Haske).

Whereas the majority of reviewers stressed the game's realism, *Wired*'s Chris Kohler remarked that the "pinpoint-precise motion-capture technology" provided "a glimpse at the future of high-end videogames" and the "hyperrealism we can expect." Kohler's use of the term "hyperrealism" evidently denotes a representation extremely close to "reality," a realism that surpasses the realism of past video games. However, the prefix "hyper," in fact, implies excess. In this way, Kohler's words entail that the "realism" he has in mind, far from promoting an objecthood of physical reality, presents an excess of realism, as the link between material reality and representation disappears. The same idea is implicit in a quotation featured two paragraphs above: If *L.A. Noire*'s Los Angeles "looks exactly the way you imagine it," the question is no longer one of imitating material or historical reality, but rather of approximating an imagined reality. Of course, my deliberations are moving toward the world of simulation and hyperreality here, whose operation is founded on "substituting the signs of the real for the real" (Baudrillard, "Precession" 2).[2]

Even though Baudrillard scholarship has repeatedly cautioned against applying the French poststructuralist's theories to fictional texts, for such a move diminishes the force of his arguments, one might argue that this process of replacing physical reality with signs of "the real" becomes especially pertinent in video games. After all, video games may not be so much "half-real," as Jesper Juul has suggested (*Half-Real*); they may rather be doubly real, creating a simulated environment that in trompe-l'œil-fashion extends to the physical space occupied by the players. This conflation of different layers of reality is also implicit in Espen Aarseth's remark that video games "are allegories of space" which "pretend to portray space in ever more realistic ways but rely on their deviation from reality in order to make the illusion playable" (169). Aarseth pictures a breakdown of accepted relations between the sign and its referent. Apparently, he "leaves the principle of reality intact," for "the difference [between reality and pretense] is always clear" (Baudrillard, "Precession" 3). However, Aarseth actually suggests that videogames rely on the substitution of reality, the creation of a hyperreality. Yet the implied extension of gamespace into material reality goes even further, as McKenzie Wark has noted: "The real world appears as a video arcadia divided into many and varied games.... Games are no longer a pastime, outside or alongside of life. They are now the very form of life, and death, and time itself" (006).

While these deliberations might lead one to conclude that *L.A. Noire*'s seemingly hyperreal character would advocate abandoning any notions of "truth," "original," and "reality," the video game rather seeks to re-create the experience of driving through and living in post–World War II Los Angeles in an authentic way. However, this authenticity gets usurped by the myth of Los Angeles, which frames the city as both a utopian beacon of hope and a dystopic vision of urban decay. Significantly, in the game, players do not simply read or watch the story of a do-gooder opposing the corrupt city, but they perform this (not-so) heroic role and end up in a situation in which to win also means to lose. This paradoxical conclusion, I will suggest, reinforces the mythical role of the City of Angels, which is characterized by dualisms.

Virtual Movement through Hyperreal Los Angeles

L.A. Noire puts players in control of two characters, Cole Phelps and Jack Kelso. Cole is a naïve Ivy League alumnus working for the Los Angeles Police Department, while Jack starts out as an investigator for an insurance company but later becomes one of the district attorney's investigators. Cole functions as the players' avatar for the majority of the game; only in the final three (or four, if an add-on is installed) episodes do they control Jack (the two are controlled alternatingly in the final mission). A number of flashbacks scattered over the narrative elaborate on Cole and Jack's shared past, as they both fought in the Pacific Campaign during World War II. On the one hand, these flashbacks deconstruct Cole's mythical claim to fame, for he received the Silver Star for effectively cowering next to the dead remains of a close friend during an encounter with Japanese troops. On the other hand, the glimpses into the past illustrate how Cole and Jack's relationship in the Pacific Campaign came to a shocking conclusion when one of Cole's men set on fire a cave system functioning as hideaway for Japanese civilians and left dozens of women and children writhing in pain. Cole subsequently ordered his troops to kill the injured, purportedly relieving them of their misery. One of the American soldiers, however, shot Cole in the back, only for Jack to step in, take control of the situation, and tell the troops never to mention the incident. This tension-filled relationship proves influential on the present moment, as Jack and Cole both come to Los Angeles and their paths repeatedly cross during the course of the events depicted in *L.A. Noire*.

These two temporal layers—the recent past of World War II and the (past-turned-)present moment of 1947—are accompanied by a spatial duality that pits Los Angeles against Japan. These dualities, however, quickly disappear, for the Japanese past influences the Californian present, as experienced by Cole and Jack. This combination of spatial and temporal dislocation is typical of Los Angeles fiction, as David Fine has observed: "In Los Angeles fiction the counterpoint is not between the present and past of *a* place but between a Southern California present and a past carried from some *other* place" (16; original italics). Yet *L.A. Noire* complicates these temporal and spatial geographies by highlighting the early twenty-first-century cultural artifact's anchoring in the United States of the post-war years in general and in 1947 Los Angeles, in particular, adding another dimension to the mix. This interrelation between 1947 and the present moment of the early twenty-first century becomes evident when players drive around the sprawling metropolis in one of the historical car models and hear bits from 1947 radio programs and news, such as *The Jack Benny Program* (1932–1955), Ed Herlihy reporting on the Hollywood HUAC hearings, and Ben Grauer informing the public about the effects of nuclear waste. These soundbites are, however, just one element in *L.A. Noire*'s mining of historical reality. Other references to the "real" past include Richard Nixon's campaigning posters scattered across the city and the street layout of the virtual city, which mirrors its real-world sibling.

In addition, since the game's narrative centers on crime in the City of Angels, it makes heavy use of real-world crimes. The "Red Lipstick Murder" case, for example, draws on the killing of Jeanne French, while "The White Shoe Slaying" references the murder of Laura Trelstad, both of which happened in February 1947. All of these cases are based on real-world incidents, but fictionalize the events, blurring historical reality and fiction. This process becomes most apparent in connection with the most prominent real-world case referenced in the game—the Black Dahlia.

In our worldly reality, Elizabeth Short was torn into two pieces and her nude body subsequently left in a vacant lot in Leimart Park. The gruesome reality of the murder stoked the public imagination, which is why the public knowledge of the case is intricately connected to fictional accounts in different media. From speculation linking the Black Dahlia Murder to the murder of Jeanne French to the possible connections between the Dahlia and Lipstick Murders in Chicago, the Black Dahlia case has transcended the sphere of historical reality and entered the realm of myth, a micro-myth that feeds into the larger myth of Los Angeles, in particular the myth of how the years following World War II were plagued by crime, perpetuated by recent movies such as *Hollywoodland* (2006) and *Gangster Squad* (2013), TV shows such as *MOB City* (TNT, 2013),[3] and popular novels such as James Ellroy's L.A. Quartet series (1987–1992), along with the cinematic adaptations of two of the books in the series (1997; 2006). What "really" happened is thus no longer of significance.

Accordingly, *L.A. Noire* can play around with the tale of the Black Dahlia Murder and add another story to the myth. In *L.A. Noire*'s version of the tale, the Black Dahlia Killer did, indeed, also kill Jeanne French's fictional stand-in, Celine Henry, and four other women. *L.A. Noire*, however, does not simply embrace and simultaneously cannibalize and feed into the mythic post–World War II Los Angeles; rather, it highlights the constructedness of this mythic age by offering its interpretation of the story, which not only mixes a fictional form with historical reality, but also introduces anachronistic objects into its world that, historically speaking, would not be seen in 1947 Los Angeles. These anachronisms only add to both the proliferation and conflation of spatial and temporal layers in *L.A. Noire*.

Yet another element may have an even more profound impact on these spatial and temporal levels. Whereas Fine discusses books and motion pictures in his monograph *Imagining Los Angeles* (2000), *L.A. Noire* is a video game. This point is of some significance, for "videogame play offers a very different temporal experience than our other media" (Atkins 251). Playing "has a basic sense of happening *now*," Jesper Juul explains in an essay and continues, "Pressing a key influences the game world, which then logically (and intuitively) has to be happening in the same *now*" ("Introduction" 134; italics in original). As Juul's words indicate, the temporal "conflict between the now of the interaction and the past … of the narrative" ("Games Telling") entails the transgression of spatial dimensions, for "the virtual environment is incorporated into the player's mind as part of her immediate surroundings, within which she can navigate and interact," while, simultaneously, "the player is incorporated … in the virtual environment" (Calleja 169).

As an interface between the physical reality occupied by players' bodies and the virtual space inhabited by their avatar, the PC or video game console becomes an analogy for the virtual cars players drive in virtual L.A. Deborah Lupton has observed that "[w]hen one is driving, one becomes a cyborg, a combination of human and machine" (59). The vehicular extension of the human body (the "becoming-car," if you will) does not create a reality that displaces the realm of physical existence, but this bodily extension is required in order to truly experience Los Angeles. Accordingly, driving around virtual Los Angeles elicits an immersive feeling that, in fact, depends on highlighting the interface between virtual reality and material reality.[4]

When writing about the interrelations between movies and late twentieth-century "reality," Jean Baudrillard argued that "there is an inverse negative relation between the cinema and reality," for the two "evolve in asymptotic line towards one another: cinema attempting to abolish itself in the absolute of reality, the real already long absorbed in cinematographic (or televised) hyperreality" ("Evil Demon" 98). James Donald has echoed this argument, claiming that the city "has been learned as much from novels, pictures and half-remembered films as from diligent walks" (7), as the connection "between the urban fabric, representation and imagination fuzzies up the epistemological and ontological distinctions and ... produces ... the imagined city where we actually live" (10). However, rather than capitulating vis-à-vis the sheer overpowering force of hyperreal Los Angeles, *L.A. Noire*'s self-aware *re*-creation of post–World War II Los Angeles, which consciously garnishes historical reality with anachronisms and combines historical with fictional narratives, draws players' attention to both the construction of the past and the imaginary creation of the city. As Benjamin Fraser notes in *Digital Cities* (2015), "Prose dealing with cities ... allows us to construct the city in our mind's eye and teach us that cities are always imagined this way, that the image of a city is ... always constructed" (25). Yet their medial affordances allow video games such as *L.A. Noire* to add a crucial layer to this message, for they emphasize not only the ways in which cities are, indeed, imagined, but that the ways in which we experience metropolises such as Los Angeles constantly interrelate the imagined city to the built environment of the urban space. The interplay between these apparent dual opposites thus shapes both our experience of urban spaces and the ways in which cities are imagined.

The Good and the Bad

However, the interrelation between the material reality of the city and the city as an imagined space is merely one of numerous dualisms at the heart of Los Angeles. In his review of *L.A. Noire*, Brad Shoemaker proclaimed that the game "isn't [the] kind of game" where players "grab a Tommy gun and wreak havoc in [the] city," as it focuses "on good, clean police work" (n. p.). While the game does, indeed, emphasize the importance and value of "clean police work," players and the characters they control repeatedly find themselves in situations in which the evidence they have collected does, in the end, not matter or in which they are forced to employ not-so-clean measures in order to get the intended (and/or expected) results. This emphasis on corruption is typical of the Los Angeles noir style the game text embraces. Fine's differentiation between classic crime stories and noir fiction is worth quoting at length in this context:

> The classic detective story posits an essentially rational and orderly society; crime is an aberration, usually the act of a single deranged person. The detective, using powers of logic and observation beyond the reader's scope, solves the crime the way an intricate puzzle is solved....
> By contrast, in the brand of detective fiction ... anchored in Los Angeles..., crime is not just an aberrant act—a murder in the vicarage or country estate—but a pervasive feature on the urban landscape, a network that crosses neighborhood, class, and racial divisions. The city itself is corrupt, and the private detective is not there as meliorist assuring readers that society ... is correctable and essentially sound but as a social critic ... battling forces of urban corruption rooted in the rich and powerful. No longer the rational problem-solver, the detective ... digs for answers in the urban muck ... and often comes away without really "solving" anything [119].

While Cole's struggles with the established structures in both Los Angeles and the Los Angeles Police Department are hinted at as early as the tutorial case, they become especially pertinent once he is promoted to Homicide. On their way to their first crime scene, Cole's new partner Rusty Galloway, "a fine lawman of the old school," notes that by being teamed up with Rusty, Cole might "learn something about how a real cop operates." He goes on to stress that "90% of murders are domestic." As a result, it comes as no surprise that when some time later Cole and his partner are informed that their latest female victim "was reported missing by her husband th[at] morning," Rusty suggests, "Just grab the husband, take him downtown, and work him over—we could have this wrapped up by lunchtime." Cole becomes confused and irate and shouts, "What about not making assumptions and going on the evidence?" Players may likewise question the morality of the characters they are asked to cooperate with. In this sense, *L.A. Noire* presents a textbook example of what Miguel Sicart has called "closed ethical game design" (213), for the players' lack of agency asks them to "live the values of the system" and, accordingly, "reflect upon its consequences and meanings" (163).

During his time in Homicide, Cole becomes increasingly disillusioned, a process which culminates when he comes to understand that he and Rusty arrested several purported murderers who, in fact, had not killed anyone. However, Captain James Donnelly makes it abundantly clear that "[t]he department will not survive the scandal if we have to let them all go." Apparently, the LAPD's reputation is much more important than justice. Luckily, Cole figures out that the Black Dahlia Killer is behind all of the crimes and succeeds in uncovering the murderer's identity after a wild paper chase that leads Rusty and Cole to a number of iconic landmarks in (virtual) Los Angeles, including the fountain in Pershing Square, the La Brea Tar Pits, the L.A. County Museum of Art, and the (temporally and spatially misplaced) set of D.W. Griffith's movie *Intolerance*. But identifying and killing the murderer only seems to complicate matters. While Rusty is enthused about solving the "case of the century," Captain Donnelly explains that "there won't be any press briefings or commendations," as the killer "is the half-brother of one of the most highly elected officials in this country."[5] When Cole protests that he is unwilling to cosign the sentencing of innocents, Donnelly elaborates that there will be a "bit of missing evidence at the Grant Jury[,] [a] procedural error here, a mistake there. They'll all be quietly let go." Apparently, this is the way law is enacted in the Los Angeles depicted in the game—Cole (and the player) may act on the symptoms, but the disease plaguing Los Angeles, the urban corruption, cannot be counteracted by a single individual. While *L.A. Noire*'s depiction of the LAPD as a kind of state-sanctioned mafia may be considered pure imagination, corruption undercut the L.A. police force between the 1930s and William H. Parker's appointment in 1950: "The law was where you bought it," James Bultema distraughtly diagnoses in his book on the history of the LAPD and explains that "[c]ross the mayor and you are out" was the established practice for police commissioners during those days (ch. 17). With corruption running wild, many policemen were deeply involved in criminal actions.

This complex crime web becomes most evident in the game's concluding episodes. When Cole uncovers the involvement of several high-ranked people in a crime network, he is suspended from duty for adultery, thus exposing the "higher authority" of the police force as "immoral and manipulative" (Švelch 59). Cole's minor misconduct of sharing the bed with a woman subsequently overshadows the corruption that apparently keeps Los Angeles running.[6] Cole is demoted to the Arson Squad until his review hearing. During his time there, he starts to understand that the crime network he thought he had uncovered is much more complex than he had ever imagined. Through the intermediary of his German lover, Cole sets his fellow World War II veteran Jack Kelso on the trail of a real estate magnate who is part of the crime network. Eventually, the two former soldiers and Cole's lover find themselves in a shootout in the Los Angeles River tunnels. Cole and Jack save the German singer, and Cole just barely gets Jack out of harm's way when the tunnels are flooded, but the water sweeps Cole away. While he is posthumously reinstated, the concluding cinematics clarify that corruption still holds Los Angeles under its sway: Cole's former partner Roy Earle, a slime ball implicated neck-deep in the criminal network, gives the eulogy at Cole's funeral, in which he proclaims that Cole "never lost his faith in the LAPD and the system." Roy clarifies that Cole "fought to expose the evil corruption of the murderous Dr.

Harlan Fontaine and the rapacious property tycoon Leland Monroe." However, the dead Dr. Fontaine and the apparent scapegoat Leland Monroe were merely the tip of the iceberg; the implications of the LAPD in the crime ring have not only been brushed under the carpet, but—so the ending implies—they are still in operation.

The game's narrative thus backs Neon Kelly's assertion that the game "plunges you into the violence, the corruption, and the sadness of post-war Los Angeles." Kelly's emphasis on the pastness of the Los Angeles depicted in *L.A. Noire* hints at nostalgia for this time, a seemingly simpler time when things, however, were not so simple; a time of corruption and rampant racism (as evidenced by the Zoot Suit Riots in 1943, the first of many major race riots to erupt in the City of Angels[7]). Nostalgia, as Baudrillard stressed, is a yearning for a "lost referential" that never was but always could have been ("History" 43). However, implicitly, this "what if"-scenario played out in *L.A. Noire* segues into reality, for the game's narrative ends with the hero's sacrificial death and the corrupt system still in place. In this way, the video game suggests that the criminal network running Los Angeles is not a thing of the past. As the wife of a B-movie producer remarks at one point, "This is Hollywood—there's always a deal to be done!" Thus, the video game's depiction of the criminal undercurrents of Los Angeles not only draws on fictional representations of the City of Angeles, but also nurtures the utopian dreams and promises invested into the city further and thus highlights the paradoxes at the heart of Los Angeles. As *L.A. Noire*'s opening voiceover puts it against the visual backdrop of a Western shoot that contrasts the pro-filmic reality of a fake horse and a background painting with the realism constructed by the camera: "The city of dreams, where Hollywood will shape the thoughts and desires of the entire planet."

Playing to Win ... and to Lose?

Beyond exposing the paradoxes defining Los Angeles, *L.A. Noire*'s tragic ending counters established notions about the workings of digital narratives. Marie-Laure Ryan has, for example, argued that "interactors would have to be out of their mind ... to want to submit themselves to the fate of a heroine who commits suicide as the result of a love affair turned bad." Jesper Juul has advanced a more nuanced understanding of tragic endings, suggesting that "the question of game tragedy is not either/or" (*Art of Failure* 99). In his book *The Art of Failure* (2013), Juul discusses the ending of *Red Dead Redemption* (2012), a game that "can only be completed by letting the protagonist die" (103), and highlights two particularities about the game's conclusion: first, the avatar-protagonist "dies for a cause" (105). Second, players "are powerless spectators to his murder" (105), as the protagonist is killed in a cut-scene—when players do not control the character.

L.A. Noire's final hours play out the players' movement away from identification with Cole in a similar way: Cole is exposed as an adulterer, then players assume control of Jack Kelso, and, eventually, Cole's death is part of a cut-scene. Players do not have the power to avert Cole's tragic exit, as the game subjects player agency to narrative needs in an attempt to transform Cole's heroic actions in the present into a compensation for his past failures. As such, Cole's death signposts his failure to ameliorate life in (past-turned-)present-day Los Angeles. To L.A. Noire's players, to win the game thus means to kill the protagonist and to accept the paradoxes of virtual Los Angeles. The final moments of the playing experience thus come to mirror the dualisms characteristic of Los Angeles, the shiny surface and the dirt beneath.

When virtual cities began to feed the public imagination in the early 1990s, they were imagined as a means for "decontaminating ... urban landscapes, redeeming them, saving them ... from the diesel smoke of courier and post-office trucks, ... from billboards, trashy and pretentious architecture, hour-long freeway commutes" (Benedikt 3). Twenty years later, however, L.A. Noire had left these utopian ideas behind and came to embrace the filthy, polluted, and unpleasant aspects of metropolitan life. Billboards across the virtual city feature realty tycoon Leland Monroe's smirk and promote his company's latest development projects, whose business strategy squarely rests on the displacement of the poor. Getting from the corner of Olympic Boulevard and Santa Fe Avenue to Hollywood Boulevard will take players (if they do not skip the driving) about twenty, uneventful minutes in real time. These rather dull minutes allow "you [to] really get a feel for the game's vivid urban landscape: the architecture, the cars, the fashion, the light, the mood. You'll drive past a diner and see people inside, eating hamburgers and reading newspapers" (A. Kelly). Indeed, spending time in (virtual) cars mirrors the Los Angeles experience, in which cars act as extensions of the human body. Similarly, driving from Beverly Hills to the inner city feels like entering an entirely different place, as the natural, green surroundings are gradually replaced by gray brick blocks. Indeed, L.A. Noire's Los Angeles is at a far remove from the clean virtual city imagined in the early 1990s. However, the uncovering of the city's dark sides simmering beneath the superficial glitter makes the gameworld so much more attractive and immersive. This aspect was diagnosed by numerous critics after the game's release. In his review for *Videogamer*, Neon Kelly, for example, opined, "As you stoop to inspect the naked body of a mutilated young woman, as you shakedown a gambling racket in a dusky backroom, as you pick through the skeletal cinders of a burnt-out building... as you do these things, you'll silently admit the truth:

you don't want to stop the bleakness, you want to *revel* in it" (italics and ellipses in original).

This reveling in the city's darkness highlights misery, sorrow, and despair as part and parcel of the attraction emanating from the City of Angels. As Kevin R. McNamara puts it in his introduction to *The Cambridge Companion to the Literature of Los Angeles* (2010), "Los Angeles is less a city, county, or 'metropolitan statistical area' than a state of being" which may represent "grace, fear, emergency, or exception, depending on whom one reads" and which draws its significance and meaning from "the collective imagination of utopia, dystopia, and, more recently, the urban future" (1). *L.A. Noire* does not simply highlight these interrelated images of progress and decay in its depiction of Los Angeles; the game also underlines how the popular imagination feeds our experience of the city. Los Angeles, the game suggests, has a dark and dirty undercurrent, but if you are willing to ignore these realities, you may build your future among the city's refuse.

Notes

1. See, for example, the website *L.A. Noire: IRL* (http://www.beneluxe.net/LA/index.html) for comparisons between in-game images and real-world photographs.

2. With only a few exceptions, game scholars have been quick to point out that the simulation Baudrillard discusses is not the simulation they have in mind when employing the word. Noah Wardrip-Fruin and Pat Harrigan, for example, stress that "[t]he simulation discussed by [Baudrillard] is a cultural phenomenon, not a computational one—and as such is fully existent in old media as well as new" (71). In one of the rare positive assessments of the values of Baudrillard's theories to game studies, James Campbell notes, "[I]t is precisely because Baudrillard's version of simulation is a cultural rather than a merely digital phenomenon that it has important implications for computer game studies" (187). As he continues, "Ludology does occasionally fall into the trap of divorcing games from the cultures that produce them; if these cultures include simulation as a nondigital condition as well as a digital occurrence, it need not mean that discourse about the digital must limit itself to simulation as a pure feat of computer engineering" (187–88).

3. Real-life gangster Mickey Cohen is the main antagonist in both *MOB City* and *Gangster Squad*. In *L.A. Noire*, he appears as Cole's main foe during his time in the Vice Department.

4. A similar process is at work in the more recent iterations of the *Grand Theft Auto* franchise. Driving around virtual cities and listening to the local radio stations undoubtedly are important elements in immersing players in the virtual cities the game's narratives are set in. However, there is a key difference between *L.A. Noire* and the *GTA* games. The Los Angeles streets in *GTA V* (2013), for example, are filled with action and players will from time to time miss some of the gameworld's minute details if they do not travel around virtual Los Angeles by foot. *L.A. Noire*, on the other hand, very much forces players to drive around the virtual city, thus highlighting the significance of the car to imagining and experiencing Los Angeles.

5. In the context of mixing of historical reality and fiction, it may be noted that the killer's family name, Mason, points to Lowell Blake Mason, the Federal Trade Commissioner under President Harry Truman from 1945 to 1956.

6. The case in question is tellingly called "Manifest Destiny," transforming the paradoxes with which Cole is confronted into an allegory about the paradoxes that define the American national project.

7. Of course, one should not forget about the Chinatown (or simply "Chinese") Massacre

48 Part I: California Under Construction

of 1871, which "led contemporary newspapers to label the city a 'bloodstained Eden'" (Rasmussen).

WORKS CITED

Aarseth, Espen. "Allegories of Space: The Question of Spatiality in Computer Games." *Cybertext Yearbook 2000*. Ed. Markku Eskelinen and Raine Koskimaa. Jyväskylä: University of Jyväskylä, 2001. 152–71. Ebook.
Atkins, Barry. "Killing Time: Time Past, Time Present and Time Future in *Prince of Persia: The Sands of Time*." *Videogame, Player, Text*. Ed. Geoff King and Tanya Krzywinska. Manchester: Manchester University Press, 2007. 237–53. Print
Baudrillard, Jean. "The Evil Demon of Images." 1984. Trans. Paul Patton and Paul Foss. 1987. *The Jean Baudrillard Reader*. Ed. Steve Readhead. New York: Columbia University Press, 2008. 84–98. Print.
_____. "History: A Retro Scenario." 1978. *Simulacra and Simulation*. Trans. Sheila Faria Glaser. Ann Arbor: University of Michigan Press, 1994. 43–48. Print.
_____. "The Precession of Simulacra." 1978. *Simulacra and Simulation*. Trans. Sheila Faria Glaser. Ann Arbor: University of Michigan Press, 1994. 1–42. Print.
Benedikt, Michael. "Introduction." *Cyberspace: First Steps*. Ed. Michael Benedikt. Cambridge: MIT Press, 1991. 1–26. Print.
Bultema, James A. *Guardians of Angels: A History of the Los Angeles Police Department*. West Conshohocken, PA: Infinity, 2013. Kindle.
Calleja, Gordon. *In-Game: From Immersion to Incorporation*. Cambridge: MIT Press, 2011. Print.
Campbell, James. "Just Less Than Total War: Simulating World War II as Ludic Nostalgia." *Playing the Past: History and Nostalgia in Video Games*. Ed. Zach Whalen and Laurie N. Taylor. Nashville: Vanderbilt University Press, 2008. 183–200. Print.
Davis, Mike. *Ecology of Fear: Los Angeles and the Imagination of Disaster*. 1998. New York: Metropolitan, 2013. Ebook.
_____. *Planet of Slums*. London: Verso, 2006. Print.
Donald, James. *Imagining the Modern City*. Minneapolis: University of Minnesota Press, 1999. Print.
Fine, David. *Imagining Los Angeles: A City in Fiction*. 2000. Reno: University of Nevada Press, 2004. Print.
Fraser, Benjamin. *Digital Cities: The Interdisciplinary Future of the Urban Geo-Humanities*. Basingstoke: Palgrave Macmillan, 2015. Kindle.
Gangster Squad (2013).
Haske, Steve. "*L.A. Noire* Review." *Cheat Code Central*. 17 May 2011. Web. 28 January 2016.
Hollywoodland (2006).
Hurel, Matthieu. "Test de *L.A. Noire*." *Gamecult*. 26 May 2011. Web. 28 January 2016.
Juul, Jesper. *The Art of Failure: An Essay on the Pain of Playing Video Games*. Cambridge: MIT Press, 2013. Print.
_____. "Games Telling Stories? A Brief Note on Games and Narratives." *Game Studies* 1.1 (2001): n. pag. Web. 23 May 2011.
_____. *Half-Real: Video Games Between Real Rules and Fictional Worlds*. Cambridge: MIT Press, 2005. Print.
_____. "Introduction to Game Time." *First Person: New Media as Story, Performance, and Game*. Ed. Pat Harrigan and Noah Wardrip-Fruin. Cambridge: MIT Press, 2004. 131–42. Print.
Kelly, Andy. "The City of *L.A. Noire*." *PC Gamer*. 25 November 2015. Web. 28 January 2016.
Kelly, Neon. "*LA Noire* Review." *Videogamer*. 16 May 2011. Web. 28 January 2016.
Kohler, Chris. "Review: Searching for Meaning in the Faces of *L.A. Noire*." *Wired*. Web. 16 May 2011. 28 January 2016.
L.A. Noire. Team Bondi, 2011. Xbox 360. Video game.
Lupton, Deborah. "Monsters in Metal Cocoons: 'Road Rage' and Cyborg Bodies." *Body & Society* 5.1 (1999): 57–72. *SAGE Journals*. Web.

McNamara, Kevin R. "Introduction: Landmarks." *The Cambridge Companion to the Literature of Los Angeles.* Ed. Kevin R. McNamara. New York: Cambridge University Press, 2010. 1–11. Print.
MOB City (TNT, 2013). TV show.
Rasmussen, Cecilia. "A Forgotten Hero from a Night of Disgrace." *Los Angeles Times* 16 May 1999. Web. 12 October 2016.
Ryan, Marie-Laure. "Beyond Myth and Metaphor: The Case of Narrative in Digital Media." *Game Studies* 1.1 (2001): n. pag. Web. 23 May 2011.
Shoemaker, Brad. "*L.A. Noire* Review." *Giant Bomb.* 16 May 2011. Web. 28 January 2016.
Sicart, Miguel. *The Ethics of Computer Games.* Cambridge: MIT Press, 2009. Print.
Švelch, Jaroslav. "The Good, The Bad, and The Player: The Challenges to Moral Engagement in Single-Player Avatar-Based Video Games." *Ethics and Game Design: Teaching Values through Play.* Ed. Karen Schrier and David Gibson. Hershey, PA: IGI Global, 2010. 52–68. Print.
Videogameszone. "*L.A. Noire.*" *Videogameszone.de.* 20 May 2011. Web. 28 January 2016.
Wardrip-Fruin, Noah, and Pat Harrigan. "Critical Simulation." *First Person: New Media as Story, Performance, and Game.* Ed. Noah Wardrip-Fruin and Pat Harrigan. Cambridge: MIT Press, 2004. 71–72. Print.
Wark, McKenzie. *Gamer Theory.* Cambridge: Harvard University Press, 2007. Print.

"Feed the hole"
Alienation, Neo-Marxism and the Real in Richard Kelly's Southland Tales

Elizabeth Lowry

What happens when we are overtaken by our excesses? What happens when we are consumed by consumerism? How will the world *really* end—and is it worth saving? Can we, a nation of what Hunter S. Thompson once referred to as "killer whores,"[1] be saved by a counter-culture comprised of porn-dependent ideologues? By considering the twisted ethos of a cell of Los Angeles Neo-Marxists, I explore how such questions become central themes in Richard Kelly's *Southland Tales*.

In Kelly's *Southland Tales*, a darkly comic sci-fi thriller, it is 2008: a year in which nuclear bombs dropped on Texas have precipitated World War Three. The film opens with the grainy lopsided footage of a home movie depicting a Fourth of July barbecue. Family figures sit on a lawn drinking beer, eating hotdogs, and watching their children play. And then, all at once, the camera travels to an image of a mushroom cloud. The people at the barbecue are stunned, staring at the brown cloud growing bigger and bigger in the summer sky—a clear signal that the end is nigh. Following this scene, we learn that an updated Patriot Act has given rise to a government surveillance program known as U.S.-IDent. U.S.-IDent, described as "the brainchild of the Republican party," controls the Internet, and its expansion is promoted by the Republican presidential candidate, Robert ("Bobby") Frost.[2] Frost's wife, Nana Mae, presides over U.S.-IDent, always clad in black dresses reminiscent of those of the evil queen from Disney's *Snow White*. U.S.-IDent employees work in an enormous, sterile-looking open plan office and wear white windbreakers that look like hazmat gear. These employees operate both as scientists who will find cures to the myriad social diseases plaguing America and as factory workers who—on command—engage in rudimentary calisthenics at their workstations. Such is the state of American political and civic life.

The film's opening sequence is narrated by Pilot Abilene[3] (Justin Timberlake), a disfigured Iraq war veteran who outlines the genesis of World War Three, U.S.-IDent, and a series of shady international deals for Fluid Karma, an alternative fuel source. Abilene explains that the trouble with this fuel source (likened to the "soul" of the planet) is that its extraction is causing the Earth to rotate more slowly on its axis. This deceleration in the Earth's rotation causes people to go mad—and also heralds an impending environmental disaster. (Fluid Karma, in a more distilled form, is also a highly sought-after street drug that allegedly endows its users with clairvoyant and telepathic powers.) Moreover, Fluid Karma poses another problem—its extraction has caused a rift in the spacetime continuum over Lake Mead in Nevada, which will have a catastrophic (though not fully explained) effect on human life.

Abilene's soft, measured voiceover comes in sharp contrast to its accompanying imagery: A lurid series of banners, talking heads, screens within screens, and headlines catalogue the events leading up to World War Three. The war has been sponsored by Bud Lite and Hustler, whose ads adorn the army tanks rolling through the streets. Eventually, the camera pans out to Abilene, who sits at a gun turret above Venice Beach alternately reading from the Book of Revelation and quoting from T.S. Eliot's "Hollow Men." Two of Eliot's best-known lines read: "this is the way the world ends—not with a bang but with a whimper." However, Abilene changes the order of the verse's final words, declaring that the "world ends not with a whimper but with a bang." While T.S. Eliot envisioned the world fading away as a result of all humanity having been crushed beneath the weight of its own meaninglessness, Abilene sees humankind as having taken an active role in its own destruction. In an effort to find meaning through excessive consumption, human beings have ensured an inevitable disaster: the world's dramatic demise.

Having set this unhappy scene, Abilene begins to recount more intimate stories—personal narratives of various Los Angeles denizens. Abilene describes an actor, Boxer Santaros (Dwayne Johnson) and his lover, a porn star named Krysta Now (Sarah Michelle Gellar). Santaros and Krysta have written a screenplay together, entitled *The Power*. But while at work producing *The Power*, the lovers find themselves embroiled in a conspiracy involving access to Fluid Karma. Santaros will eventually realize that he has traveled through time via the rift in the spacetime continuum and that he is in fact his future self. Santaros and Krysta's stories matter because, in their screenplay, the two of them have essentially predicted "how the world ends" signaling that the boundaries between fact and fiction have become impossibly blurred.

Finally, Abilene highlights another element of this apocalyptic scenario: a cell of Neo-Marxists who are determined to disrupt the 2008 election. The presidential race is in full swing, and an anarchic angst pervades the city, perpetuated by the Neo-Marxists, whose signature slogan "Feed the Hole," often appears as an accompaniment to stenciled images of Karl Marx.[4] Significantly, Neo-Marxist sympathizers are invited to feed literal holes: a series of secret dropboxes intended for the delivery of information serving to undermine the conservative agenda. However, viewers only see one such dropbox, which is embedded within an image of Marx situated above a toilet in the ladies' room of a bar.[5] The slogan "Feed the Hole" suggests that in an imperfect (capitalist) world, rising up against one's oppressor is a moral imperative— however, the slogan leaves us to wonder what it means to be an anarchist within a social system that is already unraveling. Who are the Neo-Marxists and what exactly do they want? I argue that the Neo-Marxists are, in Slavoj Žižek's terms, a "symptom" of late monopoly capitalism,[6] and that the "hole" referenced in the slogan is, in turn, a symptom of Neo-Marxist ideology. The "hole" is the void, the sense of lack that tells us that we desire something, that we need something—but we do not know what. And if indeed this is the case, how do we "Feed the Hole"?

Neo-Marxism as a Symptom of Late Monopoly Capitalism

In the diegetic world of *Southland Tales* an enormous wage gap has concentrated power in the hands of the über-wealthy, leaving Los Angeles to devolve into the kind of dystopian nightmare that the nineteenth-century economist and philosopher Karl Marx struggled to avert. In more directly Marxian terms, capitalism has bred a widespread sense of "alienation" (Marx *Economic* 60). That is, workers are no longer working for themselves—they work to make the ruling class wealthy and to ensure that the ruling class stays in power. An "alienated" worker finds that their labor is meaningless insofar as it is disconnected from their personal life. As cogs in the capitalist machine, workers lack autonomy and (in such a system), social inequality abounds, as does a prevailing sense of discontent. Because of this feeling of disenfranchisement, people turn to crime—either out of material necessity or in a desperate bid for power. In the Los Angeles of *Southland Tales*, crime is rife.

In her work on constabulary rhetoric, Jordynn Jack discusses Kenneth Burke's observation that establishment figures typically attempt to resolve crime in two significant ways: first via a process of "symbolic bridging and merging" and second by "law making" (Burke qtd. in Jack 72). When Burke speaks of "symbolic bridging and merging," he suggests that the establishment attempts to cope with the alienated subject by encouraging him to "bridge the gap between his private impulses and ... social norms" (Burke 179–80). That is, Burke uses the metaphor "bridging the gap" to describe the subject's perceived need to transcend his situation (Burke 180). According to Burke, in Western culture, such "transcendence" is believed to be attainable through various forms of ritual behavior—namely, psychoanalysis. Through the ritual of psychoanalysis, one is expected to cultivate a sense of self-awareness that will help one to adapt to the status quo. Hence, Burke argues that "bridging the gap" is a form of social coercion. And in *Southland Tales*, the notion of coercion becomes imminent as the "establishment" floods the streets with Urban Peace Units (UPUs). Urban Peace Officers act as law-enforcers as well as security guards and surveillance operatives, but the idea of a "Peace Unit" is an example of ironic branding: decked out in combat gear, the Peace Officers do not look in the slightest bit peaceful, and do not seem likely to calm an agitated populace. But there are other ways of soothing social anxiety and helping people to adapt to their changing environment: the establishment promises yet more goods and capital as well as a vast and vapid entertainment complex to distract the public from its woes.

Evidently, the Neo-Marxists of *Southland Tales* have no desire to "bridge the gap" between their personal impulses and the world around them. Instead they hope to challenge the status quo. The Neo-Marxist leadership consists of porn producer Cyndi Pinziki (Nora Dunn), and her cronies, Zora Carmichaels (Cheri Oteri), Dream (Amy Poehler), and Dion (Wood Harris). As self-proclaimed counter-cultural agents, the Neo-Marxists claim to despise all emblems of the capitalist establishment, particularly its methods of law enforcement. However, the Neo-Marxists are unable to effectively expiate their feelings of alienation and to productively express their animus toward an aggressively capitalist social order because that social order is already in the process of collapse. The Neo-Marxists need capitalism in order to exist as an effective counter-culture. Or, arguably, Neo-Marxism and capitalism are parts of the same system. In *Southland Tales*, this symbiotic relationship is highlighted by the Neo-Marxists' involvement in pornography—and is significant insofar as scholars have argued that the porn industry is an inevitable product of a consumption-driven culture (Restivo and Cante 162). In *Southland Tales*, the porn industry—an icon of objectification and abuse—is represented by historically oppressed subjects: women and African Americans—that is, Cyndi, Zora, Dream, and Dion. Since the Neo-Marxist cell is funded by porn money, the material existence of the Neo-Marxists is literally reliant on the system that they purport to fight.

As the capitalist order crumbles, the Neo-Marxists find that they must resort to ever more dramatic counter-cultural tactics in order to draw attention to their cause. This means engaging in increasingly risky criminal behavior. However, the Neo-Marxists are unable to create a sense of political exigency because their efforts are rendered meaningless in the face of the apocalyptic atmosphere pervading Los Angeles. As a result, the Neo-Marxists find themselves dispossessed not only from the capitalist mainstream, but also from themselves—they simply cannot keep up with what is taking place in the world around them; they cannot "sync with cultural change" (Jack 74). As capitalist subjects, the Neo-Marxists are doomed to repeat a series of fruitless attempts to make meaning within a broken system. Such attempts to make meaning seem to echo the counter-cultural nostalgia following the gradual implosion of the 1960s-era hippie revolution. Following the turn of the twenty-first century, the dialectic between establishment and revolutionary has become increasingly blurred. This uncomfortable relationship between the status quo and anarchy is further symbolized by the "twins," Ronald and Roland Taverner. Roland is an UPU officer who becomes friends with Boxer Santaros, while his brother Ronald is an itinerant rogue. Later, we discover that they are actually the same person. Ronald and Roland are the anarchist and the "peacemaker" bound up into one entity.

Referencing Jacques Lacan's psychoanalytic theories, Žižek asserts that we (as subjects) make meaning within broken systems of communication by developing a "symptom"—that is, a psychological coping mechanism—a way to "avoid madness" (74–75). The "symptom" Žižek says, is intended to "fill out a void" in the Other—the Other being the politically, economically, and socially dominant "Establishment" culture that repeatedly fails to serve its subjects (74–75). Žižek's theory of the symptom suggests that essentially we cannot help behaving the way we do. We may be aware that our behavior does not make sense or that it is destructive, but we have been socially conditioned to continue replicating certain kinds of behavior because of our unconscious desires. When Žižek says "enjoy your symptom" he means that since you are complicit in the production and manifestation of your symptom, you might as well enjoy it because it will somehow always be there—a part of you that you can neither identify, nor control (Bogost n.p.).

In one of *Southland Tales'* most memorable scenes, Pilot Abilene actually tries to "enjoy his symptom." Sex, violence, drugs, and alcohol have become the spiritual conditions that define his daily life. His poignant awareness of this is conveyed to the film's audience by a bizarre musical number in which Abilene—high on Fluid Karma—lip synchs to The Killers "All the Things I've Done" in an arcade on the Santa Monica Boardwalk. The sequence begins with Abilene drinking a Budweiser. He wears dog tags, army fatigues and a white T-shirt that looks as if it is stained with blood around the neck and shoulders. Meanwhile, a troupe of dancers (all Marilyn Monroe look-alikes clad in tiny red and white nurse costumes) do a series of high kicks while lying across pinball machines, and whirl past Abilene who seems to acquire fresh cans of beer simply by wishing them into existence. The Marilyn Monroe look-alikes spark a sense of nostalgia. Each dancer is identical, carefully made up to give the impression of a single Marilyn, who, like Warhol's screen prints—is repeated over and over. When one woman lies across a pinball machine and does a high kick, the others follow suit in rapid succession—the effect being that of a hall of funhouse mirrors. Thus, both Abilene and the audience are caught up in the inexorable force of the capitalist plan—one that continually reproduces and replicates itself. Capitalist values must be continuously reinscribed and, as Jameson suggests, such reinscription via repetition is in constant demand: "The atomized or serial 'public' of mass culture wants to see the same thing over and over again, hence the urgency of the generic structure and the generic signal" (14). Mass culture embraces genre-specific art forms because they are purpose-driven. That is, content is less important than form—or the production of the genre itself. The content is merely a means by which the genre can be satisfied. Genre demands repetition, but repetition does not necessarily imply an "original" as it might have in a pre-capitalist era: "for Jean Baudrillard, for example, the repetitive structure of what he calls the simulacrum (that is, the reproduction of 'copies' which have no original) characterizes the commodity production of consumer capitalism and marks our object world with an unreality and a free-floating absence of referent ... utterly unlike anything experienced in any earlier social formation" (Jameson 12). The absence of an original referent suggests a lack of meaning and context—but the consistently repeated image creates its own meaning—one that is both purpose-driven and culturally specific, designed to manipulate consumers in ways that advance a commodity-driven social agenda.

But Abilene is too aware of how he is being manipulated to enjoy his symptom. At first, Abilene appears to be having fun, but then he begins to look troubled, tugging at his dog tags and raising his middle finger to the camera. As the invigorating rock number ends, a softer eerier tune begins, and Abilene looks dejected—as if something were weighing on his mind. When high on Fluid Karma, one is supposed to be able to enjoy one's symptom fully—but Abilene cannot. Instead, he is troubled by an awareness that there is a part of himself he cannot escape, a part of himself that is oddly generic. Like Abilene, the Neo-Marxists oscillate between a painful awareness of the hopelessness of their situation and a dogged adherence to their ideology. Thus, as a cultural phenomenon, the Neo-Marxist underground emerges as a "symptom" of a "lack" in the "Other"—or in this case, as a symptom of a capitalist plutocracy defined by relentless discourses of fear and fantasy.

The "Hole" as a Symptom of Neo-Marxism

Inside the Neo-Marxists' loft, the camera lingers on a chair that is shaped like a giant left hand. The hand is open, palm up, with the fingers curving as though they are holding an invisible object. The word "IDEATH" has been crudely painted across the fingers of the hand—a DEA on the middle fingers, and a TH on the thumb. (This implies a reference to U.S.-IDent—the surveillance complex fronted by the Republican Party—along with an embedded critique of the Drug Enforcement Agency.) The walls behind the chair are covered with graffiti, including a giant bright blue painting of Karl Marx's head. There's a fluorescent orange triangle on Marx's forehead, inside of which is an eye. This same icon appears on the dollar bill, where the eye of the pyramid symbolizes the eye of God. The pyramid and eye are part of the "Great Seal of America," which was created in 1782. The thirteen steps on the pyramid symbolize the thirteen original states of America. On the dollar bill, the thirteen steps of the pyramid suggest that the pyramid is unfinished, signifying the country's potential ("Symbols"). However, in *Southland Tales*, the pyramid on Marx's forehead is complete, suggesting that America has exhausted its potential. These symbols imbue the Karl Marx icon with additional layers of meaning that can be used to code and recode an updated 2008 Neo-Marxist vision.[7]

Marx's head looks like a screenprint made from a stencil that has no doubt been reproduced on many walls. Stencils make for easy replication. The proliferation of these Marxian images acts as propaganda to counter the capitalist images with which we are bombarded daily—images of sex, cars, and energy drinks. Capitalist images function to spur consumption—they awaken our desires and then convince us that those desires can be sated by whatever product is being sold. Ironically, mass-produced images of Marx fulfill the same function. The images of Marx both imitate a capitalist mode of production and subvert it: Marx's head on a poster advertises the revolution, meaning that the revolution itself becomes a commodity. Images of Marx's head repeatedly seduce and recruit, their function being to produce more Marxists—to imbue the Neo-Marxist underground with as much a sense of inevitability as the capitalist machine.

Drawing on the scholarship of Guy Debord, Jameson writes, "the ultimate form of commodity reification in contemporary consumer society is precisely the image itself" (5). The image is the primary means by which we turn ideas and behaviors into objects and objects into commodities—or sexualized "Others." Jameson continues: "the new model car is essentially an image for other people to have of us, and we consume, less the thing itself, than its abstract idea, open to all the libidinal investments ingeniously arrayed for us by advertising" (5). In *Southland Tales*, the notion of a car as an abstract idea of who we wish ourselves to be is stripped away by a commercial depicting two anthropomorphic Hummers engaging in sex. The product no longer stands in for the "Other" as the unexpressed desires of the capitalist subject, rather it has begun to eclipse the capitalist subject altogether—just as identical images of Marx's head are used as placeholders for potential Neo-Marxist recruits.

As subjects of late monopoly capitalist society, we are unable to understand our dependency on the "Other" because we are constructed by it, and implicated within it. Our subjectivity is determined by our unconscious, but our unconscious constitutes what Lacan described as a "lack"—in other words, we cannot know our unconscious and therefore we cannot understand our relationship to the "Other."[8] An inability to articulate our relationship to the "Other" becomes the "hole" that challenges our subjectivity, and our agency as cultural subjects (Žižek 116). Neo-Marxists are aware of this "hole" insofar as they are aware of the communicative failures of capitalism and they realize that the "hole" can never be sated. What they do not realize, however, is that the "hole" itself is an integral part of who we are—more specifically, evidence of our imbrication within the capitalist system. We feed the "hole" primarily through sex and violence because we are aware that somehow the "hole" is related to the ineffable—to a primal or (or indeed transcendent) state of being—a sense of meaning that exists beyond our perception. Put another way, the "hole" signifies an unrealized and repressed sense of need. For instance, in his *Atlantic* article on the bizarre allure of the McDonald's McRib sandwich, Ian Bogost explains that our desire for the McRib is not about the McRib itself—but that eating at McDonald's addresses a hidden desire: "McDonald's sells what it does not sell: the conditions of predictability, affordability, and chemico-machinic automated cookery that make its very business viable. When we eat at McDonald's we don't eat its food—Quarter Pounders or Big Macs or what have you—so much as we consume the mechanical predictability of its overall offering" (n.p.). In the same vein, I argue that Neo-Marxism "sells what it does not sell." That is, a potential recruit's attraction to the Neo-Marxist underground is not necessarily spurred by an affinity for Marxist philosophy, rather by the promise of a potential solution to the existential angst that afflicts us all.

Žižek argues that the psychoanalyst hopes to reach our hidden desires because these hidden desires manifest as "symptoms." We may treat the symptom as problematic, but in reality, the symptom is our best coping mechanism within rigid, and often punitive social systems (74). However, Neo-Marxism has failed at being representative of a "symptom" because the impending apocalypse means that the "Other" no longer designates lack—rather, it has become lack itself. There is no "void" in the "Other" to "fill out" because the "Other" has collapsed into the void. If the lack or the "void" in the "Other" can be equated to the Neo-Marxist "hole" and the hole subsumes all, then the hole cannot be "fed" via the production of a symptom. The Neo-Marxist dropbox in the bathroom wall leads to nothing and nowhere.

Which Symptom Is Real?

There is a bigger threat to the people of Los Angeles than nuclear attacks and widespread anarchy, but no one (except maybe for Abilene) seems to be aware of it. A fissure in the spacetime continuum could literally result in the world ending (in T.S. Eliot's words) "not with a bang, but a whimper." This idea—coupled with that of not being able to stay in step with cultural change—is emblematized in a scene where Boxer Santaros (who has been sent through time) realizes that he can never catch up with himself as he crawls through the desert after his future-self clone. Santaros is not aware of being a time traveler—only of odd coincidences that give him an unsettling sense of déjà vu. Aptly, the narrative trope of the spacetime continuum becomes a metaphor for the alienation that arises when our social apparatus cannot keep up with cultural change.

Divested of the bikinis and lingerie she usually wears for her film and TV spots, Krysta sports a baggy blue shirt and pair of horn-rimmed spectacles. She looks serious. Her tone is earnest: "Scientists are saying that the future is going to be far more futuristic than they originally predicted." When Krysta Now says so, she is suggesting that we are too limited to imagine the future's possibilities. She is talking about the Real—that is, that which exists beyond language and outside of all symbolic systems; the Real cannot be imagined, articulated, or perceived. Krysta's demonstration of the limits of language in conveying the meaning of the term "futuristic," is compounded by her earnestness—and underscored by a sense of the absurd that Kelly uses to elicit laughter from his audience.

Here, Santaros and his girlfriend Krysta Now invite UPU officer Ronald Taverner into Krysta's home, where Santaros explains the concept of the screenplay he and Krysta have written together:

> SANTAROS: I play an LAPD cop who isn't who he seems. He's a paranoid schizophrenic who has a supernatural gift. He sees things. He senses a change.
> KRYSTA: Crime suddenly skyrockets for no apparent reason. The world is coming to an end. He's the only one who can see the truth.
> TAVERNER: What's the truth?
> SANTAROS: My character, he realizes that the apocalyptic crime is because of global deceleration. He realizes that the rotation of the earth is slowing down … each day, disrupting the chemical equilibrium of the human brain.

As the narrative unfolds, the viewer realizes that Santaros is entering the world of his own screenplay—which is, in fact, reality. He and Taverner acknowledge that they have met somewhere before—and Taverner shares characteristics with Jericho Cane, the protagonist in Santaros and Krysta's screenplay. As fact and fiction begin to blur, not only does Santaros enter an already anticipated future, but he echoes (and comments on) the past via elements of *The Power* (Santaros and Krysta's screenplay) as well as the storyline for *Southland Tales*, both of which allude to a 1999 Arnold Schwarzenegger movie entitled *End of Days*. (For instance, *End of Days* involves a rift in the spacetime continuum, a climate of widespread anarchy and a main character named Jericho Cane). In some respects, *Southland Tales* counters the *End of Days* and the biblical apocalypse by suggesting that the devil will not cause our demise, we will do it ourselves through our inconceivable excesses—our sense of "lack" that becomes the "Real" (Žižek 162). But what are the implications of an apocalypse that fails to be religiously charged? We hope to make sense of the apocalypse through religion because then (at least) the End of Days would be meaningful—it would suggest that there is divine plan; that we lived and died for a reason.

Conclusion

Alienation and dispossession do not emerge from discourses of labor and materialism alone, "but from the symbolic or spiritual conditions of a social order that is no longer in sync with cultural change" (Jack 74). Kelly's dystopic portrait of Los Angeles reveals a populace that is so distracted by images of sex and violence, that it simply does not know how to think, what to believe, or how to react to genuine chaos. Traumatized by recent nuclear attacks, the American people participate in an apocalypse of sorts, but this apocalypse is quite different from the (almost) comfortingly familiar apocalypse described in the Book of Revelation. How can we make meaning of our lives on Judgment Day? Capitalism is certainly not the answer, but then neither is its opposite. This cultural change is so profound that nobody can "sync" with it (Jack 74). Thus, in *Southland Tales* we repeatedly see the failure of the Neo-Marxists to draw meaningful attention to the social failures of capitalism. Hence, the concept of "Feeding the Hole" comes to signify not only our unavoidable lack of awareness and our symptomatic desire to account for what seems to be missing, but the way in which "feeding the hole" only seems to increase the hole's appetite—the hole must be fed still more and more, until it literally consumes itself.

Notes

1. This term appears in Hunter S. Thompson's *Kingdom of Fear* as part of a critique of American involvement in the Middle East (Thompson 66).
2. Senator Bobby Frost's campaign motto, "the road less traveled," is a reference to ex-poet laureate Robert Frost's poem "Stopping by the Woods on a Snowy Evening." The irony of Senator Frost's motto is that he does not "take the road less traveled"—rather his campaign is predictably derivative of so many preceding this one, signaling servitude to corporate interests, greed, and fear-mongering. The "road less traveled" may also refer to the alternative history and the specific vision of the future created in *Southland Tales*.
3. Pilot Abilene's name could have been inspired by several sources: Pontius Pilate, the man who allegedly sent Jesus to his death, and Pilate Dead, a character in Toni Morrison's *Song of Solomon* who acts as a storyteller and a guide—a voice of wisdom and experience that attempts to transcend the chaos of everyday life. Pilot Abilene tells the story of the apocalypse alternately from a detached omniscient perspective and from the perspective of someone who is deeply implicated in bringing about humanity's demise. Further, Abilene is one of the Texas cities said to have been decimated by nuclear bombs, and the "Abilene Paradox" refers to a social situation in which reluctant individuals participate in a particular activity because they believe that they must bend to the will of a perceived majority.
4. The slogan brings to mind the Bible's directive to feed the hungry suggesting a parallel with Marx's proposal to eradicate poverty by promoting social equality. However, Marx famously rejected religion, suggesting that, as an "opiate" for the masses, the church reinscribes social hierarchy by metaphorically sedating the populace (King James Version, Matthew 25.35; Marx, *Critique* 3).
5. The association of the toilet to the "hole" serves to remind viewers of a more scatological aspect of consumption, the implication being that consumption produces waste—lots of it. Feeding the mouth-hole inevitably means feeding the toilet-hole.
6. The term "monopoly capitalism" is used here because it more aptly describes capitalism in the United States in the twenty-first century than Marx's capitalism, which refers to nineteenth-century Europe. "Monopoly capitalism" emphasizes the idea of corporate conglomerates that eliminate competition and dominate the market.
7. The pyramid may also be interpreted as evidence of the Neo-Marxists' connection to a hippie counter-culture: the pyramid symbol (explored enthusiastically by conspiracy theorists) has become the key motif of Anton Wilson and Robert Shea's counter-cultural classic, the *Illuminatus Trilogy*. The cult status of the *Illuminatus Trilogy* is discussed in Damien Thompson's work on charisma and apocalypse (Thompson 103).
8. Here, Žižek draws on Lacan's concept of the "Other" as outlined in *Four Fundamental Concepts of Psycho-Analysis* 44–47.

Works Cited

"Attitudes toward History." *Rhetoric Society Quarterly* 38.1 (2008): 66–81. *JSTOR*. Web. 4 Mar. 2016.
Jameson, Frederic. *Signatures of the Visible*. London: Routledge, 2007.
Lacan, Jacques. *The Four Fundamental Concepts of Psycho-Analysis*, London: Harmondsworth Press, 1979.
Marx, Karl. *Critique of Hegel's Philosophy of Right*, Transl. Joseph O'Malley. Oxford: Oxford University Press, 1970.
_____. "Estranged Labour." *Economic and Philosophic Manuscripts of 1844*. Overland Park: Digireads Publishing, Neeland Media, 2014.
Restivo, Rich, and Angelo Cante, "The Cultural-Aesthetic Specificities of All-Male Moving Image Pornography." *Porn Studies*. Ed. Linda Williams. Durham: Duke University Press, 2004.
Southland Tales. Dir. Richard Kelly. Darko Entertainment, 2006.
"Symbols on American Money." *Philadelphia Fed*. Federal Reserve Bank of Philadelphia, n.d. Web. 4 Mar. 2016.

Thompson, Damien. *Waiting for Antichrist: Charisma and Apocalypse in a Pentecostal Church.* Oxford: Oxford University Press, 2005.
Thompson, Hunter. *Kingdom of Fear: Loathsome Secrets of a Star-Crossed Child in the Final Days of the American Century* New York: Simon & Schuster, 2003.
Žižek, Slavoj. *The Sublime Object of Ideology.* London: Verso, 1989. Print.

Tension of Exclusion
On Death Grips and the Californian Ideology

BENJAMIN HALLIGAN

California Light, 1969

The Pirelli calendar shoot of 1969 can be read as exemplifying the use of the light of California. Each photograph is presented as mounted above the car number plate CALIFORNIA PIR 1969, stamping the slightly washed-out aesthetic of the beach images, which draws on sunlight and the colors of illuminated sand and sea, with location, brand and date. Blondes in bikinis were Pirelli's stock in trade but for the 1969 shoot (on Big Sur), photographer Harri Peccinotti, designer Derek Birdsall and Art Director Derek Forsyth crudely calibrated and synchronized a number of themes. In this portfolio, oral sex and orality (the celebration of the year of '69; the first image is the numerical figure on the t-shirt of a jumping blonde, and subsequent shots feature open mouths, or mouths with bottles, ice pops or cigarettes), as a relatively "sophisticated" sense and pastime of pleasure, is writ large across the presentation of California and its beach-dwelling, sun-kissed denizens.[1] The late 1960s light is seen to gloss the State of California and warm the images of pleasure and freedom. And the wealth and well-being needed for pleasure and freedom, that seem intrinsic to the idea of California more generally, are often presented as intimately connected to Californian sunshine.

To darken this sense of California is to consider those excluded from this vision of a secular utopia—those not illuminated by or luxuriating in Californian beach sunshine—and a darkened California is the concern of this essay: not in respect to those who failed to party across the late 1960s (although that legacy also figures here), but those who proclaim themselves excluded and dispossessed, and living in a state of exile, and so dwell unseen, as if in the dark. The group Death Grips are read in this way, and the exclusion is considered in relation to a later flowering of the legacy of late 1960s California: neoliberalism and virtuality.

The Californian Ideology

Virtuality—as theorized through now quaint terms such as "the information age," "hypermedia," "the digital future," "virtual reality" and "the information superhighway"—is read as the coming condition by Richard Barbrook and Andy Cameron, writing in August 1995. And with a state of virtuality, for a "virtual class," comes the radical transformation of modes of work and life: the merging of social and professional spheres.[2] It is not clear why this turn is referred to as "The Californian Ideology." The authors identify what seems to be a coined term, but without attributing authorship to any one element of that "loose alliance of writers, hackers, capitalists and artists from the West Coast of the USA [who] have succeeded in defining a heterogeneous orthodoxy for the coming information age: the Californian Ideology" (Barbrook and Cameron). However, in any intellectual history of Californian culture, two parallel tracks are held as dominant: the counterculture, particularly around the Summer of Love of 1967, and its utopian and communal concepts and ideals of freedom; and a venture capitalist/information technology culture, as originating in part in that counterculture (the Homebrew Computer Club of the mid–1970s, for example), with its utopian and communal concepts, and libertarian ideals. In the Californian Ideology, these two tracks entwine: countercultural positions meet anti-statist positions.

Thus, one could think of moving to a situation of historically unprecedented levels of personal freedoms for individuals (through progressive legislative elements of decriminalization, the "rolling back" of state control, freedoms of movement, speech, thought and choice, and so on), but as co-existing with a regime of near total surveillance of the individual. For those who once baulked at Ronald Reagan's position as governor of California (1967–1975), especially in respect of Reagan's strategic attempts to gain political traction, as achieved via attacks on the countercultures around Berkeley campus (see Kahn), the Californian Ideology is a placating combination of radical and conservative perspectives (Barbrook and Cameron, n.p.). The common denominator or foundation for this new alliance, and one that Reagan articulated when he chastised academics and students on the grounds of their lack of responsibility, was taken to be individual agency.

What the Californian Ideology considers in respect to the coming state of virtuality is the way in which such agency is to be computer-facilitated. To put it in very vulgar terms, this agency is not the freedom granted to slaves once their chains have been removed: freedom of movement, freedom of choice, freedom to work for, in part, their own financial gain (and freedoms which seem to resonate across the myths of California in the late 1960s). Rather, this agency is the freedom that is possible for those who remain enslaved or choose enslavement—that is, surrendering their lives to the forensic and archived surveillance of the computer-city. "Freedom is slavery" write Barbrook and Cameron (n. p.). And insurrection, for those "off the grid," is not merely just a matter of (as many 1970s science fictions had it) destroying or shutting down the central computer. Rather, the physical focus or target of insurrection is itself lost: there is no central computer, but an infinitely interconnected grid with no center. That "central command" "thing" has, in a neoliberal maneuver, vanished.

One is tempted to pick an argument with this continuum: libertarian positions often tend to center on individual freedom, whereas the counterculture's concept of freedom was often communal. Indeed, the counterculture was to a far degree about communing: happenings, orgies, music festivals, squats, communal living, communes.[3] But the erosion of that sense of the mass or (to use a later term) multitude,[4] can be seen as occurring during the dying days of 1960s. This shift is often imagined, in a clichéd and journalistic way, as the ending of the Summer of Love, or death of the counterculture, around an eruption of violence associated with Charles Manson and his followers in August 1969, with five members of the Bel Air/Hollywood set seemingly ritually murdered. More arrestingly, this cliché is understood to have resonated in a changed or changing cultural sensibility of the time, for the perceptions around the music festival, and the entire "culture" of culture itself, as argued by Wright, or sexual subcultures, as argued by Halligan and Wilson. Here, communalism comes across as vulnerability, and the heightened potential for things going wrong rather than a joyous coming together. One immediate solution to such danger was the social apartheid of the Californian gated community, which is often traced to the intrusion of Manson's associates; or the refashioning of recreation to the individual him or herself—"bowling alone," as Robert Putnam put it. And, beyond this, comes communalism-in-isolation: something achieved via the interconnection of isolated individuals via virtuality, and institutionalized via social media.

Of course these protective tendencies refer pretty much exclusively to the upper strata of class and wealth. Barbrook and Cameron remain aware that the coming neoliberal city of the Global North is one that contains the Global South at its borders, or within it—in its public spaces (the homeless and destitute), or in its business spaces (a service industry of precariat or grey collar works, from cleaners to sex industry workers). And the Californian Ideology is also exclusionary. Those "techno-booster" ideologues and evangelists "are at the same time reproducing some of the most atavistic features of American society, especially those derived from the bitter legacy of slavery. Their utopian vision of California depends upon a wilful blindness towards the other—much less positive—features of life on the West Coast: racism, poverty and environmental degradation" (Barbrook and Cameron).

Barbrook and Cameron footnote this comment with a reference to West Coast rap, and list a number of figures who, since their gangsta rap early/mid-90s heydays, have all gone on to become pillars of the entertainment establishment (even specifically extolling the hedonistic virtues of the State of California).[5] But the point is usefully made, and makes for a cultural critique of the unenviable situation of the excluded majority. A mid-point in this downward trajectory in respect to gangsta rap, or a text indicative of the way in which criminal routes out of racism and poverty are then subsumed into bourgeoisie culture, can be found in Tupac's "California Love."[6] The first verse lists the benefits of the titular new Wild West: a city characterized by eroticism, with good quality marijuana, full nightclubs, efficient pimps focused on making money, and endemic bling as emblematic of new and crass wealth.

Unlike Tupac, Ice-T is listed by Barbrook and Cameron. His 1989 album *The Iceberg (Freedom of Speech … Just Watch What You Say)*—the very subtitle of which points to the paradox mentioned above of freedom and surveillance—opens with the track "Shut Up, Be Happy": a millennial, dystopian vision consisting of doom metal chords under a shouted monologue by Jello Biafra, formerly of the hardcore punk group Dead Kennedys. Biafra adopts the position of a threatening newsreader declaring martial law for reasons of national security: all rights have been suspended, a curfew is being enforced, gatherings are prohibited, and DNA material will be collected from everyone. Instructions not to think (which risks depression), and to remain calm, and to continue to take prescribed medications, are repeated throughout. Biafra's satirical twist, as per the track's name, is that this then is the coming state of happiness where, finally, all needs are catered for by unnamed external agencies. One surmises that the material that follows, on *The Iceberg*, then represents the mindset of the rebels against this state—but the cultural critique one derives from this is often reactionary and trivial.[7]

Death Grips

The music of Death Grips, the Sacramento punk/rap/noise/electronica group,[8] can be read as exemplifying this tension of exclusion. But, rather than boast of strategies of personal resilience, or complain in respect to infringements of liberties, or even simply articulate narratives along these lines, Death Grips seem to prefer to act out the material conditions and resultant mindset of exclusion. In these respects, Death Grips find some common ground with outsider art—artifacts presented from the psychologically/mentally distressed and damaged, in which avant-garde tendencies seem to be manifest (as a break with the rules of artistic form meets and matches a tendency to break all rules in general, and hence the exclusion of such "madmen"), particularly for connoisseurs of Modernist art. The artifacts are offered as indicative of clinical conditions. For Death Grips, then, their music indicates madness, a turn to cultism, or occultism, or primitivism (as shall be argued), and suicidal tendencies or preoccupations. Death Grips present themselves as victims of the process identified as the Californian Ideology rather than, as with Tupac of "California Love," its outriders and innovators.

And the group, as with Ice-T and David Bowie, introduce themselves into the dystopia with spoken word, albeit via turning up, as it were, with Manson in tow. "Beware," the first track on their first release, the mixtape *Exmilitary* (2011), opens with the sampled audio of an interview with Manson.[9] He talks singingly and charismatically, recalling his thoughts before his imprisonment, and he advances his argument or defense in a way that now sounds like a rapper dissing his detractors—pre-empting criticisms, rising above a fray perceived to be beneath him, bigging himself up, questioning the grounds of others' questioning. Thus, in a one-side dialogue to a "he," Manson claims, seemingly on the subject of his personal and professional connections to the Beach Boys in 1968–1969, to have been in a state reminiscent of imprisonment, even when at his freest, as arising from his interactions with the industries around popular entertainment as they lustily courted him. The "he" seems to refer to a star-making entertainment executive, perhaps keen to further cash-in on the West Coast sound during the Summer of Love, and so seeking to recruit Manson as a folk singer. But the fame offered here seems a trap, and the narrative is reminiscent of the story of the temptation of Christ by Satan in the Judean desert.[10] Like Christ, Manson claims to see through the material riches on offer, understanding that the price for their gain is the loss of his soul. Such an impression is sustained until Manson then notes that fame, or fortune, was in fact unnecessary—not because such promises are hollow but because his needs were already amply catered for: several women, he claims, are available to him (one assumes sexually), the money he has at his disposal, and how this puts him in a primary position in respect to the cultural/political underground, and exerts his control over it.[11] In this respect, Manson seems to blend cult leader with a Lenin-style figure, as if his actions were undertaken during the tumult of a pre-revolutionary situation, and perhaps then with the Bel Air murders configured as an October 1917 moment, or the execution of the Romanov family.

After the sample has run its course, MC Ride flatly intones several verses and choruses that—in their apocalyptic scenarios, self-obsession, and occult references—would seem to suggest an attempted entry into, or recreation of,

Manson's stream of consciousness. After the burning of a house, the promo video mostly consists of a shirtless, bald, bearded, and heavily tattooed MC Ride, in what looks like the Mojave Desert—with the imagery intercut with (seemingly) blurry, 1980s videotape footage, overlaid with 1980s psychedelic computer effects. One could surmise that this would have been the line of flight for the Manson family: destruction of the Bel Air house, and exile, and contemplation. The lyrics swing between what sounds like a psychotic state of mind and a sense of the physical body under extremes of stress or in hostile conditions: a body stripped of skin to reveal the skeleton beneath, hunger, and bones then pulverized, and a reprise that suggests a blind lunge against and an attack on an enemy.[12] This introduction to Death Grips sketches out what would then become a constant theme: the degraded biological and psychological conditions of those excluded from the wealth and well-being envisaged along the Summer of Love/Californian Ideology axis. The oppressed and befuddled subject is then one who is given over to a demagoguery that makes the self-aggrandizement of other MCs seem trivial. And the sense of the rude presence of this individual locks such a subjectivity into, as it were, the "really existing" conditions of California: those way below the upper strata, or outside the virtual bubble/gated communities, that seem to have grown within and around the hippie commune as was.

In this respect, the group attempt a framing of Manson and his family's activities that seems to seek to account for such behaviors—without condemning Manson or reacting with revulsion (which then spurred, as noted, perceptions of the "ending" of the countercultural 1960s, and an architectural/urban planning reaction), or indeed the pulpy modish recreation of the narrative against a montage of civil strife and Vietnam footage, as with Sonic Youth's "Death Valley '69" or in various faked Mondo and "snuff" films from the 1970s.[13] The framing offers the kind of correction that the above-quoted proviso from Barbrook and Cameron invites: the tracking of the continuum from the dispossessed then to the dispossessed of the present, rather than from the hippies to the techno-boosters. These dispossessed, in a literal sense, make for that hinterland of the homeless and the poor, the excluded and the broken, whose hunger and limited life expectancy are somehow beyond solution for Californian capitalism. But such precarious conditions seem to creep upward too, so that dispossession becomes, in a psychological sense, a background fear for those only a few disasters away from the street, or those whose security is tenuous. The dispossessed, for Death Grips, offer a counter-narrative, or altermodernity, to the modernity, and postmodernity, of the aspirational end of the Californian Ideology: the jumble of occult and dark psychedelic ideas aping, or holding a dark mirror to, the techno- and psycho-babble of high digital capitalism. And while the modernity of the Californian Ideology is one of disappearance and virtuality (the centerless network, the "hollowing out" of civil and state institutions in the name of neoliberal outsourcing), this altermodernity is one of an unavoidable materialism: the sense of the actualité or presence of the body under stress. What more need be said, or what further metaphorical elaboration is required, in respect of a straightforward statement of need and deprivation?

This particularly physical stress is to be found in MC Ride's shouting-strained voice and his gasps for breath. And one senses that the paranoia of his lyrics is physically manifest too: pushing the body into a state of high agitation.[14] And indeed the voice contrasts sharply with the actualization of technobabble in the electronic soundscapes, which sounds like computer crashes or information overloads, or will break with a certain groove without warning, or "jump cut" to shards of found sound or noise, or seem to be so rough as to be first or spontaneous or even autopilot mixes. The result could push weary listeners away, or could be configured as a test of willingness to rise to the challenges of such expanded sounds (or just evidential material for those who wish it to be noted by their peers that they have risen to such challenges). This is in sharp contrast to the disco-era utilization of machine music, which often found a lulling smoothness in repetition, merged with the human voice and, at its most suggestive, sought to link body and computer together—as if the latter melding was a near-future erotic technology.[15] The human/computer dynamic here is one of difference and disparity, if not a form of mutual sonic warfare. And Death Grips make a virtue of such material presentness too; the way in which, for the "No Love" (2014) promo video, Zach Hill pounds his drums with his fists and hands—a flattened thump from his skin impacting on drum skin—negates access to his musical skills for this extraordinary drummer. And Hill's blood-gorged flesh reputedly features again on the cover of *No Love Deep Web*: it is a shot of his erect penis, with the album title scrawled along it in black marker pen. For a section of "No Love," Hill lugs a loudspeaker around on his shoulder in a way which, iconographically (and not least in terms of Hill's appearance and pained expressions), mimics images of Christ shouldering the cross on his journey to Calvary.

Such material presentness has been much in evidence in live performance. Live, the trio or duo of Death Grips is hyper-energetic—even to the extent of, as with thrash metal groups, needing to radically curtail standard set lengths. Their Manchester concert of 6 November 2012, in Sound Control, began gradually. Hill arrived alone, and proceeded to set up and tune his drum kit, and change aspects of his clothing, and footwear, as if oblivious to the crowd packed into this small venue. It was only with the gradual assembly of the full "band" (drums, laptop/keyboard, video screens), and the belated arrival of MC Ride, that the concert proper started. The laptop/keyboard-generated sounds and samples were constant and maximal—a battery of noise—and Hill's athletic drumming can be described as very apparently indebted to math's rock: constant beats (that is, filling all beats in the bar) and minimal cymbal work, delivered with click-track precision despite the speed, and with Hill almost doubled-over his kit, as if crouched into himself, rather than the grandstanding of some drummers.

MC Ride, upon arrival, both in Manchester and for a concert some months later for the Primavera Sound festival (in Barcelona, for the night of 23 May 2013), appeared as if a cult leader, adopting a Messianic pose, as if in a trance-like state: expressionless, motionless for jarringly long periods, despite the growing crescendo of the electronic soundscape, the storm of lighting and smoke, and the cheers and whooping of the expectant audiences. His motionlessness seemed to whip those audiences into a frenzy, placing on them the need to create a kinetic energy, or to yell loudly enough to rouse MC Ride from his passage-into-trance and, state now altered, to begin the performance. It is a technique that is particularly reminiscent of Artaud-derived ideas in operation in the 1960s theater, both in terms of trance-like states (the Living Theater would experiment with performers staring at the audience for indefinite periods), and in terms of frantic, dervish-like activity, with the performer seeking to channel the psychic energy of the massed crowd into the performance (as with Jim Morrison of The Doors).[16] And, again, this is in sharp contrast to the majority norm of vamping an entrance and beginning with a bang—and straight into a hit song, and so winning over an audience, rather than risking their alienation and irritation. The demand is that the audience communicate to the presence in the same space, and find a shared wavelength, independent of or cutting through the soundscape chaos and samples and looped digital visual displays. The hand reaches out to the hand, metaphorically speaking: human contact is needed to activate the performance. Or, for a concert at the Manchester Academy some years later (on 16 October 2016), for the audience to act as midwife, and "birth" the start of the show: MC Ride began with utterances of basic sounds, as if learning a language for the first time, and so needing to repeatedly articulate the guttural tones of parts of words. The effect was akin to a slow-motion stammer, or listening to someone attempting to speak again, as can be the case with those who suffer from aphasia after a stroke. That concert offered no support act but, rather, an electronic buzzing around the darkened concert hall, lasting an hour and a half.

MC Ride's sweat-drenched naked torso, his undulating and convulsive movements, his barked, chanted and intoned lyrics, running between shouting and glossolalia, and staccato-delivery in the manner of a military drill instructor, his rolling around on the floor and lolling head, seem to suggest explosive demonic possession—as if he were in the throes of some kind of occult ceremony. The substantial pentagram tattoo on his chest directly invites such a connection. And the propensity of Death Grips live for very low lighting levels (typically blues and purples, and no spotlight on MC Ride), denying the audience the ability to watch a performer perform (in the sense of facial expressions, and to be seen singing or rapping) ensures that the performance is about this shadowy, sinuous figure (seen in silhouette, or on occasion flash-illuminated for milliseconds by bursts of white light). As a stage presence strategy, MC Ride at times recalls Public Enemy's Flavor Flav, who renders an almost pantomime-like racist grotesque of the drink-crazed or drug-addled African American hobo. The implications are troubling, especially as performed for, one would surmise (at least from the three concerts discussed here), the predominantly educated and seemingly white audiences: as if an African-American who, pushed to and then beyond his limits, returned to some sort of "savage" state, blathering incomprehensibly, squinting or glowering, dancing "tribally."[17] What kind of performance has been activated? One that seems to implicate the prejudices of the audience? That performs an Uncle Tom–esque victimhood? That critically undermines the ways in which famed African-American artists obscure their otherwise demeaning performances with ideas of empowerment, individuality and "fierceness"? If so, then the condition of this victimhood is one of self-abasement—as if he were "forced" to dance and entertain in ways that reinforce the existing structures of exclusion. Shortly after the first period under discussion here (2012–2013), Death Grips went through a brief phase of failing to turn up to scheduled concerts (Bychawski n. p.), as if moving to the next stage of their "unacceptable" live strategy and dramaturgy. Touring again in 2016, on the other side of considerable critical acclaim, their rebarbativeness was somewhat tempered: something of a "greatest hits" set was delivered, albeit buried in the uninterrupted 80 minutes of constant noise, for which MC Ride would at times orchestrate or conduct the audience as it chanted or shouted along. Elsewhere, the harsh electronic soundscapes that interjected shards of beats into distorted samples, and with no discernible hook or time-signature to allow for an easy access into the music, left that audience (perhaps curious as to the source of the critical acclaim) immobile, or exiting, and seemingly baffled, or bored. In this context, a track such as "Bubbles Buried in This Jungle" from *Bottomless Pit* (2016)—which was the second song of the 2016 concert—works to marshal the freeform noise chaos into a discernible structure for finite periods by imposing a shouted punctuation of words across it for each chorus.

Subjectivity and Radical Refusal

In such ways, the live performances very directly suggest that Death Grips seek to illustrate, rather than critically comment on, the condition that is here read in terms of the divisive nature of the Californian Ideology. As Corrigan notes, the band are adept at expressing the alienating conditions of contemporary life, but without being able to advance any concrete reading of such conditions or their amelioration, or effective resistance to them. And the illustration, embodied live and in their recorded material, can be read as the materialization of the effects of contemporary social conditions in respect to presenting the body under stress, and a besieged and desperate subjectivity within it. The title *Exmilitary* itself suggests, for the post–9/11 period, homeless war veterans, suffering post-traumatic stress disorder, self-medication via drink and drugs, and the fatal consequences of blowback from those on "our" side. Such materialization of the effects of social conditions is one that drags with it a sense of where power resides: institutions of the Californian Ideology still physically exist. "All motherfuckers have addresses," as The Invisible Committee note (76) in respect to anti-capitalist activism. The later album, *The Powers That B*, suggests an engagement with, as the cliché of the title has it, the self-determined authorities. These lyrics are not confessional so much as accusatory: it is the deracinated "I" (of MC Ride) which is positioned in respect to the effects of oppression. And yet this positioning, as if an end in itself, occurs again and again: one scans the lyrics sheet of *No Love Deep Web* and notes the endless, obsessive "I's."

The limit of this approach, in Death Grips, resides in the sense of an individual subjectivity, and with their avant-garde tendencies tied, in a Modernist way, to an exploration of that individual subjectivity. Hardt and Negri note that individual refusal to the demands of contemporary capital may be taken as an "absolute purity": to decry and reject the impossible demands made on one, and so to track and chart "lines of flight from authority." Refusal has determined the relation of Death Grips to the conventions of the dissemination of music, record company allegiance, and performance. But refusal is, in itself, effectively a dangerous position for Hardt and Negri: to "continuously tread" (in the literary examples they chose, from Herman Melville and J. M. Coetzee) "on the verge of suicide." Radical refusal, in political terms, is "a kind of social suicide": isolating, disempowering and immiserating (Hardt and Negri 204). "Come Up and Get Me," which opens *No Love Deep Web*, dramatizes just such a dynamic: the protagonist seems physically isolated and surrounded by hostile forces, lingering on the verge of self-destruction or death. Death Grips excel, perhaps uniquely in recent years, and certainly to enormously disconcerting effect, in presenting such a precarious position, and mining its tensions in and for their work.

NOTES

1. The portfolio is reproduced in Pirelli.
2. "Virtuality" is typically defined as a condition arising from an immersion into technologically enabled simulations of life that then come to replace non-virtual (i.e., "real") life

itself: events, emotions and courses of actions as all increasingly determined and informed by life-simulators—as with, to turn to a typical example, one whose social interactions with the world are mostly via (and feel more authentic or real or manageable via) online social media. Such a state, where life is diminished by being mediated through or by the media of technology, is seen as a movement from human interactions and communications to that of "excommunication" (see Galloway, Thacker and Wark). For an extensive definition of virtuality in respect to music, see Whiteley and Rambarran 1–3.

3. Most famously in the film *Easy Rider* (Dennis Hopper 1969); see also sociological / investigative writing from the time, and after; Roberts and Miller 327–51, respectively.

4. On the use of "multitude" in respect to subcultural movements, see Mueller 65–78.

5. Barbrook and Cameron also see in this the circumstances for new forms of artistic expression, of a "new machine aesthetic," and briefly question what such forms have to tell us about the coming condition. For my discussion of this aspect of their writing in respect to electronic dance music, see Halligan 529–50.

6. The single, which features Dr. Dre and Roger Troutman, was released in 1995 and appeared, in a different mix, on the 1996 Tupac LP *All Eyez on Me*.

7. David Bowie's *Diamond Dogs* (1974), which also opened with a spoken monologue concerning the future dystopia of "Hunger City" (at least for the album's original vinyl version: the monologue was removed at the point of the reissuing of the album), made for a much more progressive case, in terms of difference (along gender rather than "gangsta" lines) and rebellion.

8. I would not immediately or predominantly associate the group with rap, despite the use of rhythmically delivered spoken word; this association, typically made for Death Grips in journalistic writing, seems more to do with the presence of their African American frontman, MC Ride. Similarities, in terms of music styles, seem closer to The Last Poets (sometimes claimed as proto-rap) or, in terms of fractured, polyrhythmic soundbeds, soundscapes or sound collages, and a strained vocal delivery that often obliterates comprehension, to the Salford post-punk group The Fall.

9. The album is a mixtape in the sense that the sonic foundation mostly consists of samples; original contributions seem to consist of MC Ride's rapping and Zach Hill's drumming, and with Andy Morin credited with keyboards and programming. "Beware" is reminiscent of "Punk Rock," the opening track of Mogwai's LP *Come On, Die Young* (1999). This also presents or reproduces a found speech from Iggy Pop (in fact, supposedly extracted from a 1977 television interview: the band claimed this audio originated from a video cassette found on sale in a garage). Manson and Pop are presented as iconoclasts, defining their times, and talking passionately, and on a roll. This suggests the essential context for understanding the newer music about to come: as a continuum with the spirit of the iconoclasts of yesteryear. I am unable to ascertain the origins of the Manson interview, but his physical appearance in the video clip from which this audio is sourced suggests 1980s or 1990s footage, seemingly made for legal reasons—perhaps as part of a failed bid for parole.

10. The biblical verses for this story are Luke 4:1–13 but it is also mentioned in the Gospels of Matthew and Mark.

11. The particularity of the metaphors deployed here, and the ways in which the dialogue seems structured around imaginary questions or interjections, are available with reference to the lyrics of the track.

12. The minimalism, fragmented state and earthiness of the lyrics recall at times something of the poems of Sam Shepard of the 1970s.

13. The single, which featured and was co-written and co-produced by the New York punk figure Lydia Lunch, was released in 1984 and again in 1985, and was included on the album *Bad Moon Rising* (1985). The video, directed by Judith Barry and Richard Kern (associated with the New York-based "Cinema of Transgression"), includes a re-enactment or recreation of the moments immediately following the Bel Air murders.

14. This is not to say that the group are, like the outsider music associated with Wild Man Fischer, somehow genuinely outside the entertainment market and the material benefits that affords. Their second album, *The Money Store* (2012) was released by one of Sony's main record labels, Epic, and *The Powers That B* (2014) and *Bottomless Pit* (2016) by Harvest. Epic

dropped the group after they leaked *No Love Deep Web* (2012) online, seemingly frustrated by the label's negative reaction to it and unwillingness to release it. As with many groups of their cultural and critical cache around these years, Death Grips were pictured with A-list stars, and yet their record label's name, and website's URL—thirdworlds.net—hubristically appropriates such an insulting term in striving for, one assumes, a sense of difference from the mainstream.

15. For a fuller discussion, particularly around the pioneering disco production of Giorgio Moroder, see Halligan. It should be noted too that Death Grips have also released instrumental collections: *Fashion Week* (2014) and *Instrumental 2016* (2016).

16. For a discussion of connections between Morrison and The Living Theater, and the shared interest in Artaud's theories of performance, see Milton.

17. For a straightforward use of such an horrendously racist stereotype, see the film *Predator* (John McTiernan 1987).

Works Cited

Barbrook, Richard, and Andy Cameron. "The Californian Ideology." *Alamut: Bastion of Peace and Information*. August 1995. Web. 1 March 2016. Available at http://www.alamut.com/subj/ideologies/pessimism/califIdeo_I.html.
Bychawski, Adam. "Fans Destroy Death Grips' Equipment After Lollapalooza No Show." *NME*. 2 August 2013. Web. 1 March 2016. Available at http://www.nme.com/news/death-grips/71829.
Corrigan, Zac. "Death Grips' *No Love Deep Web*: A terminally destructive message." *World Socialist Web Site*. 13 December 2012. Web. 1 March 2016. Available at https://www.wsws.org/en/articles/2012/12/13/deat-d13.html.
Death Grips. *Black Google*. Self-released compilation, 2011.
_____. *Bottomless Pit*. Third Worlds, Harvest, 2016.
_____. *Ex-Military*. Self-released mixtape, 2011.
_____. *Fashion Week*. Third Worlds, 2015.
_____. *Government Plates*. Third Worlds, Harvest, 2013.
_____. *The Money Store*. Epic, 2012.
_____. *No Love Deep Web*. Self-released, Third Worlds, Harvest, Epic, 2012.
_____. *The Powers That B*. Third Worlds, Harvest, 2015. (Disc 1 of *The Powers That B* was first self-released as *Niggas on the Moon* in 2014.)
Fanon, Frantz. *The Wretched of the Earth*. Preface by Jean-Paul Sartre, trans. Constance Farrington. New York: Grove Press, 1963. Print.
Galloway, Alexander R., Eugene Thacker, and McKenzie Wark. *Excommunication: Three Inquiries in Media and Mediation*. Chicago: Trios / University of Chicago Press, 2013. Print.
Halligan, Benjamin. "Mind Usurps Program: Virtuality and the 'New Machine Aesthetic' of Electronic Dance Music." *The Oxford Handbook of Music and Virtuality*. Ed. Sheila Whiteley and Shara Rambarran. New York: Oxford University Press, 2016. 529–50. Print.
Halligan, Benjamin, and Laura Wilson. "Use/Abuse/Everyone/Everything: A Dialogue on LA Plays Itself." *Framework: The Journal of Cinema and Media* 56, issue 2, article 4 (2015): 299–322. Print.
Hardt, Michael, and Antonio Negri. *Empire*. Cambridge: Harvard University Press, 2001. Print.
The Invisible Committee. *To Our Friends*. Cambridge: MIT Press / Semiotext(e), 2015. Print.
Kahn, Jeffery. "Ronald Reagan Launched Political Career Using Berkeley Campus as a Target." *Berkeley News*. 8 June 2004. Web. 1 March 2016. Available at http://www.berkeley.edu/news/media/releases/2004/06/08_reagan.shtml.
Miller, Timothy. "The Sixties-Era Communes." *Imagine Nation: The American Counterculture of the 1960s & '70s*. Ed. Peter Braunstein and Michael William Doyle. New York: Routledge, 2002. 327–51. Print.
Milton, Daveth. *We Want the World: Jim Morrison, the Living Theatre, and the FBI*. Birmingham Bennion Kearny, 2012. Print.

Mueller, Charles. "Were British Subcultures the Beginning of Multitude?" *Countercultures and Popular Music*. Ed. Sheila Whiteley and Jedediah Sklower. Surrey: Ashgate. 65–78.
Pirelli Ltd. *The Complete Pirelli Calendar Book*. Introduced by David Niven. London: Pan Books, 1975. Print.
Putnam, Robert. *Bowling Alone: The Collapse and Revival of American Community*. New York: Simon & Schuster, 2000. Print.
Roberts, Ron E. *The New Communes: Coming Together in America*. Upper Saddle River, NJ: Prentice-Hall, 1971. Print.
Whiteley, Sheila, and Shara Rambarran. *The Oxford Handbook of Music and Virtuality*. New York: Oxford University Press. 2016. Print.
Wright, Julia Lobalzo. "The Good, the Bad, and the Ugly 1960s: The Opposing Gazes of *Woodstock* and *Gimme Shelter*." *The Music Documentary: Acid Rock to Electropop*. Ed. Robert Edgar, Kirsty Fairclough-Isaacs and Benjamin Halligan. London: Routledge, 2013. 71–86. Print.

PART II: CALIFORNIAN MONSTERS

"Wolf howls and the roar of police sirens"
Fractured Identities, Lycanthropy and the Streets of Los Angeles in Toby Barlow's Sharp Teeth

CARYS CROSSEN

The city of Los Angeles is almost literally a fractured one. Built on the San Andreas fault-line, and subject to numerous earthquakes, it is an unstable city. Located in California, at the very edge of the United States, bordered by the Pacific on one side and the U.S.-Mexican border on the other, it is a liminal city. These boundaries are geographic, but also metaphorical: L.A. is synonymous with Hollywood and its numerous movie studios, a fantasy land where the line between reality and the imaginary can blur with disconcerting ease. Divisions occur among its population also: the infamous 1992 race riots and the notorious street gangs such as the Bloods and the Crips ensure that violence is indelibly associated with the mean streets of L.A. Despite the borrowed glamour of the film industry, L.A. has a darker side. As Richard Lehan observes: "Probably no city in the Western world has a more negative image: one vast freeway system, enshrouded in smog, carrying thousands of dreamers to a kind of spiritual and physical dead end. In this world, we shift easily from a sense of promise to the grotesque, the violent and the apocalyptic" (257).

From the fairy dust of movie stars and Hollywood to gangs, drugs and drive-by shootings, L.A. has always been a two-faced city. Such a location would be a perfect habitat for the most two-faced of monsters, the werewolf, and recent novels such as John Farris's *High Bloods* (2009), Kirk Lynn's *Rules for Werewolves* (2015) and most particularly Toby Barlow's *Sharp Teeth* (2007) do indeed portray werewolves in Los Angeles. Werewolves in this context are quite literally humans who turn into wolves, or at the very least creatures who resemble wolves. All three novels depict lycanthropes as an outbreak, an epidemic almost, or to use a non-medical metaphor, as gangs of rioters or criminals. In *High Bloods*, werewolves are second-class citizens controlled by law enforcement and, as it fails, hunted for sport by wealthy Californians. In Lynn's novel, the werewolves form large packs and live off suburbia the way their wild counterparts live off the land, foraging for food and living in abandoned houses (and taking violent revenge on anyone who does them harm, though they are generally peaceable). Barlow presents yet another take on the contemporary werewolf, depicting his lycanthropes as street gangs jostling for power in the L.A. underworld.

Before we proceed, we must ask the question: what is a werewolf? The basic definition of the werewolf is a straightforward one. It is, quite simply, a human being who turns into a wolf, or a lupine creature. This is the description offered by Chantal Bourgault Du Coudray in her monograph *The Curse of the Werewolf: Fantasy, Horror and the Beast Within* (1) and also by Charlotte F. Otten in *A Lycanthropy Reader: Werewolves in Western Culture* (1). Of course, such a simple definition offers endless opportunities for re-interpretations and re-imaginings but the werewolf's role in Western popular culture, until the 1980s at least, has been surprisingly limited. Since the nineteenth century, werewolves have largely been depicted as the beast within, the representative of mankind's dark, violent and irrational instincts, the raging id let loose to savage unfortunate victims. Their most famous portrayals, in films such as *The Wolf-Man* (1941) and *An American Werewolf in London* (1981) have added to this popular perception. The werewolf is also strongly associated with darkness and the Gothic throughout its history. The cinematic werewolf typically transforms under the full moon (visible only at night) and both literary and cinematic werewolf display a tendency to lurk in forests and out in the wilderness, living in shadow and concealment. Lycanthropy in many texts is a stigma, something to be hidden at all costs, such as is the case with the figure of Remus Lupin in J.K. Rowling's *Harry Potter* series, where it is surrounded by the darkness of ignorance rather than the light of knowledge.

Nonetheless, in recent years authors (Toby Barlow among them) have begun to explore new ways of depicting the werewolf. In the novels by Barlow, Lynn and Farris, werewolves are used as a metaphor for dispossessed, alienated individuals, and often represent an upsurge in violent energy seeking an outlet amid urban confines. In all three novels, the endless suburbs, beaches, gated communities and mean streets of L.A. become the backdrop for these new types of werewolves. This newness is not necessarily linked to their appearance—they are not a new biological breed of werewolf. Barlow does not describe the appearance of his lycanthropes in any great detail, but as at least one werewolf manages to masquerade as a family pet, their appearance must be more canine than lupine. There does not appear to be a specific L.A. "look" with regards to the werewolves—although it is worth noting that Kirk Lynn offers virtually no description of his werewolves in *Rules for Werewolves* either. Anonymity is a powerful weapon in the werewolf's fight for survival in Barlow and Lynn's novels: less so in Farris's where their uncontrollable violence is impossible to conceal.

What is new in these depictions of werewolves is their social structure—itself a revolutionary development, as for decades the werewolf has been the most solitary of monsters. L.A. has exceptionally strong associations with images of riots and gangs, and the werewolf is the perfect metaphor to express this repressed, disturbing energy. As Julian Murphet comments when analyzing the works of an L.A. poet, Wanda Coleman, "the wolf ravages from within, he is the very condition of possibility of the riot as such" (106). All three novels mentioned above certainly depict ravening wolves and the riots that result from their presence. In *High Bloods* lycanthropy is an infectious disease that causes no small amount of trouble for law enforcement when werewolves transform and wreak havoc. In *Rules for Werewolves*, the lycanthropes are depicted as disaffected, disillusioned beings who reject the American Dream (particularly its consumerist ideology) and search for an alternative, wilder, more satisfying existence, initially in the suburbs and later in the wilderness, away from the urban sprawl. The crucial distinction between the two is that Farris's novel is told from a perspective of a (human) police officer, who is charged with defending human society, so the city of L.A. is perceived as worth protecting. In Lynn's book, human society and suburbia are soul-crushing dead ends akin to that described by Lehan, and the lycanthropes struggle, sometimes violently, to find an alternative.

Likewise, Toby Barlow's blank verse novel *Sharp Teeth* presents werewolves as an outbreak, a collective threatening law and order, and always on the edge of violence. The novel focuses on a wide range of characters, at the center of whom is down-on-his-luck Anthony (the closest thing the story has to a hero). As the novel opens, Anthony manages to find employment as a dogcatcher, a job he despises but sticks at because he likes dogs. At the same time as Anthony begins work, ambitious gang leader Lark is making plans to consolidate his hold on L.A. by eliminating two of his rivals, while a tough cop named Peabody investigates his activities and the murder of a dogcatcher who previously held Anthony's job. Lark and Anthony's worlds collide when Lark sends his only female gang member (who remains nameless throughout the novel) to integrate herself into Anthony's life and affections. It seems a peculiar move, given Anthony is a humble dogcatcher and no criminal. But it begins to make sense with the revelation that Lark and his gang (or pack) are werewolves and want a man/wolf on the inside of the local dog pound—

to release any of their number who get caught, or to make sure members of their pack are placed with wealthy or influential individuals looking for a loyal pet. Problems arise when the She-Wolf actually falls in love with Anthony, Peabody gets a little too close to the truth, and Lark loses his control over his pack. The novel culminates in a catastrophic final fight among the lycanthropic gangs. The conclusion features Peabody closing the case but accepting he will never have all the answers. Lark has lost all his power and influence but survives and starts a new werewolf pack. Anthony (by now also a werewolf) and the She-Wolf find one another again, having been separated earlier in the novel, and the conclusion depicts them living happily as wolves on the beaches of L.A., hunting to feed themselves and living a much simpler but more fulfilling existence than they experienced at the start of the novel.

That Barlow's werewolves serve as a metaphor for gangs and gang-related violence is obvious—although his lycanthropes are unusual in that they do not wield guns, instead preferring to fight with tooth and claw. One review identifies "the radical separation from conventional, law-abiding society, the constant threat of violence" as characteristics werewolves and gang members have in common (Robshaw n.p.) Contrary to this assertion, recent werewolf fiction has increasingly presented werewolves as desirous of acceptance into mainstream human society. Popular book series such as Carrie Vaughn's *Kitty Norville* books (about a werewolf radio DJ), Maggie Stiefvater's *Wolves of Mercy Falls* series (in which werewolves fight desperately to remain human) and, of course, Stephenie Meyer's *Twilight* series all depict lycanthropes as living among and interacting with humans. However, it is undeniable that even werewolves who live and make their living among humans maintain a certain distance from the human populace. The *Twilight* werewolves, all Native Americans, live on a reservation and prominent werewolf character Jacob Black does not attend mainstream high school. Anne Rice and Glen Duncan, two of the most prominent authors of recent years who have treated the werewolf theme, depict werewolves coming together and forming their own communities. The former in *The Wolves of Midwinter* series depicts the werewolves as a family living in a large, isolated mansion, and the latter in *The Last Werewolf* trilogy portrays the lycanthropes as a peripatetic group that avoid establishing any meaningful links with the human populace or a particular geographical location. While both Rice and Duncan present their werewolves as wealthy, patrician and civilized (apart from the odd savaging of some unfortunate human) and about as far from the dog-eat-dog world of the inner city as possible, werewolves in popular culture are presented as living on the fringes of society and in some cases being desirous of maintaining a distance from the remainder of humanity.

Barlow's werewolves are no exception, with none of them (excepting the She-Wolf, who falls passionately in love with Anthony) exhibiting any real desire to establish true relationships with humans and human institutions, unless they stand to profit by them. The werewolf pack therefore serves as an apt metaphor for the L.A. street gang—staking out territory on the streets, frequently engaging in violence and arousing the suspicions of law enforcements. But for all their wolfishness, they remain partly human, their identities divided between human plotting, scheming, rivalry and manipulation, and the much more instinctual drives and behavior of wolves. Like the city of L.A. itself, the werewolves are fractured, torn between two modes of being, as they have been in the majority of pop-culture depictions of them. So what implications does their dual nature have for their identity—and how does this link back to Barlow's presentation of the fractured urbanity of Los Angeles?

Werewolves, L.A. and Identity

Against the fractured backdrop of L.A., divided by race, wealth and of course the San Andreas Fault line, identity is almost inevitably a complicated affair. In an examination of how society has changed since the 1800, Lawrence N. Friedman observed that increasing urbanization in America had a dramatic impact on how people presented themselves to others: "The social fact of spatial mobility has enormous consequences. One of them, which is relevant here, is that for the first time, *identity* becomes problematic.... The growing towns and cities are full of people who have come from somewhere else. They present themselves, they parade a certain identity. But can we believe them? It has become very easy to lie. It has become very easy to invent a new self" (376, original italics). It has always been particularly straightforward for werewolves to invent a new self, as all they have to do is shape-shift into a wolf, or back into a human. But re-invention of the self has become a much more complex affair for the werewolf in recent years. Its very figure is undergoing a re-invention, as since the 1980s the lycanthrope has been represented as a subject.

The werewolf has traditionally been presented as the beast within, the divided self, in such famous films as *The Wolf-Man* (1941) and *An American Werewolf in London* (1981) and in books such as *Wagner the Werewolf*. The werewolf, in its transformed state, was pure violence, pure bloodthirstiness and pure instinct, leaving no capacity for rational thought or reflection. But in recent fiction, most particularly that dated from the 1990s onward, this has begun to change, with the werewolf increasingly being depicted as retaining their conscious mind, their rationality and their sense of self rather than temporarily being consumed by a monster, no matter what form they assume. This development has been made possible by the werewolf's increasing sociability and the introduction of the lycanthropic pack in werewolf fiction. Throughout its history in literature and film, the werewolf has been presented as a solitary monster, isolated from both humanity and Nature. This began to change in the 1980s and '90s, when the werewolf pack began to appear in fiction such as Cheri Scotch's *The Werewolf's Kiss* (1992). Conversely, the werewolf's developing subjectivity has been made possible by its gradual integration into society, whether that society is human or lycanthropic. In an examination of subjectivity, Nick Mansfield argues that "the subject is always linked to something outside of it—an idea or principle or the society of other subjects. It is this linkage that the word 'subject' insists upon. Etymologically to be 'place (or even thrown) under.' One is always subject *to* or *of* something. The word subject, therefore, proposes that the self is not a separate and isolated entity, but one that operates at the intersection of general truths and shared principle" (3, original italics). The advent of urbanization has arguably hastened the dawning of subjectivity for the werewolf. When living in the wilderness, isolation is a viable mode of existence for the werewolf—but if they wish to live in the city, turning into a monster come the full moon and eating the neighbors would inevitably cause a few problems! If the werewolf wishes to live in the city, they might be able to get away with a few judicious murders, but violent rampages in the manner of *An American Werewolf in London* are not conducive to their survival. The subjective werewolf is the only kind of werewolf suited to life in the big city.

It is this subjective werewolf that Barlow has chosen to depict in his epic poem. This is a remarkable development for the monster which almost throughout its entire history has not possessed an identity to reinvent. The contemporary werewolf, particularly the female werewolf, is considered by critics to represent a new mode of subjectivity that moves beyond the established social order and represents new modes of being—particularly as the werewolf often violates gender norms simply by existing (Pulliam 100). A dark segment of the novel features the She-Wolf remembering her previous life before becoming a werewolf, in which she suffered at the hands of an abusive boyfriend. She reflects that "she doesn't need the men/she could do plenty of damage/all by herself./She has the blood for it" (12). She-Wolf has left her old self behind: far from being a victim of violence, she has crossed the line from the hunted to the hunter. Traditionally, the werewolf has been the representative of a nature at war with itself, the id versus the ego, to borrow a Freudian analogy. Divided between the polarities of guilt-racked human and ravening beast in such Hollywood productions as *The Wolf-Man*, the traditional mode of presenting the werewolf as the beast within would seem appropriate for a novel set in the divided city of Los Angeles. But the subjective werewolf possesses an identity to reinvent, in keeping with the anonymity Friedman identifies as synonymous with the city, and it is this ability that makes possible many of the plot strands in Barlow's texts.

Lark, for instance, spends a large segment of the novel posing as a friendly dog named Buddy, adopted by career woman Bonnie. Of course, reinvention of the self goes much deeper in Barlow's novel, and occurs in multifaceted ways. That Barlow's werewolves are unlike any others in popular culture is emphasized throughout the story. As the omnipresent narrator comments about the She-Wolf, "she is her own brand of beast" (40). The city of L.A., in keeping with Friedman's assessment, is what allows the werewolves to lie about themselves. It provides numerous settings, environments and scenarios, all of which require different personas, actions and patterns of behavior. Lark is simultaneously a gang leader, a stylish gambler and a loyal pet. The She-Wolf is both a savage predator and loving live-in girlfriend to Anthony, who spends her time cooking and cleaning in old-fashioned housewife mode. Her re-invention is not purely tied to violence: one of the most important aspects of the novel is the romance between Anthony and the She-Wolf. Contrary to her previous relationship, Anthony and the She-Wolf form a loving and mutually supportive bond and the novel concludes with their reunion. Both She-Wolf and Lark represent the fractured existences that can be led within the vast sprawl of L.A., where anonymity is easy to find—another contradiction in a city that is home to some of the world's most recognizable faces from the film and music industries.

The contradictory, fractured identity of L.A. resonates strongly with how Barlow chooses to depict his werewolves. A divided city, it reflects the divided nature of the werewolves: human and wolf, civilized and savage, urban and wild. Despite these divisions, the werewolves manage to embody the restless, sometimes violent energy that has become synonymous with L.A., shown in its endless freeway systems, the tremendously powerful film industry and even the riots that have occurred throughout the city's history. But what is this energy composed of? Is it a vigor and vitality that originates in the city, or is it the expression of a different sort of wildness altogether?

Werewolves, Nature and the Urban Jungle

The appearance of vast cities and the urban sprawl overtaking the wilderness has also had a dramatic effect on lycanthropic identity. Werewolves were, and still are, strongly associated with wildness, nature and the untamable, with Bourgault Du Coudray going so far as to suggest that the werewolf in modern fiction is a conduit for wildness, an agent for allowing humanity to reconnect with Nature (140–41). In *Twilight*, despite the novel's setting on the West Coast, the werewolves are very much associated with the forest and the mountains, their ancestral home. City life is reserved for the more patrician vampires. Yet although some texts depict the werewolf reconnecting with Nature (it is more popular in film, such as the 1981 *Wolfen* and the 1994 *Wolf*) the geographical movement of the contemporary fictional werewolf has largely been toward the city. Novels by authors such as Barlow are increasingly turning away from the wilderness toward the metropolis, which in many respects is just as savage as Nature. Popular book series, such as Vaughn's *Kitty Norville*, often adopt urban backgrounds. Vaughn sets her stories against the backdrop of Denver, but also features Las Vegas and London as the settings for the adventures of her lycanthropic heroine. Likewise, Yasmin Galenorn's *Otherworld* series, featuring a lycanthropic private eye, is set in Denver, Cheri Scotch's *The Werewolf's Kiss* is set in New Orleans, and Kristopher Reisz's *Unleashed* (2008) is set in the rough streets and abandoned factories of Detroit. On one level this is purely practical: true, isolated wilderness is becoming increasingly rare in both America and Europe, and it makes sense for the werewolf to begin migrating into the cities, along with humanity. But simultaneously these contemporary werewolf texts suggest that something vital is missing from modern human life in the city. Scotch and Reisz's texts both feature restless teenagers who, dissatisfied with the safe but predictable lives mapped out for them, find fulfillment in lycanthropy.

The werewolves in *Sharp Teeth* differ considerably from those portrayed by Scotch and Reisz in that they are too busy struggling for survival to devote much time to existential teenage angst. Barlow's werewolves are also typically from low-income backgrounds, possibly raised within the city and as such do not experience such teenage rebellion, which sociologists such as Amy C. Wilkins identify as a middle-class phenomenon (28). Moreover, the L.A. setting is vitally important to Barlow's text, with the city almost becoming a character itself. The beach, the suburbs, rickety back alleyways all play their part in the action of the story. Nonetheless, the liminality of Barlow's werewolves and their determination to remain on the fringes of society are strongly reminiscent of the hunting techniques of wild wolves. Barry Lopez, in a detailed examination of the wild wolves, observes that their preferred prey tends to be the very old, very young, diseased or injured among their prey species. "Individuals the prey population can conveniently do without," Lopez notes unemotionally (58). Barlow's werewolves function in much the same manner, picking their victims carefully. Struggles over territory, such as Lark's plotting to take out two rival lycanthropic packs, are also similar to the behavior of wild wolves—or street gangs, a metaphor Barlow makes ample use of. The werewolf pack brings the wildness of the wolf pack into the city, and it simultaneously brings an element of tribalism, associated with street gangs, into the petrified structures of civilization. Although not a direct product of nature, tribalism—in which members of a tribe assist one another and stay together for protection—is reminiscent of a pre-industrial world when people lived by hunting and agriculture, of a time when they had a closer connection with the land and Nature.

This bringing of the wilderness, of Nature, into the city through lycanthropy is an increasingly prominent theme in popular culture. In her analysis of the werewolf in film, Barbara Creed suggests that "the genre seems to argue that humanity lost something important in the processes of evolution—that is, the wild and savage part of human nature. The individual who becomes a werewolf hunts and eats human flesh. The lost wildness is thus restored" (130). This interpretation of the contemporary werewolf in popular culture (literature *and* film) certainly has plenty of evidence to back it up, with films such as *Wolf* and novels such as *River* (2006) by Skyla Dawn Cameron emphasizing that humankind has undermined its essential connection to Nature, and that the werewolf is the conduit for returning it to modern life. Certainly, Barlow emphasizes that "there are still some watchful creatures/whose essence lies unbound by words./There is still a wilderness" (40). The theme of bringing Nature into the midst of the city is also prevalent in much literature set in Los Angeles. J. Scott Bryson asserts that "the natural world pervades the city's literature" (167) and that it is emphasized in L.A. fiction that Nature remains strange and chaotic, and refuses to be tamed by humanity. This is certainly true of Barlow's werewolves: strange, chaotic (despite Lark's best efforts to impose some order), they refuse to be tamed—especially not by the rather ineffective city police and other social organizations, which, like L.A. street gangs, they exist firmly outside of. They also exist outside of conventional gang structures in Barlow's novel. Although he bases his werewolf pack on gang culture, Barlow keeps a safe distance between human gangs and his werewolves throughout the narrative. In this sense, Barlow's werewolves and by extension the space they inhabit is very much a wilderness.

The construction of the space the werewolves inhabit as a wild, untamed area is ironically made possible by the fact that the werewolves have moved into the city, which is teeming with both human and lycanthropic inhabitants. According to J. Patrick Williams, "space is always socially arranged, structured by the expectations people hold for how others should behave" (153). Traditional expectations of the werewolf is that they will run amok and savage numerous unfortunate victims. Wild wolves are regarded in a similar suspicious manner, as a threat. Likewise, gangs are perceived as dangerous entities that must be contained. Barlow's werewolves/gang members take the city for their hunting grounds, and humans for their prey. In one darkly humorous sequence, it is described how one werewolf terrorized a fried chicken restaurant, eating humans and chicken alike. "It's either retreat/or adapt," the narrator notes sagely, briefly contemplating the impact of mass surveillance and safe streets upon the werewolves (45). In order to survive, they have had to adapt—not by leaving their essential wildness behind, but by bringing it with them into the city. However, categorizing the werewolf as representative of Nature in *Sharp Teeth* would not be wholly accurate either—the werewolf may be *supernatural*, but natural it most certainly is not. Barlow devotes a brief section of his novel to the origins in his werewolves, detailing their evolution, their struggle to survive in the wild, and after that the natural world is seldom invoked, either literally or as metaphor.

But the werewolf, as I have demonstrated, is entering upon a form of existence that is stunningly new by struggling to achieve subjectivity and a new form of identity. A new identity, fractured and manufactured, can be achieved most successfully in the environs of the huge, anonymous sprawl of L.A.—particularly if the werewolves keep to the edges of the social order, which is not difficult to do if, as Lark's werewolves do, you form yourselves into a street gang.

Werewolves, Gangs and Crime in L.A.

Werewolves are liminal beings in *Sharp Teeth*, existing very much on the fringes of human society and banding together for some form of companionship and protection, though this existence is fundamentally unstable and prone to disruption through power struggles and attempts by members to leave for a new, solitary life. The werewolf pack, in short, bears a distinct resemblance to an L.A. street gang. Gangs are comprised of those individuals, male and female, who have little status or interest in society. As James Diego Vigil comments, "basically, the street gang is an outcome and marginalization, that is, the relegation of certain persons or groups to the fringes of society, where social and economic conditions results in powerlessness" (7). This is an apt description of Barlow's werewolves, albeit most of them cannot be accurately described as powerless. Lark has culled his werewolves from the edges of society, just as the wild wolf pack hunt their prey from the outcasts among the herd, or gangs recruit new members who are alienated from mainstream society. It is also strongly reminiscent of Meyer's presentation of her werewolves in the *Twilight* series. The Quileute werewolves are an ethnic minority (Native American), live on a reservation and are economically disadvantaged. Their all-male society (with the exception of Leah, a very reluctant female werewolf) is also strongly reminiscent of a gang, as is their propensity toward violence. One book even contains a disturbing suggestion of domestic abuse, when it is revealed that one werewolf lost his temper and permanently scarred his girlfriend in a rage.

Vigil also observes that gang members have few links to conventional social structures such as schools or a stable home, and this is also true of

Barlow's werewolves. The She-Wolf has left an abusive relationship, Anthony the dogcatcher lost his father to a car accident when he was still a child, and even human Bonnie is shown slapping her nephew and arguing with her sister (not to mention her story concluding with her implied transformation into a werewolf).

The concept of the werewolf pack as street gang does not correspond entirely as to how gangs, particularly notorious L.A. gangs such as the Bloods and the Crips are perceived by the general public. Tim Lucas observes that L.A. gangs were largely perceived as a racial issue by the general public in the U.S. during the 1990s (152). He also identifies what he terms the moral panics surrounding gangs as a youth issue, linked to increased public fears regarding juvenile delinquency (152). Barlow does not pay much attention to racial issues, although several of his characters are Hispanic. Also, his werewolves are not teenagers: although Barlow does not specify their ages, the life experience of most werewolves implies they are no longer adolescents. Their similarity to gang members stems primarily from their marginalization from (human) society and their desire for companionship. As J. Patrick Williams suggests, when analyzing research into what caused gangs to form in the first half of the twentieth century in the U.S., "gangs were not caused by psychological abnormality, but rather by sociability and a shared sense of excitement" (22). The werewolf pack has only recently begun to appear in lycanthropic fiction, with the werewolf prior to the 1990s being very much a solitary creature. The werewolf pack/gang has been made possible by the advent of lycanthropic subjectivity, enabling them to live alongside one another and with the human population.

However, the werewolf, like L.A. gang members, is still constructed as the other. As Lucas observes in his study of Californian gangs and moral panics, associating gangs with a specific geographic area allows the normalized community to impose a literal and metaphorical distance upon gang members (150). The distance in Barlow's novel is not a literal one (he does not confine his packs to specific locations, despite Lark identifying possible rival packs in Long Beach and San Pedro). A metaphorical distance definitely exists between his werewolves and the human population, however. They bring an undeniable wildness into the city, living and hunting as wolves whenever they wish. Despite their ability to pass themselves off as human, Barlow's werewolves are a breed apart, and even the decent dogcatcher Anthony, who is born human and turned into a lycanthrope, leaves human existence behind by the conclusion to the novel. Significantly, he and the She-Wolf live in the liminal space of the beach, located between land and sea, an appropriate area for beings who either cannot or do not wish to live among normal humans. Although the werewolf has begun to attain subjectivity and to move into the city in contemporary popular culture, it is still too wild and wolfish, still too other, to be fully accepted and integrated into human society and for that reason must live on its fringes, as a pack, or even as a gang, with fellow marginalized beings.

Conclusion

In a city that is fractured by its very nature, the werewolves are also fractured in nature—but their unceasing energy and vitality, which has found expression in the fights they participate in and L.A.'s never-ending urban sprawl, has the potential to cause even more damage to the city. For this reason Barlow's werewolves are relegated to the side-lines of the city, to cull the humans who will not be missed. They do their best to be invisible, to stick to the shadows and live a shadowy existence. Although the werewolf has existed outside human society for centuries, *Sharp Teeth* depicts the lycanthrope at a transitional moment. Caught between human society and the pack, having left the wilderness behind but not quite absorbed fully into the city either, Barlow's lycanthropes are fractured beings, neither one thing nor the other. But one aspect of his novel's climax is worth noting. While the werewolf in popular culture frequently dies at the end of whatever story or film it features in, a number of Barlow's lycanthropes are permitted to survive past his novel's closure. While they cannot be assimilated into mainstream L.A. society just yet, the werewolf serves as an excellent metaphor for the gangs that populate its streets and even the city itself. Divided, conflicted and fierce, they are simply too suited to life in the big city to be exterminated altogether. Werewolves in *Sharp Teeth* stick to the shadows, but are undaunted by what they find there, too busy living and fighting to be frightened. As Barlow phrases it, "life goes on. The light asks little from those who send the darkness away" (45).

Works Cited

Anderson, Sam. "Hair of the Doggerel." *New York Magazine*. New York Magazine, 4 February 2008. Web. 2 March 2016.
Barlow, Toby. *Sharp Teeth*. London: Random House, 2007. Print.
Bourgault Du Coudray, Chantal. *The Curse of the Werewolf: Fantasy, Horror, and the Beast Within*. London: I.B. Tauris, 2006. Print.
Bryson, J. Scott. "Surf, Sagebrush and Cement Rivers: Reimagining Nature in Los Angeles." *The Cambridge Companion to the Literature of Los Angeles*, ed. Kevin R. McNamara. Cambridge: Cambridge University Press, 2010. 167–76. Print.
Creed, Barbara. *Phallic Panic: Film, Horror and the Primal Uncanny*. Carlton: Melbourne University Press, 2005. Print.
Friedman, Lawrence, M. "Public and Private Eyes." *Law and Popular Culture: Current Legal Issues 2004*, ed. Michael Freeman. Vol. 7. Oxford: Oxford University Press, 2005. 375–84. Print.
Frost, Brian J. *The Essential Guide to Werewolf Literature*. Madison: University of Wisconsin Press, 2003. Print.

Lehan, Richard. *The City in Literature: An Intellectual and Cultural History.* Berkeley: University of California Press, 1998. Print.
Lopez, Barry. *Of Wolves and Men.* New York: Scribner, 2004. Print.
Lucas, Tim. "Youth Gangs and Moral Panics in Santa Cruz, California." *Cool Places: Geographies of Youth Cultures,* ed. Tracey Skelton and Gill Valentine. London: Routledge, 1998. 145–60. Print.
Mansfield, Nick. *Subjectivity: Theories of the Self from Freud to Haraway.* New York: New York University Press, 2000. Print.
Murphet, Julian. "The Literature of Urban Rebellion." *The Cambridge Companion to the Literature of Los Angeles,* ed. Kevin R. McNamara. Cambridge: Cambridge University Press, 2010. 101–10. Print.
Otten, Charlotte, "Introduction." *A Lycanthropy Reader: Werewolves in Western Culture,* ed. Charlotte Otten. Syracuse: Syracuse University Press, 1986. 1–17. Print.
Pulliam, June. *Monstrous Bodies: Feminine Power in Young Adult Horror Fiction.* Jefferson, NC: McFarland, 2014. Print.
Robshaw, Brandon. "Review of *Sharp Teeth* by Toby Barlow." *The Independent.* The Independent, 23 October 2011. Web. 6 November 2015.
Vigil, James Diego. *A Rainbow of Gangs: Street Cultures in the Mega-City.* Austin: University of Texas Press, 2002. Print.
Wilkins, Amy C. *Wannabes, Goths and Christians: The Boundaries of Sex, Style and Status.* Chicago: University of Chicago Press, 2008.
Williams, J. Patrick. *Subcultural Theory: Traditions and Concepts.* Cambridge: Polity Press, 2011. Print.

Stuck Here Forever
Los Angeles as Purgatory
in American Horror Story

ROSE BUTLER

City of Lost Souls: American Horror Story and Los Angeles

Combining the talents of writer/director duo Brad Falchuk and Ryan Murphy—known for their collaborations on *Nip/Tuck* (FX: 2003–2010), *Glee* (Fox: 2009–2015), *Scream Queens* (Fox: 2015–) and *The People Vs. O.J Simpson: American Crime Story* (FX: 2016)—anthology series *American Horror Story* (hereafter *AHS*, 2011–) has, over five interconnected seasons, explored the dark underbelly of past and present American culture.

The retroactively titled *Murder House* (2011) follows a suburban family to a restored—and haunted—Los Angeles mansion in a last-bid attempt to reconcile their failing marriage; *Asylum* (2012) focuses on the crumbling psyche of the staff and residents at Briarcliffe Manor—the titular asylum—in Massachusetts; *Coven* (2013) takes us to post–Katrina New Orleans and follows the patriarchal oppression of two rival covens of witches; *Freak Show* (2014) comments upon the discrimination facing the cast of one of Florida's last remaining curiosity acts, while *Hotel* marks the series' return to California and Los Angeles. This collection is concerned with depictions of California's dark side, and the two seasons of *AHS* that utilize a Californian setting a notable for playing with many of the staple themes of dark fiction centered on Los Angeles; the fictionalized L.A. of *Murder House* and *Hotel* has a particular lure for the sinful and corrupt. Enticed by the excess and decadence that the city offers, they become trapped by its insidious web of lies; both seasons comment on celebrity and the pursuit of fame as synonymous with death or—for the few lucky characters—a painful rebirth. *AHS*' imagined Los Angeles, then, is everlasting and unforgiving: a revisionist depiction of purgatory.

Los Angeles has traditionally been conceived as either a heavenly vision or a hellish nightmare. Typically seen as a polarizing city, it has been described as "the city of the Big Dream, but ... also a city in which dreams can disappear in a moment" (Scruggs 82). A sunny, golden-hued haven, it is often positioned at either end of a spectrum: "redolent of paradise," or a grubby cesspool of corruption and vice, "stinking of hell" (Sullivan 2). However, Sullivan interrogates the city's apparent polarity, investigating this alleged formulation of Los Angeles as a site existing "at one or another end of a continuum." Rather, he argues, "that every point along the continuum exists within Los Angeles" and ultimately, the city exceeds, "supersedes and sunders" this spectrum to exist outside of this strict dichotomy, shaking off "conceptual straightjackets" (2) to stand as a place tethered to each imagining. Sullivan is not alone in suggesting that Los Angeles holds an uncommon duality, as Balazs also notes "it has come to play the role of both utopia and dystopia," alluding to a schizophrenic space of both good and evil. L.A. is a town at odds with itself; as Balazs continues, "while it is the source of our notion of glamour, it is also blamed for the failings of our morals." It is, he argues, "the same place as heaven and hell" (12).

Despite academic research suggesting that the cultural formulation of L.A. sits somewhere on a vast scale, depictions in media and fiction perpetuate binary oppositions in their interpretations of Los Angeles. In one of the earliest conceptions of L.A. as a place synonymous with evil, Brecht and Weill's satirical ballet *The Seven Deadly Sins* (1933) uses American cities to represent each of the cardinal sins. While the first city goes unmentioned, the protagonist meets Pride in Memphis, Gluttony in Philadelphia, Lust in Boston, Greed in Tennessee, Envy in San Francisco and Wrath—typically regarded as the most abhorrent sin—in Los Angeles. The satire is clearly influenced by early theological works in art and literature, predominantly Dante's *Divine Comedy* (1320), separated in to its three parts: *Inferno*, *Purgatorio* and *Paradiso*; Chaucer's *Canterbury Tales* (1475), particularly Fragment X: *The Parson's Tale*; Bosch's painting "The Seven Deadly Sins and the Four Last Things" (approx. 1500), Spenser's *The Faerie Queene* (1590) and Milton's *Paradise Lost* (1667) with its pedagogical telling of biblical tale, "The Fall of Man." Referring to contemporary examples such as *City of Angels* (1998) and *Constantine* (2005), Solomans observes that the imagined L.A. respectively functions in these texts as a heavenly port and a literal hell on earth (6). Through such fictional constructions, Los Angeles takes cultural shape only as a city of the blessed or the damned; a place that can make dreams come true, or one that has "abused and destroyed, disappointed and enraged many of the people who have lived in, or known it" (Shiel 17).

Traditionally, then, Los Angeles has either been perceived as a paradise or a netherworld; for *AHS*, it is most closely aligned with Sullivan's framework, falling somewhere in between as a modern imagining of the city as an eternal purgatory for the tormented. It is a text that does not polarize L.A. in the same manner as many modern fictional depictions of the city; Los Angeles is not heaven nor hell, but a place of continuous anguish—a reimagined purgatory.

Of course, the dominant form of Christianity in American culture is Protestantism, which has given birth to a number of other prolific denominations including Evangelism and Baptism. American horror fiction—and particularly the horror film—has often demonized Catholicism and its doctrines, including the concept of purgatory as a transitory and terrible place for malevolent and harmful spirits. As Curtis suggests, "The Protestant response to the Catholic category of Purgatory and the scope that it gave for a space between life and death was to assert that all spirits were demonic in origin and that they were manifested by conjuring and manipulation" (175). California, however, has a particular connection to Catholicism that is not common across much of the rest of the United States thanks to its association with Hispanic and Latino cultures; the territory was claimed for the Kingdom of Spain in 1542 by Portuguese-born explorer Juan Rodríguez Cabrillo, and today just under half of the city's residents are of Hispanic or Latino origin; the city's name, of course, literally translates to "The Angels." So while the title *American Horror Story* strongly connotes white Protestant culture, the strong historical bonds of Catholicism with California—the wider location of *Murder House* and *Hotel*—explains the series' focus on depictions of the afterlife in Los Angeles. I would argue that the addition of purgatory to the conceptual rhetoric of *AHS* seems not only justified, but also essential in highlighting the city's uniqueness on the map of American culture.

To understand *AHS*'s interpretation of purgatory, it is important to contextualize its conception in Catholic cosmology. Catholic theologian Gary Anderson posits that "when one sins, something concrete happens: one's hands may become stained, one's back may become burdened ... and the verbal expressions that render the idea of forgiveness follow suit: stained hands are *cleansed*, burdens are *lifted*." This concept, typically referred to as the "final purification," exists in a number of fictionalized representations of the afterlife that reinforce purgatory as a place of forgiveness and repentance. Such accounts also suggest that until guilt "has been engaged and dealt with ... that thing that sin has created will continue to haunt offenders" (4, original italics). The primary function of purgatory is the spiritual cleansing of unholy souls so that individuals may become "holy and thoroughly upright in spirit and character" (Walls 4). Purgatory, then, has been traditionally theorized as a place for sinners to atone for their transgressions in life; to show remorse and receive forgiveness. More importantly, purgatory is traditionally assumed to be temporary. Heaven and hell are eternal; purgatory, by its very definition, is not. It is a transient state, a midpoint between the paradise of heaven and the everlasting torment of hell, a place where "only the most vile are irrevocably damned" (Van Scott 240).

The traditional view of purgatory is revised in *AHS*, where the purgatorial realms of Los Angeles' haunted mansions and decaying hotels remove the opportunity for expiation and penitence. When a character dies within the boundaries of the Murder House and the Hotel Cortez, they remain locked in that netherworld forever; they are, in short, holding pens for L.A.'s sinners. With no chance of spiritual purification, their souls become trapped in perpetual misery. Balazs suggests that the siren city of Los Angeles represents a "Mecca for the damned" (1996, 247), but while many works of art centered on L.A. imagine it as hell on Earth, *AHS* figures it as a void between reality and damnation; here, the transitory purgatory of orthodox Catholicism is replaced with indefinite waiting in cages that offer no cleansing of the soul, no purification, no atonement—only boredom and misery. Traditional purgatory is defined by time; *AHS*' purgatory, then, is the site of eternal contemplation of sins committed in life with no hope of forgiveness: a wretched and eternal time warp.

Reading *AHS*' Los Angeles as a modern vision of purgatory reveals a great deal about the cultural perception of America's "Dream Factory" and reinforces Katherine Gin Lum's observation that California is representative of a "damned nation" (9). Subverting popular portrayals of the city as a "Dreamland" (Anger 12), Murphy and Falchuk's vision is a cesspool of decay and lies in which the dead are imprisoned with no hope of escape. L.A. is thus rendered as a place of never-ending perdition for those unfortunates who fall for California's false promises. In turning Los Angeles into a living nightmare, Falchuk and Murphy build upon Solomans' dualistic idea of the city's "continually fascinating dark charms as both the city of angels and place of apocalyptic despair" (7) ultimately aligning it with Andre Balazs' perception of L.A. as "the most terrifying town in America" (247).

"You're gonna die in here": The Murder House as Californian Purgatory

In the series' first visit to Los Angeles, *Murder House* follows therapist Ben, his wife Vivien Harmon (Dylan McDermott and Connie Britton) and their teenage daughter Violet (Taissa Farmiga) as they move to California for a "new start" after Vivien's discovery of Ben's infidelity. After falling in love with the West Coast lifestyle—"Even the light is different out here!" ("Pilot"

1:1)—and a suspiciously inexpensive mansion, the Harmons soon move in. Despite their realtor recalling that the previous owners died in an apparent murder/suicide, the family refuses to be swayed by the house's grisly past. They have barely unpacked before they begin to encounter the doomed ghosts of many former residents, who appear in tangible form; there are approximately fifteen ghosts trapped in the house when the Harmons first arrive, each with distinct connections to specific parts of the building's history.

Much like the festering interior of the Cortez in *Hotel*, the Murder House's ornate Victorian exterior masks the true extent of its internal horror. In an allusion to the aforementioned striking artifice of golden Los Angeles, the mansion is beautiful and opulent on first impression, boasting large stained glass windows, mahogany paneling, Tiffany & Co fixtures and expensive period fittings. But the building itself and its surrounding grounds are concealing something that cannot be hidden for long: Vivien quickly starts to renovate the house, peeling back wallpaper to uncover a disturbing original mural, while Ben builds a summer house in the back yard to conceal the burial site of a number of bodies.

The building—like so many literary haunted houses—becomes a character of its own; Violet even remarks, "I love our house, it's got soul" ("Murder House" 1:3). In his monograph on the cinematic haunted house, Barry Curtis asserts that the haunted house is "deeply implicated with humanity" with its "uncanny animation and flexing of margins ... the structure itself is prone to metamorphosis and agitation" (10–11). This is most apparent in *Murder House* when Violet eventually finds out that she too has died in the house (1:10). When she desperately tries to leave, the mansion's corridors and doors morph into dead ends and endless hallways, trapping her in an inescapable suburban nightmare.

Though they range from being sorrowful and wretched to malevolent and destructive, the house's trapped spirits all share a common connection: they are representative of one of the Seven Sins. Moira (Frances Conroy) represents lust and is able to manipulate her image; she appears to Ben—and a young, male property developer—as a seductress (Alexandra Breckenridge) while to Vivien and Violet she is an elderly housekeeper. Original owners Charles Montgomery (Matt Ross) and his wife Nora (Lily Rabe) are embodiments of gluttony, fixed in the decadence and excess of the 1920s. Gay couple and former owners Chad (Zachary Quinto) and Patrick (Teddy Sears) are symptomatic of greed: materialistic and covetous, they bicker over the remodeling of the home, making snide remarks about Vivien's apparent lack of style. Neighbor and one time resident Constance (Jessica Lange), the only living character to represent a sin, is the season's incarnation of pride, a once fame-hungry young would-be starlet who is now embittered and ageing; she states, "I knew I was destined for great things. Person of significance ... but my dreams became nightmares" ("Afterbirth" 1:12). She visits the house constantly in attempts to see two of her children who died there: Beau (Sam Kinsey) and Tate (Evan Peters), both of whom she favors over her living daughter, Adelaide (Jamie Brewer). Tate is the season's emphatic embodiment of wrath: a psychopathic murderer responsible for a high-school shooting reminiscent of the Columbine High School massacre, he cannot accept his death. He manipulates Ben and Violet, and in one of the season's most horrific acts, rapes Vivien.

In the first of a series of flashbacks littered throughout the season, we meet the Murder House's youngest ghostly residents in the pre-credit sequence of the first episode ("Pilot" 1:1). An intertitle reads "1978," and a shot of the house reveals it is in a state of decay; vines have trailed over the brickwork and windows are broken. Two pre-teens run up the garden path and past a young Adelaide who ominously warns: "You are going to die in there." Ignoring her, they rush inside to wreak havoc, throwing firecrackers and swinging baseball bats. Outside, Addie repeats "You're gonna regret it." Sure enough, before the credits roll, they meet their demise in the basement. In cuts to the present day, the two boys are now captured in perpetual adolescence and continue to play pranks on the living residents of the house, throwing eggs at Ben's car ("Halloween, Part 1" 1:4) before irreparably damaging it in a later episode ("Birth" 1:11).

Through its depiction of its ghosts, *Murder House* utilizes a revisionist approach to purgatory and the afterlife. Throughout the season, little information is given regarding the history of the eponymous haunted mansion; we are not privy to where its apparent curse came from or why. It is only revealed that those who meet their end on the property are destined to stay there; in fact, the only time the ghosts can leave the grounds is during the season's two-part episode set on Halloween night ("Halloween, Part 1" 1:4; "Halloween, Part 2" 1:5). The apparitions are able to choose if they interact with—or are "seen" by—the living and in doing so, much like the vampires of *Hotel*, they occupy a position between life and death—and by extension, heaven and hell. Trapped inside the house, they are caught in a microcosm of L.A. society, suspended in time and forced to watch the lives of the existing tenants unfold around them.

The ghosts function, then, as Tom Ruffles suggests is true in the case of many on-screen specters, as striking "reminders of mortality," invoking a "fear of what is *beyond* death" (3, original italics). *Murder House*'s resident ghosts certainly act as fearful reminders of what awaits in the afterlife. While Ruffles argues that the cinematic ghost may occupy one of two binary positions—to frighten or to console—the fact that such phantoms suggest "that death is not the end" (1) is precisely what is so frightening and simultaneously sorrowful about the ghosts of *Murder House*. In the extended purgatory of

AHS, what lies beyond is, at best, perpetual boredom or, at worst, eternal misery.

Many of the building's ghosts—such as Tate and Hayden (Kate Mara), the envious student with whom Ben was having an affair—fail to accept responsibility for their sins, and become the house's most tormented spirits. They are haunted by their wrongdoings in accordance with Anderson's claim that those stuck in purgatory carry guilt with them (4). Their crimes are all the more horrific because they never truly accept responsibility; Tate is even confronted by the ghosts of his victims during Halloween. They demand an explanation for their deaths; Tate does not give them one. Only when challenged by Ben in the final episode ("Afterbirth" 1:12), does he admit to shooting his classmates, murdering Chad and Patrick and attacking Vivien. Even so, he fails to show any repentance or remorse. Ben, once but no longer Tate's therapist, quashes his empty, last-ditch attempts at atonement: "I'm not a priest. I can't absolve you" ("Afterbirth" 1:12).

During the final episode, we see the mansion's ghostly inhabitants—who appear to have paid for their sins and, perhaps more significantly, accepted their fate—dressing a Christmas tree in the house. Vivien and Ben are reunited and cooing over their stillborn son, Violet is contentedly hanging "ancient" ornaments on the tree, while Moira reminds her that "the word 'ancient' will lose all its meaning when your entire existence is one long 'today'" ("Afterbirth" 1:12). The Harmons and Moira have reached a degree of contentedness through their acceptance and admittance of their sins, with Ben and Vivien actively scaring away the next potential family to move in, and Moira admitting: "I would've made a good mother if I hadn't been such a little tramp" ("Afterbirth" 1:12). As the camera tracks backward, there is a shift to the darkness where Tate and Hayden are watching the festive scenario from outside. They are literally fenced out by iron bars at the window, while figuratively ostracized from those inside who have accepted their fate. For some—but not all—of the building's spirits, a haunted house has become a haunted home. They have not been forgiven, but they have accepted that it is their fate to remain trapped together forever.

Nobody Checks Out: Vampires and Eternal Punishment in Hotel

Following three seasons set elsewhere in the United States, *AHS: Hotel* marks a return for the series to the thematic concerns of *Murder House* as well as a geographical return to Los Angeles. Its plot centers around two narrative threads. The first is the elusive Cortez hotel in Downtown L.A. and its transient residents: the vampire Countess (Lady Gaga), her lovers Donovan

(Matt Bomer) and Tristan (Finn Wittrock), manager Iris (Kathy Bates), bartender Liz Taylor (Denis O'Hare), drug addict Sally (Sarah Paulson) and the Cortez's undead founder, James Patrick March (Evan Peters). The season's second plotline follows Detective John Lowe (Wes Bentley) and his investigation of a series of brutal murders, apparent revenge for violations of each of the Ten Commandments. As the season progresses, John's enquiries lead him to the inevitable, joining the two narrative strands together in the Hotel Cortez.

Much like *Murder House*, the backstories and interconnected relationships of *Hotel*'s characters are revealed through numerous flashbacks. *Hotel* also continues to connect earlier seasons together in the same way that *Freak Show* had done the previous year; a young Countess—Elizabeth Johnson—was once married to March (a clear nod to Chicago's serial killer and hotelier H.H. Holmes). In a flashback to 1926, she visits Charles and Nora Montgomery at season one's Murder House to undergo an abortion, creating a clear link between the Hotel Cortez and season one's house of horrors.

The Murder House and the Hotel Cortez share a number of similarities, most notably a sense of artifice and a tangible decay underneath the pretense of grandeur. In *Hotel*, the malevolent souls spend their eternity trapped inside the cavernous decaying building: a "no-tell motel" ("Checking In" 5:1). The 1920s Cortez is heavily indebted to previous cinematic depictions of horror hotels, particularly those adapted from the work of Stephen King; Falchuk and Murphy not-so-subtly borrow the carpet design of the Overlook Hotel in *The Shining* (Kubrick 1980), while its volatile Room 64 mirrors both *1408* (Håfström 2007) and *The Shining*'s ominous Room 237. The constant use of fish-eye lenses and repeated tracking shots of the Cortez's labyrinthine hallways are inspired by the claustrophobia and terror of Kubrick's famous sequences following young Danny peddling his trike along the Overlook's endless corridors.

Like the Overlook, the once opulent and decadent Cortez—with its gilded chandeliers, plush carpets and grandiose staircases—has now fallen into decay and disrepair. The building's deterioration seeps through its corridors; an almost living, breathing entity, it rots from the inside out. Festering rooms with blood-stained carpets and bodies under beds present the hotel as an updated *House of Usher* (Corman 1960). Here, the stench of death and damnation seems to seep down the hotel's every corridor; the perfect setting for eternal punishment.

Importantly, *Hotel* does not just return to *Murder House*'s Los Angeles setting, but also expands one of the thematic concerns at the heart of the earlier season: a socio-cultural critique of an unfortunate obsession with celebrity and fame. While this was a minor thematic concern in *Murder House*—primarily communicated through Lange's bitter and twisted Constance and

Mena Suvari's portrayal of Black Dahlia victim Elizabeth Short—2015's *Hotel* would give this theme a new and central prominence, the probable result of having cast pop sensation and cultural icon Lady Gaga in the season's central role.

Hotel provides constant reminders of L.A.'s symbiotic relationship with the movie industry and the metaphorical immortality which comes with being captured on celluloid. Numerous episodes include subtly playful but glaringly obvious nods to cinema: the Countess and Donovan pick up victims at a midnight drive-in screening of *Nosferatu* (1922) ("Checking In" 5:1); we see behind-the scenes filming of 70's Blaxploitation films called "Slaughter Sister," "Silky Fine" and "Bride of Blackenstein" ("Mommy" 5:3), clear nods to exploitation pictures such as *Blacula* (1972) and *Blackenstein* (1973); the Countess appears as a 1920s Hollywood chorus girl in a flashback to Hollywood's Golden Age ("Flicker" 5:7); and silent film star Valentino (Wittrock) is turned into a vampire at the hands of non-other than *Nosferatu* director F.W. Murnau, who in reality met a suspicious death at the wheel of an automobile in California's Santa Barbara.

Though it is more clearly concerned with fame than *Murder House*, *Hotel* also maintains the earlier season's theistic concern with endless purgatorial punishment for sins and transgressions in life. The unseen antagonist—the "Ten Commandments Killer"—is a serial murderer clearly influenced by Kevin Spacey's portrayal of Joe Doe in David Fincher's *Seven* (1995). Here, the killer prowls Los Angeles dishing out corporeal punishment to those who flout Christian doctrine, replacing *Seven*'s punishment of the Deadly Sins with brutal retribution for disobeying the Ten Commandments. *Hotel*'s crime scene set-pieces are suitably gruesome and also replicate those featured in Fincher's film, including the crucifixion and disembowelment of two male twins who have disrespected their mother and father; the sexual assault on and bludgeoning of a movie fan and film reporter slaughtered for his worship of false idols; and the mutilation of two gossip site editors, their tongues pulled out and nailed to their desks as part of righteous punishment for bearing false witness.

Combining an overarching theme of sin with another haunted location in the Cortez, *Hotel*—in contrast to *Murder House*—widens its repertoire of monsters. While season one represents those doomed for an apparent eternity solely in the form of ghosts stuck inside a cursed mansion, the Hotel Cortez plays host to a group of resident vampires in addition to its own group of spirits, all of whom died in or on the grounds that surround the building. Falchuk and Murphy utilize the vampire myth and its associations with eternal life as a metaphor through which they extend the season's thematic concern with eternal purgatorial suffering.

The Gothic figure of the vampire is one of transcendent reality; it represents a frightening fusion of the living and the dead. Traditionally, the vampire in popular culture has "[allowed] for a continuing fascination with something beyond human life, a seemingly constant curiosity of the human soul" (Murnane 150). Writing about the vampire's link to our perception of the afterlife in her monograph *The Gothic Imagination*, Linda Bayer-Berenbaum states that "like the saint or savior, he is all suffering, a perverted Christ figure who offers the damnation of eternal life in this world rather than the salvation of eternal life in the next. Life after death has been transposed into a living death" (35). Building upon Bayer-Berenbaum's assertion, the vampires—and by extension, ghosts—of *Hotel* are not only representative of this "living death," but they are damned to eternal suffering, metaphorically trapped by their unnatural existence and literally trapped inside the confines of the Hotel Cortez. There does exist an alternative and largely contemporary conception of the vampire as "a kind of dark angel, a help to humankind, a hero or savior" (Hallab 133) who uses their eternal life to atone for their past wrongdoings. Unlike the heroic undead of modern vampire fiction, though, *AHS*' vampires are the very embodiment of human sins and weaknesses; similarly to previous literary depictions, such as master vampire Stephen Barlow in Stephen King's *Salem's Lot* (1975), they are "the emblem and fulfilment of the very human envy, greed and lust" (Hallab 133).

While the ghosts must wander its moldering halls, the hotel's penthouse is reserved for the vampires. Ageless, rich, and impossibly beautiful, the undead residents of the Cortez represent the lifestyle that motivates so many of *AHS*' narcissistic and aspirational characters, all of whom find themselves in Los Angeles. Here, the vampires do not bite, but cut; they sip their victims' blood from decanters while writhing in a blood-soaked sexual ecstasy, confirming that "vampires appeal to two of the only constants in life: sex and death" (Murnane 150). As embodiments of the vices of L.A., the vampires represent the resounding emptiness of the city obsessed with beauty. When the fictionalized Murnau transforms silent film stars into creatures of the night ("Flicker" 5:7)—lamenting the coming of sound as "the death of the gods"—he remarks that "eternal life is endless youth," the most bankable commodity in Los Angeles. As a result *Hotel*'s vampires are the most astute criticism of the city's rank artifice. Just like the imposing mansion of *Murder House* and the opulent 1920s décor of the fading Cortez, they appear to be beautiful on the outside—but beyond their veneers, they are symbolic of our worst weaknesses: greed, lust, envy and wrath. In *Hotel* they are also representative of the eternal punishment in *AHS*' revisionist depiction of purgatory; here, vampires are rendered as the living dead, trapped among death and decay in the form of the hotel's ghosts. They watch patrons check in, knowing that they themselves will never check out.

"No Refunds—Welcome to America": Los Angeles as the Center of Sin

Both *Murder House* and *Hotel* are aligned by a construction of Los Angeles as a place of ultimate evil. It is important to note that while *Murder House* takes its cues from haunted house narratives and *Hotel* draws on the vampire myth, both seasons also make reference to several real-life incidents of horror and suffering and transpose them to a nightmarish vision of L.A., creating a drastic reimagining of the Golden State. *Murder House* alludes to the infamous Manson Family slayings ("Home Invasion" 1:2) and the Black Dahlia murder ("Spooky Little Girl" 1:9). In its allusion to the Black Dahlia, *Murder House* incorporates one of America's most infamous unsolved murders, for which Americans have developed "a healthy appetite" (James 182), as it offers its take on the story of a woman who "had come to Hollywood to break into movies," while several months later, "in the pre-dawn hours ... her dismembered body—she had been cut in half—was carried from a black car, and deposited in an empty lot" (182). These links to the grisly cultural history of L.A. and the reappropriation of Los Angeles as a "Nightmare Factory" center on a depiction of the city as a pit of crime and decay. In trapping the season's unfortunate souls within walls that have witnessed some of the most atrocious crimes in California's history, *Murder House* underlines its vision of Los Angeles as a purgatorial space that ensnares all with its illusionary charm: the antithesis of the City of Angels.

Murder House also makes direct reference to violent incidents that occurred outside of California, chiefly the Columbine High School massacre of Littleton, Colorado, during which Eric Harris and Dylan Klebold—two high-school seniors—killed fifteen people including themselves during an armed assault. The final stage of the massacre in the school's library is directly alluded to in a flashback sequence of Tate's own killing spree, here relocated to a Californian setting ("Piggy Piggy" 1:6). In a direct connection to the season's religious themes, on the day of the shooting Klebold wore a t-shirt emblazed with the word "Wrath."

Hotel, too, plays on the horrifying history of the United States both within and without the state; the most obvious inspiration for the hotel itself is clearly the Hotel Cecil in Downtown L.A., notorious for renting rooms to serial killers Richard Ramirez in 1985 and Jack Unterweger in 1991. The hotel would make international headlines following the suspicious death of student Elisa Lam in 2003. *Hotel* is also heavily influenced by H.H. Holmes' "Murder Castle"; opened in 1893, Holmes' Chicago hotel was designed for the primary purpose of trapping and killing its guests; the secret passageways and hidden rooms in *Hotel* certainly emulate this. Similarly, in *Hotel*'s Halloween episode

("Devil's Night" 5:4), America's most notorious serial killers arrive at the hotel for an annual meeting: Richard Ramirez, Aileen Wuornos, John Wayne Gacy, Jeffrey Dahmer and the unnamed Zodiac Killer are all in attendance. Of course, these predators operated all over the United States; while Ramirez and the Zodiac Killer committed their crimes in California, Wuornos, Gacy and Dahmer stalked prey in Florida, Illinois and Milwaukee, respectively. Regardless of the fact that these killers hail from all over the nation, it is, of course, Los Angeles that plays host to their annual meetings: a city of the damned.

As a place of doomed souls, *AHS'* fictional Los Angeles becomes a purgatorial but everlasting prison for the transient spirits of America. Subverting traditional readings of the afterlife, the series creates a nightmarish vision of an eternal purgatory in contrast to its theorization in traditional Christian doctrine; a place where the deceased are caught in an eternal loop of misery and perpetually trapped somewhere between the living and the dead. Through their religious themes of sin, guilt and punishment, as well as the inclusion of both iconic creatures in the form of vampires and phantoms, and human monsters in dramatized versions of the nation's serial killers, *Murder House* and *Hotel*'s Los Angeles is a fictional ghost-town: America's dead end.

WORKS CITED

Aardweg Van Den, Gerard. *Hungry Souls: Supernatural Visits, Messages and Warnings from Purgatory.* Tan Books, 2009. Print.
Anderson, Gary. *Sin: A History.* New Haven: Yale University Press, 2009. Print.
Anger, Kenneth. *Hollywood Babylon: The Legendary Underground Classic of Hollywood's Darkest and Best Kept Secrets.* London: Arrow Books, 1975. Print.
Balazs, Andre, ed. *Hollywood Handbook: Chateau Marmont.* New York: Universe Publishing, 1996. Print.
Bayer-Berenbaum, Linda. *The Gothic Imagination: Expansion in Gothic Literature and Art.* Madison: Fairleigh Dickinson University Press, 1982. Print.
Braudy, Leo. *The Hollywood Sign.* New Haven: Yale University Press, 2011. Print.
Brodman, Barbara, and James E. Doan. *Images of the Modern Vampire: The Hip and the Atavistic.* Madison: Farleigh Dickinson University Press, 2013. Print.
Casey, John. *After Lives: A Guide to Heaven, Hell and Purgatory.* New York City: Oxford University Press, 2010. Print.
Curtis, Barry. *Dark Places: The Haunted House in Film.* London: Reaktion Books, 2008. Print.
Di Loreto, Dante, Brad Falchuk, and Ryan Murphy, prods. *American Horror Story: Murder House.* Television series. Los Angeles: FX, 2011.
Fahy, Thomas. *The Writing Dead: Talking Terror with TV's Top Horror Writers.* Oxford: University of Mississippi Press, 2015. Print.
Falchuk, Brad, and Ryan Murphy, prods. *American Horror Story: Hotel.* Television series. Los Angeles: FX, 2015.
Gilmore, John. *Laid Bare: A Memoir of Wrecked Lives and the Hollywood Death Trip.* Los Angeles: Amok Books, 1997. Print.
Hallab, Mary Y. *Vampire God: The Allure of the Undead in Western Culture.* Albany: State University of New York Press, 2009. Print.

James, Bill. *Popular Crime: Reflections on the Celebration of Violence*. New York: Scribner, 2012 [2011]. Print.
Lum, Katherine Gin. *Damned Nation: Hell in America from the Revolution to Reconstruction*. New York: Oxford University Press, 2014. Print.
Murnane, Ben. "Exactly My Brand of Heroin: Contexts and the Creation of the *Twilight* Phenomenon." *Images of the Modern Vampire: The Hip and the Atavistic*. Ed. Barbara Brodman and James E. Doan. Madison: Farleigh Dickinson University Press, 2013. 147–61. Print.
Ruffles, Tom. *Ghost Images: Cinema of the Afterlife*. Jefferson, NC: McFarland, 2004. Print.
Scott, Miriam Van. *The Encyclopaedia of Hell*. New York: Thomas Dunne Books, 1999. Print.
Scruggs, Charles. "Los Angeles and the African-American Literary Imagination." *The Cambridge Companion to the Literature of Los Angeles*. Ed. Kevin R McNamara. Cambridge: Cambridge University Press, 2010. Print. 75–87.
Shiel, Mark. *Hollywood Cinema and the Real Los Angeles*. London: Reaktion Books, 2012. Print.
Solomans, Gabriel, ed. *World Film Locations: Los Angeles*. Bristol: Intellect Books, 2011. Print.
Sullivan, Rob. *Street Level: Los Angeles in the Twenty-First Century*. Dorchester: Dorset Press, 2014. Print.
Walls, Jerry L. *Purgatory: The Logic of Total Transformation*. Oxford: Oxford University Press, 2012. Print.

Dreams Require Sacrifice
Fame, Fortune and Body-Horror in Starry Eyes

CRAIG IAN MANN *and* LIAM HATHAWAY

I Left My Soul in Los Angeles: Fame and Its Discontents

What is the cost of fame?

In the last five years, a cohesive group of horror films have emerged which link the pursuit of stardom—largely in California and particularly in Los Angeles—with the total degradation of the human form in a modern interpretation of a sub-genre that is most often associated with the 1970s and 1980s: body-horror. This contemporary wave of body-horror films uses disgusting images of bodily insurrection as a subversion of the engineered ideals of Hollywood beauty, and as a metaphor for the psychological and emotional trauma inflicted by the relentless pursuit of fame and fortune. All of these films—including *Antiviral* (2012), *Eat* (2014), *Excess Flesh* (2015) and *The Neon Demon* (2016)—are immeasurably important to the understanding of a dominant cultural conception of Hollywood celebrity, but none more so than the sophomore feature of co-writers and co-directors Kevin Kölsch and David Widmyer: *Starry Eyes* (2014), which sees an aspiring young actress transgress personal, social, moral and legal boundaries to secure celebrity status. In the process her body physically decays and is born anew as she is compelled to destroy her previous life so that she can become a member of the Hollywood elite.

Perhaps it is no surprise that fame has become a source of inspiration for the contemporary horror film; celebrity culture has exploded in the twenty-first century. The selected few who are lucky or unfortunate enough to be popularly known as "celebrities" have always been ubiquitous courtesy of their myriad appearances on magazine covers, television, radio, cinema screens and in various forms of advertising. Their aggrandizement has been further bolstered by contemporary society's increasingly intense relationship with fame and the famous, a relationship that is perpetuated endlessly by tabloid journalism, celebrity endorsements and, more recently, the rise of social media. Today, as Chris Rojek observes, "audiences are addicted to celebrities. They mainline on the aura of celebrity and rummage through the media for truffles of stardom" (Fame viii). We are now constantly encouraged to measure our appearances, lifestyles and ambitions against the standards of beauty and success we see on television and movie screens.

Hollywood, both as an entertainment industry and the celebrity capital of the world, is certainly not a place for the weak-minded and vulnerable. And yet, year in and year out, it continues to draw in countless young and expectant people who dream of recognition and success. As Kieron Connolly observes: "While a heady mix of wealth, power and ambition has always been the oxygen that fuels Tinseltown, the industry doesn't simply attract pretty people in search of fame, it *requires* them. And, like a fairytale, the lives of those so blessed can be radically remoulded" (7–8, original italics). However, for every actor, model, artist, or entertainer who is lucky enough to gain the recognition they crave and carve out a successful career, there are thousands of starry-eyed hopefuls who stumble away from Hollywood with nothing to show but a handful of shattered dreams. Why, then, are Hollywood's privileged few so alluring? Why do so many of us study them, follow them and wish to be one of them? We are often unable to actually meet them in person (and, if we do, more often than not the moment is fleeting and transient), but they can still have a profound influence on our lives.

Rojek observes, "We like to think [celebrities] have risen from the rank of ordinary mortals" (Fame 7). These are individuals who are idolized for their ascension from humble beginnings to a life in which they can do what they please, the world at their feet. This notion is supported by the rise of reality television shows, such as *The Osbournes* (2002–2005), *Run's House* (2005–2009) and *Keeping Up with the Kardashians* (2007–), that claim to offer a window into the glamorous—but generally mundane—"real" lives of the rich and famous. These shows profess to realistically portray the day-to-day activities of celebrities, which are ostensibly portrayed as similar to those of ordinary people: relationships, careers and familial conflicts. But, of course, their stars are not ordinary; they are obscenely wealthy people living in lavish mansions. The struggles of celebrity families as depicted on reality television ironically seem a world away from reality. In this regard, then, these shows are not just escapist entertainment but perversely aspirational. As Laurie

Ouellette asserts, such shows construct their subjects as "models for who to be and how to live" (44).

The stature of celebrities can grow even after their passing. Hollywood icons that have been deceased for decades such as Elvis Presley, James Dean, Marilyn Monroe, or Grace Kelly are still seen as relevant because of the inimitable impact their time in the limelight has had on the development of pop culture; their reputations ostensibly enable them to transgress death. But as Rojek continues, "celebrities are constructed" (Fame 7) and, as he further explains, "their presence in the public eye is comprehensively staged" (Celebrity 13). Accordingly, rock superstar David Bowie—whose death eerily occurred merely two days after his sixty-ninth birthday and the release of his final studio album, *Blackstar* (2016)—cemented his status as a divine, miracle-working showman to fans around the world when his producer Tony Visconti released a statement via Facebook informing fans that the album's release was a "parting gift" (n.p.). As Arthur G. Neal and Helen Youngelson-Neal suggest, then, "with the passing of time, the collective memories of celebrities tend to become endowed with immortality" (155).

So at its best, fame is attractive because it offers us a shot at eternal life. But at its worst, the crushing pressures of celebrity can cause untold psychological damage. Hollywood's elite are, of course, projected to us through meticulously constructed personas created by public relations teams; beneath that veneer, it has been suggested that there is a true self hidden from the limelight. Building on George Herbert Mead's sociological concept of the "veridical" self vs. the "Me," or the self as seen by others (173–178), Chris Rojek observes that "for the celebrity, the split between the I and the Me is often disturbing. So much so, that celebrities frequently complain of identity confusing the colonization of the veridical self by the public face" (Celebrity 11).

Rojek goes on to cite examples that validate his conception of an identity crisis among those in the spotlight, revealing a discomfort toward the split between the I and the Me: Cary Grant ironically acknowledged this schizophrenic phenomenon by remarking that even he wanted to be Cary Grant, while during an infamous incident in 1999, Johnny Depp verbally attacked paparazzi when they intruded on his evening in a London restaurant; he allegedly complained, "I don't want to be what you want me to be tonight" (qtd. in Rojek Celebrity 11–12). Of course, the apparent suffering of those in the spotlight can be a fabrication itself. As Anne Rothe points out, the proliferation of "misery literature" written by or about celebrities has led to a culture in which "the lives deemed most meaningful and significant are lives, particularly childhoods, of exceptional pain and suffering, rather than remarkable achievements. Or rather, surviving and overcoming abuse, dysfunction, addiction, and illness signify the ultimate accomplishment in contemporary American culture" (88). So while fame can be destructive in itself, it also feeds on narratives of self-destruction.

I'm Just Dying to be Famous: Celebrity Body-Horror

But before the pressures of a life in the public eye can come to bear— and potentially be exploited—those desperate to reach Hollywood's apex must pay their dues. Like many filmmakers, Kevin Kölsch and Dennis Widmyer are intimately familiar with beginning a career at the bottom of the Hollywood pile. After working in various behind-the-scenes capacities on studio films, Widmyer and Kölsch founded their own production company— Parallactic Pictures—in 2003. Parallactic's first project was Chuck Palahniuk's documentary *Postcards from the Future* (2003), the success of which allowed the two budding filmmakers to make their first feature: *Absence* (2009), which was shot in 2005 but not released until four years later, the same year that saw the release of their first short film, *Identical Dead Sisters* (2009). They followed *Identical Dead Sisters* with another short: *Ext. Life* (2010). A prototype for their breakthrough feature, *Ext. Life* focuses on the struggles of an actress on the brink of stardom. After four more years of dogged determination and with partial funding raised through a successful Kickstarter campaign, Widmyer and Kölsch took *Ext. Life*'s central theme—the price of fame—into much darker and subversive territory with their uncompromising body-horror effort *Starry Eyes*, which would gain them international recognition on the film festival circuit. A caustically cynical film, *Starry Eyes* imagines Los Angeles as a rotten, economically divided town of gross excess and urban decay, while the Hollywood machine is depicted as a cutthroat industry that wants nothing more than to consume young hopefuls desperate to ascend the hallowed steps to stardom.

Of course, such an abrasive comment on the dark side of Hollywood is not without precedent, and *Starry Eyes* is essentially a continuation of cautionary tales such as *Sunset Boulevard* (1950), *The Day of the Locust* (1975), *Barton Fink* (1991), *The Player* (1992), *Mulholland Drive* (2001) and, most recently, David Cronenberg's *Maps to the Stars* (2014). All of these films satirize Hollywood's ostensibly attractive allure as a road to destruction, madness and death, concentrating on protagonists who believe Hollywood will provide the opportunities for fame and fortune they so crave and earn them the respect and admiration of millions. *Starry Eyes* is most easily categorized as a horror film, but one firmly rooted in the tradition of the Hollywood satire; its protagonist is so obsessed with the lifestyle she desires that she is willing to surrender everything she loves to obtain it. But *Starry Eyes*—like *Antiviral*,

Eat, Excess Flesh and *The Neon Demon*—should not just be understood as a scathing satire but as a modern reincarnation of the body-horror sub-genre focused on the horrors endemic to the age of celebrity.

All four films draw on the themes of bodily destruction and decay pioneered in 1970s and 1980s body-horror, primarily by filmmakers such as David Cronenberg, Stuart Gordon, Brian Yuzna and Brian Thomas Jones. The integral characteristics of body-horror—and its defining elements as a distinctive sub-genre—were identified in two articles published in a 1986 issue of *Screen* by Pete Boss and Philip Brophy. Boss observes that in body-horror, "the enduring image is of the body irreversibly self-destructing by the actions of inscrutable cellular networks operating in accordance with their own incomprehensible schedules" (17), while Brophy suggests that "it is the mode of *showing* as opposed to *telling* that is strongly connected to the destruction of the body" (8, original italics). Together, these observations outline the key conventions of an archetypal body-horror film. Definitive texts in this sub-genre such as John Carpenter's *The Thing* (1982), Philippe Mora's *The Beast Within* (1982) and David Cronenberg's *The Fly* (1986) all feature a viral contagion, genetic abnormality or another insidious force that culminates with the body of the afflicted undergoing a graphic metamorphosis and/or deteriorating via the application of tangible and viscerally gross practical effects. In short, as Brigid Cherry suggests, in body-horror "monstrosity erupts from within and graphically transforms the body ... into something disgusting" (22).

Body-horror arose during "an era of bodies" (Jeffords 24) in which, according to Jennifer Grayer Moore, emerged a "health craze defined by myriad trends and fashions" (201). The sub-genre is often speculated to have resulted from a backlash against the excessive substance abuse and perceived debauchery of the previous decades (201), further bolstered by the sudden popularity of aerobics, Dancercise, cross-training, squash and so on. Physical fitness rose to a level of unprecedented importance and such obsessions quickly permeated and proliferated into mainstream culture via successful films and popular music. *Footloose* (1984), *Flashdance* (1983) and its tie-in music video for Irene Cara's "Flashdance ... What a Feeling," as well as the music video for Olivia Newton-John's 1981 hit "Physical"—in which the singer dressed as a gym trainer attempting to motivate several overweight men to shed some pounds—all allude heavily to this widespread cultural phenomenon.

Conversely, the rise of heart disease and cancer awareness campaigns, anti-smoking initiatives and the onset of the AIDS epidemic created a substantial dichotomy of the well and the sick, further cementing the era's emphasis on health. Actor Yul Brynner—who died of lung cancer in 1985—appeared posthumously in a calculated public service announcement to urge the American public to quit smoking in a particularly powerful example of the decade's obsession with physically transformative illnesses, while the AIDS-related deaths of such high-profile individuals as Rock Hudson, Liberace and Amanda Blake provoked widespread panic. As the AIDS crisis developed, San Francisco's KPIX produced an hour-long documentary titled *Our Worst Fears: The AIDS Epidemic* (1985), which attracted the station's highest ever ratings for a public affairs program (Kinsella 223). The UK's "Don't Die of Ignorance" campaign followed: the world's first government-sanctioned AIDS awareness campaign, its first public service announcements were broadcast on British television screens in 1987, replete with an apocalyptic voiceover by John Hurt.

That the era was defined both by considerable health scares and a preoccupation with cosmetic beauty created a distinctive contrast. As Susan Sontag declares, the arrival of these health concerns—chiefly AIDS—brought considerable attention to sick bodies, the "non-us" (48). These sick bodies were the focal points of the initial body-horror cycle: vessels that were no longer representative of the limber bodies showcased on MTV. In this original cycle, normal men and women contract incurable degenerative illnesses and are presented in various stages of bodily collapse that conflict with the decade's preferred image of the human form.

Body-horror has experienced a resurgence over the last decade, and while many examples of the modern cycle still largely conform to the observations initially noted by Boss and Brophy, there have been some aberrations from their archetype in films such as *American Mary* (2012) and *Excision* (2012), where the body's degradation is not figured as the result of "inscrutable cellular networks," but rather self-mutilation or extreme body modification. And in the case of *Starry Eyes* and its ilk, body-horror is reinvigorated for the age of celebrity; it uses the slow and painful destruction of the physical form as a metaphor through which to explore the psychological torment inflicted by a relentless hunger for recognition. As Michael S. Duffy pertinently notes, "many L.A.-set films continue to harbor the underlying notion that Hollywood's dreams can ultimately end with the destruction of everything within, whether in physical or … psychological terms" (6–7). These films allegorize the experience of chasing Hollywood stardom as a hideous transformative physical experience—and take that notion to graphic extremes.

For example, in *Eat*, an actress in her early thirties resorts to autocannibalism as a coping mechanism when she begins to face professional irrelevance as her age eclipses her ambition. In *Excess Flesh*, a growing antagonism between a size-zero model and her jealous roommate leads to imprisonment, torture and mutilation inside their dilapidated apartment (we later learn that they are two sides of the same person and their violent conflict is a literal manifestation of psychological warfare sparked by a paralyzing eating disorder). In *The Neon Demon*, an intense rivalry between a naïve young model and her jealous older colleagues climaxes in an eruption of extreme narcissism and graphic cannibalism; and in the dystopian world of Brandon Cronenberg's *Antiviral*—a brazen indictment of celebrity worship—the public are free to purchase freshly-extracted viral pathogens from sick celebrities and consume them to experience a perverse sense of intimate contact with their idols. In discussing his motivations for making the film with *Rue Morgue* magazine, Cronenberg commented: "It occurred to me that a celebrity-obsessed fan might desire disease and that connection; they might see it as a way of connecting to a celebrity and that seemed like a very interesting metaphor" (qtd. in Alexander 21). These films, then, combine Hollywood satire with body-horror, utilizing bodily destruction and revolting images as metaphors through which to confront issues relating to celebrity culture, body image and an unhealthy thirst for fame and perfection.

The aptly-titled *Starry Eyes* is the apex of this particular cycle and the most successful hybrid of body-horror and Hollywood satire. As Widmyer asserts, he and Kölsch set out to produce a parable about ambition and the horrific costs of celebrity ascension (Kölsch, Widmyer and Stevens); the resulting film is a visceral and perfectly realized indictment of a contemporary obsession with stardom. The film concentrates on Sarah (Alex Essoe), a young and introverted but determined would-be starlet living in Los Angeles with her friends, all of whom exist on the fringes of Hollywood. After a series of perverse auditions for a sinister and unusual production outfit that promises to make her a star, Sarah lands the lead role in an upcoming horror film. Soon afterward, she begins to rapidly deteriorate both physically and psychologically; her body graphically decays—recalling the bodily revolt at the center of *The Fly* (1986)—and her behavior toward those who try to help her becomes increasingly hostile. For Sarah, stardom comes at the price of her mind, body and soul.

"I will do whatever it takes": Starry Eyes

Starry Eyes begins with images that succinctly sum up the nature of its troubled protagonist and its nightmarish Los Angeles setting. Sarah's character is established by an opening scene that sees her standing in underwear before a mirror, scrutinizing her own body. She stares at her hair and face, and then pinches the flesh around her hips, thighs and stomach. She is tall and slim in build, traditionally attractive and perfectly healthy; the look on her face, though, immediately reveals a deep-seated dissatisfaction with her appearance. This opening scene immediately establishes the film's concern with the contemporary cultural conception of the female body; as Hilde Bruch asserts, the slim body is often associated with power, respect—and most importantly for Sarah—professional success (xvi), while her need to scrutinize her own appearance is indicative of Maggie Wykes and Barrie Gunter's assertion that our relationship with our bodies is increasingly framed in the context of celebrities admired for their ideal forms (3).

Sarah's self-directed scrutiny and subsequent renouncing of her private insecurity corresponds with Naomi Wolf's theory regarding the concept of female "beauty," which she postulates is a normative value constructed by social patriarchy to affirm its own predominance: "'Beauty' is a currency system like the gold standard. Like any economy it is determined by politics, and in the modern age in the West it is the last, best belief system that keeps male dominance intact" (3). In assigning value to beauty—and, therefore, to women—and rendering it an imposing and impossible physical standard, the implication is that women must compete for social precedence, which breeds anxiety and fear. In the highly competitive world of acting, Sarah is succumbing to the social pressures perpetuated by Western society and media. As Wolf continues, "inside the majority of these controlled, attractive, successful working women, there is a secret 'underlife' ... infused with notions of beauty, it is a dark vein of self-hatred, physical obsessions ... and dread of lost control" (2).

From this opening shot alone, then, it is apparent that in order for Sarah to feel capable of succeeding in the competitive world of acting—in which appearances are paramount—she must first reach satisfaction with her own body image, which will come only as a result of a hideous transformation. This point is accentuated when we learn she suffers from trichotillomania: she aggressively pulls her hair when frustrated. Sarah explains that this helps her to "stay in the moment," though it is clearly an early indicator that her later success will come at the cost of self-inflicted pain and suffering. Her vulnerability—and her propensity for self-harm—will prove to be gateways through which she will ultimately be exploited by Hollywood.

Meanwhile, Los Angeles itself is introduced as a cold, grey and unwelcoming place; an establishing shot of the Hollywood Hills—complete with the famous Hollywood sign looming ominously from the hillside under cloudy skies—immediately subverts any traditional perception of Los Angeles as "an endless vista of sun, sand and surf" (Zeller-Jacques 86). This becomes a recurring motif in the film, as such overcast and oppressive images of California—tempestuous clouds brewing overhead—recur throughout the narrative. It is also immediately established as a place of polarizing social and economic divides. For *Starry Eyes*, there are only two types of people in Hollywood: those who are involved in the film industry and those who desperately want to be; the privileged and the disadvantaged; the rich and the poor.

In all cases, the film primarily concentrates on the latter. Sarah and her friends represent an underclass desperate to join the upper echelons of society. Sarah herself works in a tacky fast-food outlet operating under the distasteful moniker "Big Taters," where she is incessantly derided by her manager, middle-aged pedant Carl (Pat Healy). Her friends are either unemployed or working in similar dead-end jobs. Hollywood's high society not only represents a form of escape, then, but the *only* escape possible from this lifestyle, adhering to Hollywood's reputation as "a magical dream factory where a little bit of luck can turn a small-town nobody into a star" (Zeller-Jacques 86).

But here the Hollywood elite is not represented as a benefactor waiting to bestow a lucky break on deserving young people, but as a single and frighteningly sinister production company, Astraeus Pictures—named for the Titan-god of the stars—that puts Sarah through a series of perverse auditions ostensibly in order to cast her in a horror film called "The Silver Scream." Following a harrowing anxiety dream in which Sarah begins to bleed from her scalp and descends into hysterics in a foreshadowing of her imminent psychological and physical collapse, her first audition almost ends in rejection before Astraeus' stony-faced casting agents catch her tearing chunks of hair from her head in a bathroom stall and ask her to repeat the episode for them. She descends into a seizure of unadulterated rage accompanied by the sickening diegetic sounds of hair ripped from its follicles.

The agents are impressed; in a satire of Hollywood's propensity to carelessly chew up and spit out vulnerable young aspirants, it is Sarah's willingness to mutilate her body that lands her a second audition. On the other hand, Sarah clearly feels that she has allowed a private side of herself to be violated; she is embarrassed to talk about her habit and visibly uncomfortable when asked to harm herself for an audience ("I've never done that for anyone before"). When she returns to the street, she looks disheveled and shell-shocked, breathing heavily as she leans against a wall for support; she has taken the first step in relinquishing her identity for stardom.

Sarah's identity is already blurred before her physical and psychological transformation begins. She is often seen to withdraw to the sanctuary of her bedroom, which takes the form of a quasi-religious shrine devoted to actresses of the Golden Age. These pictures represent the idealized version of Hollywood that she so badly wants to be a part of; an altar at which to worship her idols. Rojek suggests that in contemporary society celebrities have replaced monarchies and deities as the primary subjects of our devotion (Celebrity 14); Sarah does not kneel before gods but starlets who have long since gone to their graves. Though she will find out for herself that Hollywood's heavenly veneer hides a disturbing underbelly, she is still elated to be called back for a second audition, even following her intensely frightening first experience at the hands of Astraeus. In fact, she is so convinced that her call back will be her first step toward the red carpet that she immediately leaves her menial—but secure—job to whole-heartedly pursue a dream that will soon become a nightmare.

Sarah's metamorphosis truly begins at her second audition, when she is asked to undress—though the role does not call for nudity—for a series of photographs taken using a blinding flashbulb in otherwise total darkness. At first reluctant, she is convinced to comply when she is tellingly asked, "If you can't fully let go, how can you ever transform into something else?" In the series of strobe images that follow, we see subliminal flashes presaging Sarah's physical change, including split-second shots of her face adorned with razor-sharp teeth, a bloody mouth and piercing eyes; we also see a single shot of an ominous hooded figure, a hint at Astraeus' true nature. Though she is more than a little disturbed by the experience, she immediately agrees when the company call her back in the early hours of the morning to ask her to meet a producer at his private residence.

The producer (Louis Dezeran) is a stereotypical representation of the Hollywood elite: an older, wide-eyed white male who exhibits an initially endearing but quietly terrifying intensity when talking to Sarah about the role she so desperately desires. In a metaphorical summarization of *Starry Eyes'* own themes, he describes "The Silver Scream" as a "love-letter to Hollywood," one that will explore ambition as "the blackest of human desires." He bemoans Hollywood as a place of "desperation," before, ironically, offering the desperate Sarah everything she has ever wanted: a role that will launch her career and a chance to be loved and recognized by millions. Of course, she tells him, "I will do whatever it takes for this role." Encouraged, the producer puts his hand on Sarah's leg and begins to slide it evocatively up her thigh; disgusted, she flees the room. In this scene, *Starry Eyes* constructs one of its most biting satires of the Hollywood machine; the producer is a personification of the inveigling lure and devastating consequences of fame. He compliments Sarah, filling her with confidence and hope, and then reveals his ultimate intention to exploit her both sexually and commercially to his own advantage. And, of course, his actions are not just metaphorical; executives such as Harry Cohn of Columbia, Louis B. Mayer of MGM and Darryl F. Zanuck of Warner Bros. have all been accused of abusing their positions for their own sexual gratification (Connolly 262–65).

Despite her disgust with the producer's actions, Hollywood's allure is too much for Sarah to resist; after a short-lived return to Big Taters, she eventually relents to the producer's advances. Returning to his residence, she is convinced to perform oral sex on him as part of an occult ritual as hooded figures emerge and form a circle around her. In a literal manifestation of Jean Baudrillard's "cult of Hollywood idols" (10), the terrifying nature of Astraeus is revealed, as is *Starry Eyes'* most direct indictment of the industry elite.

Behind a production company manned by stoic casting agents and lecherous producers is a dark coven of individuals who have sold their bodies and souls for fame and success, and transgressed personal, social and moral boundaries to realize their dreams at any cost.

The specific nature of *Starry Eyes*' cult is left purposefully unexplained. Astraeus later gives a pentagram pendant to Sarah, suggesting that its members have literally sold their souls to the Devil, but very little exposition is provided to explain the coven's structure or practices. What is clear—perhaps in a reflection of Baudrillard's idea that "star idolatry" is not a "media pathology" but a product of Hollywood (10)—is that Astraeus worships fame above all else. This scene, in which the cult finally reveals itself, confirms *Starry Eyes* as a horrifying satire of the Hollywood establishment, figuring the rich and famous as demons and devil-worshippers who wish to lure young, desperate individuals to their doom. "Dreams require sacrifice," the producer later whispers, "and so do we."

Having sold her soul to Hollywood, Sarah's transformation soon begins in earnest and *Starry Eyes* confirms its status as not only an astute Hollywood satire but one of the defining examples of contemporary body-horror. Over the next few days, the heroine's physical form begins to graphically deteriorate; her fingernails fall out, her eyes discolor, she bleeds from several orifices and even vomits maggots in a visual representation of her inner rot. Astraeus simply tells her that she can embrace the change or die. In a disturbing sequence, Sarah walks, now little more than a diseased husk, to the house her friends share and systematically kills—or sacrifices—them by means of suffocation, stabbing and bludgeoning. In the film's undeniably most shocking moment, she kills one victim by crushing their skull with a dumbbell (a symbol clearly evocative of gym culture and representative of the pressure placed upon Sarah to conform to Hollywood's ideal image). She has now eradicated everything that might link her with the life before stardom—her mind, body, soul and even her friends—and will soon be reborn in an idealized form.

Sarah's visceral metamorphosis has several potential meanings. The first, of course, recalls *Starry Eyes*' opening shot—of Sarah meticulously examining her own body—and relates to the crushing cultural pressures placed on women who are, or aspire to be, in the spotlight. As Wolf states, "Many [women] are ashamed to admit that such trivial concerns—to do with physical appearance ... matter so much" (1). Of course, such pressures are magnified for women constantly living in the public eye; as Kristy Fairclough suggests, "Female celebrities are constantly scrutinized and surveilled in gossip culture. Their faces and bodies are regularly pored over, searching for evidence of ageing, surgical enhancement and cosmetic modification" (90). That Sarah must be destroyed to be reformed is perhaps a metaphor for the torment of starlets who feel compelled to maintain an ideal physical appearance, whether by strictly maintaining physical fitness or undergoing cosmetic surgery.

Such a conclusion recalls Catherine Spooner's view of the female form as it is often paradoxically imagined in contemporary Gothic literature. Building on Mikhail Bahktin's concept of "The Grotesque Body" (Bahktin 317) Spooner suggests that although the body is seemingly characterized by its fixed and stable nature, it is also defined by its liminality (67); in the contemporary world, the body can essentially be broken down, rebuilt and reappropriated until it becomes what is desired. Astraeus are able to remold Sarah's body—one thing that should be constant, even if it is a source of anxiety—into an uncannily perfect vessel fit for a Hollywood actress.

Alternatively, the film's body-horror could be considered a physical manifestation of Rojek's assertion that celebrities are media constructs; Astraeus has molded Sarah into a marketable commodity that will have "an enduring appeal for the audience of fans" (Celebrity 11). In order to achieve this, Sarah has to allow Astraeus access to her private life—or her veridical self. In doing so, she loses everything that defines her but ascends to stardom. Or, alternatively, Sarah's transformation is arguably a satire of what Rothe calls "popular trauma culture" (1); in an era preoccupied with celebrities and carefully weaved stories of self-destruction, Sarah's painful transformation could be considered a parody of a disturbing modern phenomenon: the salability of pain and suffering. It is important to note that while she is compelled to join Astraeus, Sarah is not coerced; she does everything—even commits murder—of her own volition. Sarah achieves success, but she chooses to physically suffer, relinquish her dignity and destroy everything she loves in the process.

In the film's final scenes, a large group of industry professionals—including Astraeus' personnel, now clearly represented as a sinister cult—gather on the Hollywood Hills, where they bury Sarah's rotting body. The following morning, a new, eerily inhuman Sarah, hairless and with emerald-green eyes, emerges from the ground. Suddenly, the oppressively grey image of Hollywood prevalent throughout the rest of the film has been replaced by a bright color palette and beaming sunshine. In Astraeus' absence, she is welcomed into the fold by a package bearing the message "Happy Birthday," in which she finds an expensive new outfit and hairpiece. A symbolic bookend sees Sarah once again stand in front of her mirror, a vision of glamour lit with warm colors. The scene is intercut with those long-dead matinee idols who adorn Sarah's walls—no longer gods, but equals.

Starry Eyes stands at the apex of its particular cycle, an indictment of celebrity culture that expertly combines biting satire with body-horror to create a terrifying image of Hollywood as a land of nightmarish transmutations and shattered dreams. Furthermore, like *Antiviral, Eat, Excess Flesh* and *The Neon Demon*, it plays on images of gross bodily destruction to critique a culture in which many measure their lives, bodies and aspirations against celebrities whose public images are forged constructions.

In defining body-horror, Boss suggested that "what is common is the sense of disaster being visited at the level of the body itself—an intimate apocalypse" (17). In contemporary body-horror concentrated on the ills of the celebrity age, Boss' intimate apocalypse becomes more intimate still: a physical manifestation of psychological torment relating to humankind's physical appearance, self-worth and aching ambitions. It is notable that the protagonists of *Antiviral, Eat, Excess Flesh, Starry Eyes* and *The Neon Demon* all willingly endure torturous suffering in the pursuit of either worshipping a star or trying to become one. They each believe that psychological and physical hardship will result in positive outcomes: feeling closer to an idol; conforming to cultural conceptions of bodily perfection; and ultimately obtaining fame, fortune and success. But for *Starry Eyes*, torment pays only at the cost of the soul; ambition is sickness and celebrity is death.

Works Cited

Alexander, Dave. "Generation Sick." *Rue Morgue* Sept. 2012: 16–22. Print.
Bahktin, Mikhail. *Rabelais and His World*. Trans. Helene Iswolsky. Bloomington: Indiana University Press, 1984 [1967]. Print.
Baudrillard, Jean. "Beyond Right and Wrong or the Mischievous Genius of Image." *Resolution: A Critique of Video Art*. Trans. Laurent Charreyon and Amy Gerstler. Los Angeles: Los Angeles Contemporary Exhibitions, 1986. 8–14. Print.
Boss, Pete. "Vile Bodies and Bad Medicine." *Screen* 27 (1986): 14–24. Print.
Brophy, Philip. "Horrality—The Textuality of Contemporary Horror Films." *Screen* 27 (1986): 2–13. Print.
Bruch, Hilde. *The Golden Cage: The Enigma of Anorexia Nervosa*. Cambridge: Harvard University Press, 2001 [1978]. Print.
Cherry, Brigid. *Horror*. London: Routledge, 2009. Print.
Connolly, Kieron. *A Century of Greed, Corruption and Scandal behind the Movies*. London: Amber Books, 2014. eBook.
Duffy, Michael S. "Los Angeles: City of the Imagination." *World Film Locations: Los Angeles*. Bristol: Intellect, 2011. 6–25. Print.
Fairclough, Kirsty. "Nothing Less Than Perfect: Female Celebrity, Ageing and Hyper-Scrutiny in the Gossip Industry." *Celebrity Studies* 3.1 (2012): 90–103. Print.
Gunter, Barrie, and Maggie Wykes, eds. *Media and the Body Image*. London: Sage, 2005. Print.
Jeffords, Susan. *Hard Bodies: Hollywood Masculinity in the Reagan Era*. New Brunswick: Rutgers University Press, 1994. Print.
Kinsella, James. *Covering the Plague: AIDS and the American Media*. New Brunswick: Rutgers University Press, 1989. Print.
Mead, George Herbert. *Mind, Self and Celebrity*. Chicago: University of Chicago Press, 1934. Print.
Moore, Jennifer Grayer. "The Eighties." *The Greenwood Encyclopedia of Clothing Through World History: 1801 to the Present*. Ed. Jill Condra. Westport, CT: Greenwood, 2008. 195–210. Print.
Neal, Arthur G., and Helen Youngelson-Neal. *Myth-Making and Religious Extremism and Their Roots in Crises*. Jefferson, NC: McFarland, 2015. Print.
Ouellette, Laurie. *Lifestyle TV*. New York: Routledge, 2016. Print.
Rojek, Chris. *Celebrity*. London: Reaktion, 2001. Print.

_____. *Fame Attack: The Inflation of Celebrity and its Consequences*. London: Bloomsbury, 2012. Print.
Rothe, Anne. *Popular Trauma Culture: Selling the Pain of Others in the Mass Media*. New Brunswick: Rutgers University Press, 2011. Print.
Sontag, Susan. *AIDS and its Metaphors*. New York: Farrar, Straus & Giroux, 1989. Print.
Spooner, Catherine. *Contemporary Gothic*. London: Reaktion Books, 2006. Print.
Starry Eyes. Dirs. Kevin Kölsch and Dennis Widmyer. Metrodome, 2015 [2014]. DVD. Commentary track.
Visconti, Tony. "He always did what he wanted to do…" 11 January 2016, 8:49 a.m. Facebook.
Wolf, Naomi. *The Beauty Myth*. London: Chatto & Windus, 1990. Print.
Zeller-Jacques, M. "Welcome to Hell-A." *World Film Locations: Los Angeles*. Bristol: Intellect, 2011. 86–103. Print.

Anywhere-Nowhere, California
The Real, the Imaginary and the Lonely Vampire in the Golden State

SIMON BACON

Jean Baudrillard, in *Simulacra and Simulation*, sees spaces such as Disneyland, California, as indicative of a separation of the real/reality and the imagined/imaginary, where the latter replaces the former. He further extrapolates this "hyperreality" to California itself which has replaced its actuality with an imaginary, dream space (11, 21). While this imaginary space is disconnected from reality, it does, on some level, still represent California. Baudrillard sees this phenomenon as intimately tied to consumerism/late capitalism and the entertainment industry in general, but locates its heartland specifically in California. The entertainment industry, then, increases the gulf between the imaginary/imagination and the real/reality, which is seen most clearly in films that depict this Californian dissonance by not depicting California at all.

It is not coincidental then that many of such films are vampire films—putting in the spotlight a figure that inherently depicts the collision of reality and the imagined, and featuring locations that are simultaneously L.A. and its environs but that could also be anywhere or nowhere—*The Omega Man* (Sagal 1971), *Vamp* (Wenk 1986) and *Blade Trinity* (Goyer 2004) are obvious examples but more are mentioned later. This tension is also seen in a recent vampire film, *A Girl Walks Home Alone at Night* by Lily Amirpour (2014), which, although set in the fictional town of Bad City, Iran, was actually filmed in Southern California, the resultant otherworldliness of the locations meaning they could be almost anywhere. Consequently, the scenes in *A Girl Walks Home* showing run-down buildings, an anonymous suburb and even a gulley full of dumped dead bodies gain metaphorical significance, referring not just to an imagined Iran and the actual locations used for filming but, as will be argued, to the nature of the Californian entertainment industry. While, thematically, the film's connection with the vampire genre is undoubtedly dominant, the complexity of its setting will also be considered with reference to Spaghetti Westerns, which themselves were filmed in Italy and Spain while representing the American West. This interpretation of the film appears to offer little escape from the Baudrillardian simulacra; however, *A Girl Walks Home* suggests through its use of the vampire and Western genres that the reality behind the surface/signifier—as a social construct where one's individual subject position is recognized (Berger and Luckmann 45)—will never totally disappear.

The Real California

Baudrillard sees the entertainment industry and the various media utilized by it as causing an increasing separation between our daily experience of reality as shown on media devices and the real world itself. More specifically, he points to Disneyland and places like it as being responsible for a growing detachment of reality from its simulation, so much so that the representation of a place drains its source of any meaning. Given California's history in the entertainment business, it is no coincidence that all the places that Baudrillard mentions are in the Golden State, with Los Angeles and Hollywood at its core: "Los Angeles ... is no longer anything but an immense scenario and a perpetual pan shot" (11). Reality becomes replaced by its staged, filmed and edited screen representation, so much so that one is unable to distinguish between the two. This, in turn, prevents direct interaction with reality without recourse to its simulacra, and so intimates that California can only be experienced through its own simulacra. Spaces such as Disneyland further intimate a loss of individual identity that, while situated within California, and indeed seen by Baudrillard as implicitly Californian in nature, could equally be representative of anywhere, or rather can be reproduced anywhere else and retain the same meaning. Urbanist Edward Soja in *Discovering Third Space* sees much the same situation in California, where, as a result of increasing urbanization and globalization, the distancing of the signifier from what it signifies destroys any idea of the region's architectural, and by extension cultural, identity. He, too, sees Los Angeles as the ground zero of the process whereby "the local and particular are becoming simultaneously global and generalizable" (17).

Both Jameson and Soja note that Los Angeles' Bonaventure Hotel might be seen as a synecdochal representation of the late capitalist space, anonymous and vertiginous, which requires signposts while remaining "unmappable" (Jameson 44). Similarly, Baudrillard's Disneyland speaks of places that have actual geographical locations, yet their representation denies this as it takes the form of anonymous, or cookie-cutter copies that can be placed anywhere in the world.¹ The example of Disney resorts effectively shows how this works for the original Disneyland in Anaheim, California, signifying both its actual geographical location and the cinematic simulacra that is Walt Disney films; when replicated around the world, it takes both these signifiers with it, exemplifying the global generalizations discussed by Soja but with the signposting mentioned by Jameson. This is further complicated, as the bleeding of simulacra mentioned by Baudrillard reinforces the unmappability of Los Angeles spreading out beyond its own suburbs into the state of California itself. Also Mike Davis envisions such a process as driven by a soulless "economic colony of corporations and investors headquartered elsewhere" (xii) and creating a future where "it is all too easy to envision Los Angeles reproducing itself endlessly across the desert" (12).

Thus, the real California becomes replaced by a simulacrum of itself, a representation that is simultaneously real and imagined, particular but anonymous, singular yet global. The only points which connect one to the other are the signposts which tell the passenger/spectator how to negotiate the created space. It is not coincidental that, being a major contribution to the formation of such spaces, the film industry creates equivalents of this process on the screen, where imagined spaces are themselves simulacra of California, a California that is losing itself. Further, it is equally not coincidental that these imagined spaces are often inhabited by imaginary beings such as vampires.²

California, the Vampire State

The vampire is an amazingly hyperreal construction, being so excessive in nature that it cannot be contained by either life or death and so is constantly reborn as a cultural signifier into undead existence. It is human in appearance and yet distinctly not human, and as such becomes a simulacrum of life that it simultaneously consumes and replaces. In this way it seems to embody Baudrillard's notion of the imaginary that feeds off the real, eventually taking its place as a separate, autonomous entity. It is almost inevitable that the real or imagined California, or Los Angeles, plays host to many vampire films. As well as those already mentioned above, *Blacula* (Crain 1972), *Scream Blacula Scream* (Kelljan 1973), *Christine* (Carpenter 1983), *Once Bitten* (Storm 1985), *Fright Night* (Holland 1985), *The Lost Boys* (Schumacher 1987), *Buffy the Vampire Slayer* (Kuzui 1992), and the television series of the same name (Whedon 1997–2003), *Blade* (Norrington 1998), *Modern Vampires* (a.k.a. *Revenant*) (Elfman 1998), *Angel* (Greenwalt 1999–2004), *The Thirst* (Kasten

2006), *Rise Blood Hunter* (Gutierrez 2007), and *Midnight Son* (Leberecht 2011) were all filmed or located in California. Of particular note in this incomplete list are *Blade* and *Blade Trinity*. The latter, though not filmed in L.A., shows simulacrum of the city constructed in its prequel, exemplifies the vertiginous nature of the city which spreads further and further, very much in the vein of Jameson's reflection on the Bonaventure Hotel. *Modern Vampires* and *Angel*, in turn, make specific links between vampires and the vampiric nature of the entertainment industry, and as Benjamin Jacobs notes in relation to *Angel*, represent the debate "whether L.A. is indeed the American Dream fulfilled, or … the 'dystopian nightmare of Hell Town grown to gargantuan proportions'"[3] (79). The four films see vampires as being drawn to California because of its past, at the same time as manifesting that past, which *Blade* and *Blade Trinity* show as a quality that is then extrapolated into the future. The figure of the vampire in these films, then, forms a simulacrum of both California and its people, equating the land with those that inhabit it.

This idea finds expression in a recent vampire movie filmed in California where the land, and those that live on it, are locked in a vampiric cycle they seem unable to escape. *A Girl Walks Home Alone* is set in modern-day Iran and, although billed as "the first Iranian vampire spaghetti western,"[4] it was actually filmed in Bakersfield, California, which strikes a very particular chord of both dissonance and equivalence between the two locations involved. Thus, the location in which the film is set is not the real Iran but an imagined one, and yet it is not the real Bakersfield either; neither are real but simultaneously simulacra of each other, a point that is further reinforced by the fictional Iranian town being called Bad City, which rather coincidentally echoes Californian Hell Town mentioned above. The importance of this locational dissonance is further reinforced through Amirpour's use of black and white photography, reinforcing the film's art-house credentials as well as providing a link back to earlier vampire films, not least George Romero's *Martin* (1977). The latter, also shot in black and white, and located in a run down post-industrial landscape of Braddock in Pennsylvania, features a young boy that, at one point, dresses up as Dracula and, might or might not be a vampire. Not surprisingly, this equivalence of simulacra is not unusual in Californian vampire films and, indeed, the very first adaption of *Dracula* by Universal Studios worked in a very similar manner. Browning's *Dracula* has more than one location, but the Count's castle in Transylvania was actually filmed in Universal City, California, and is constructed, to mis-appropriate David Skal's phrase, in what one might call "Hollywood Gothic" style—that is, an excessive Gothic style that could be located anywhere. The strangely ambiguous scenery fails to create any real sense of place and only produces an undefined otherworldliness. Even the Count's spectacularly Gothic castle is denied its Transylvanian roots by such oddities as armadillos and possums running around the hallways.

A Girl Walks Home very much repeats this geographical ambiguity, which is seen from the very start of the film, where a young man is shown rescuing a cat from a rundown neighborhood that could be on the edge of any town. From there the camera follows him traveling back home past a grain silo, a bridge over a ravine that is full of dead bodies, and a field of oil derricks. All these scenes could be shot anywhere near agricultural land, small oil fields or dry bed ravines, i.e., California. But as in *Dracula*, this anywhere/nowhere ordinariness is unbalanced by the dead bodies that seem just carelessly thrown into the large ditch with no attempt to hide of cover them up. This simultaneously detaches the location from the real world and intimates the darkness that hovers below the surface of this particular representation—the simulation/signifier that kills the real and the real location/signified (Hell Town/Hollywood) that is built on death and murder. Such otherworldliness or the sense that the location could be anywhere continues throughout the film. The poor neighborhood where the main protagonists live, the huge mansion where the young man works as a gardener and the suburb where he later gets lost and meets the girl who will change everything are all generically American—the suburb in particular looks like the product of any urban sprawl in the U.S. These non-places only receive any kind of specificity through the sounds, and, in particular, the voices, which the film uses as the kind of signposting that was used in Browning's *Dracula*. Robert Spadoni comments on the quality of Bela Lugosi's voice with its "mellifluously thick Hungarian accent," and "succulently foreign intonations" (76), which become the sign posts to fix the otherwise otherworldly location to Eastern Europe, as Dracula's voice becomes the one point of reality that gives specificity to the otherwise anonymous, if Gothic, location of the vampire's castle, which without it is nothing but a non-place for passengers—in this case the undead Count's victims—to pass through. Something similar occurs in *A Girl Walks Home*, where language provides the only real signpost to locate the largely anonymous locations. Not unlike in Browning's movie, sound is fairly sparse throughout Amirpour's film. It is mainly limited to occasional pieces of music—often actually played in the film rather than being background music, incidental sounds, or a rising rumbling noise used to indicate particular moments of tension. Therefore, the decision to have all the actors speak Persian is a significant one. The effect is not unlike that of Lugosi's voice which instantly signposts the location to a certain geographical point—the ambiguity of the anywhere/nowhere locations in *A Girl Walks Home* is instantly given specificity: Southern California becomes the Middle East.

Amirpour's film goes to great lengths to make its characters equally nonspecific. As a result, they become both anonymous and symbolic, which echoes Soja's concerns over architectural urbanization making the inhabitants as anonymous as the space they move in.[5] Consequently, the film features characters such as Hossein, the junkie, Atti, the prostitute, and Saeed, the pimp, who perform generic roles within the narrative, and, accordingly, become part of the larger simulacrum of Bad City where they live. This background highlights the importance of the only two characters that are not designated by their name and function, that is Arash, Hossein's son, and the lonesome vampire who is known as "the girl." Arash has no function (because he does not know who he wants to be), and the girl has no name (because she waits for her individuation process to start). Arash has much background information provided for him: he lives with his father who has been a drug addict since the death of his wife[6] and Arash's mother; and he works as a gardener at a large mansion. He dresses in white t-shirt and blue jeans, and drives an American convertible car. In fact, he has something of a James Dean look to him and one can see that he is trying to imitate the Hollywood icon to some extent, which posits a form of equivalence between Hollywood/California and Bad City/Iran. Subsequently Arash is locked in the past, not unlike Bad City itself; fixed in a cycle that can be neither rewritten nor escaped from. This goes against the thoughts of memorial geographers like Graeme Gilloch and Jane Kilby who view modern cities as palimpsests that are constantly being rewritten (6). Arash, however, dreams of leaving, but his job and his father hold him where he is, in the never-ending nightmare of a simulation of real life.

In contrast, nothing is known about the girl or her past. She lives in a small apartment with the walls covered in posters,[7] and plays indie music. She wears clothes reminiscent of Audrey Hepburn in *Breakfast at Tiffany's* (Edwards 1961)—black stretch pants and a horizontally striped shirt. Not unlike Arash's, her clothes seem influenced by Hollywood films. When she is outside in the streets, she wears a long veil that covers her head, but not her face, and flows out behind her. She seems to have suddenly materialized from nowhere, as shown by the reactions of other characters who have never left Bad City, such as the prostitute who notices her for the first time. In many ways the girl seems to be a manifestation of the city itself when she addresses Atti with the words "You're sad. You don't remember what you want. You don't remember wanting. It passed long ago. And nothing ever changes." She seems to be describing Atti's condition as much as her own, and even that of the simulated city itself as seen in the endless repetition of its inhabitants. It is a lost place that has no memory and can never change. However, once on the streets, the girl is a different person—a woman that owns the night; and once she acquires a skateboard, she glides through the streets like a dark avenging angel, with her veil flapping around here like large vampire bat wings. Her autonomy on the streets at night is unusual for a woman in Iran—

indeed, in any modern urban space—and can be linked directly to her vampirism and the vampire genre itself, for "the girl," at least in looks, resembles other, earlier, urban female vampires. Michael Almereyda's *Nadja*, loosely based on Lambert Hillier's *Dracula's Daughter* from 1936, also shows a caped vampire sweeping through the urban environment in a film shot in black and white. "The girl," then, is a direct descendent of Dracula's Daughter and other female vampires such as Kathleen from *The Addiction* (Ferrara 1995) and even Miriam Blaylock from *The Hunger* (Scott 1983). The latter two characters, as noted by Stacey Abbott, "walk the streets at night with impunity, watching and absorbing the life around them rather than averting their eyes or re- treating from it. The films [noted above] emphasize the danger within the city but also the women's attraction to the city as a site of liberation…, offer[ing] women the power to take back the night and claim their place within the urban space" (147). The girl's positioning within the narrative, then, is unique among all the characters encountered in Bad City, as rather than being a victim of the never-ending world of simulation the urban space creates, she configures a simulacrum of a simulacrum—that is, she concentrates all that Bad City is in one body. Consequently, this double negative of simulation offers some level of agency and carries the potential to break out of the cycle of continual stasis.

At no point is the clashing of simulacra and the real within "the girl" more clearly seen than when she meets Arash one night as he staggers home from a party, high on drugs taken for the first time, lost in the endless anonymity of a suburb of Bad City. Arash is dressed as Count Dracula, as based on the Hollywood/Lugosi version, with fake fangs, a long cape and a high collar, and "the girl" is wearing her veil while on a skateboard. Her look is very much based on the art-house vampire films mentioned earlier. The result is a real character, Arash, dressed as a fake Hollywood vampire, meeting a real vampire dressed as a non–Hollywood vampire. Apart from exemplifying the extremely self-reflexive nature of the vampire genre, which, as noted by Ken Gelder, "is a very particular kind of genre that—for all its fascination with origins—is condemned at the same time to re-make, recycle, to copy, to plagiarize, to cite and re-cite" (vi), this scene hints at the simulated nature of film itself, as well as the excessive nature of simulacra that itself can become real. It is because in many ways this meeting also sees the real (the girl) confronting its (her) own simulacrum and a simulacrum (the girl) being as real as the real (Arash). Before configuring a way out of the endless whirls of simulacra and reality, and finding out how the simulated Iran might say something important about the real California and vice versa, it is worth considering the genre also referenced within *A Girl Walks Home*, the Spaghetti Western.

The Wild West in Iran via Italy

A Girl Walks Home has been given the tagline of the first Iranian Vampire Spaghetti Western, a curious mix for sure, and while the characters might not wear appropriate costumes or ride horses, there are many signifiers of the genre on display. Spaghetti Westerns, a sub-genre of the classic Western, were largely directed by Italians and produced in Europe on a much lower budget than their Hollywood counterparts. They are often typified by their moral ambiguity, and gritty and violent depictions of the American West at the end of the nineteenth century. One might say that Amirpour's film is a simulacrum of a Spaghetti Western, as it copies a genre that is already a copy. An important point about such Westerns, at least for this study, is the fact that while they purport to be a depiction of the American West, they were actually made in Italy and Spain, and so exemplify a similar geographical ambiguity that relies on the appropriate signposts to locate the depicted environment and, once again, voices and language play a large part in that. However, it also utilizes genre tropes to assist in this signposting so that the audience is guided by familiarity as much as it is by geographical or linguistic details. As observed by Austin Fisher, "One of the most recognizable motifs of the western is that one of the townsfolk or—more often—a skillful individual being forced to take the law into their own hands in order that justice is served" (55), which is a feature very much seen in *A Girl Walks Home*.

While the townspeople of Bad City seem unwilling to change their situation, the girl acts as the "skillful individual" that dispatches justice to those that harm or "feed off" others. Thus she stalks the streets at night, as a silent witness to all the wrongdoings that take place, selecting out those who are predators and those who are victims. After she sees Atti's pimp abusing her, the girl gets herself invited back to his house where she kills him. Similarly, she senses when Hossein is going to harm Atti, goes to the prostitute's apartment and kills Arash's father. The girl also warns off a young street urchin from copying the bad behavior he witnesses on the streets, following him one night and threatening to watch him all his life to make sure he is good. He runs away scared, leaving his skateboard behind, which the vampire then uses to glide around the streets. Her role as the dispatcher of justice closely aligns her with an iconic figure in the Spaghetti Western oeuvre, that of "The Man with No Name" played by Clint Eastwood—a correlation reinforced by her own nameless status. Matthias Stork notes that by the final film in the series he is "no longer an ordinary hero, he has become an invincible avenger, an agent of death … appearing out of nowhere to dispatch his enemies with deadly precision and superhuman skill" (211–12).[8] The girl then becomes something of an updated version of this but possessing real supernatural powers. Like her predecessor, she is subject to the same flaws that prevent her from achieving exactly what she wants. Christopher Frayling notes how Eastwood's character is driven by desires he cannot fully control and states, "The Man with No Name's dream of settling down to retire on his own ranch is shattered by his own greed, his obsessive urge to grab (rather than spend) in excess of a few dollars more ... or revenge" (189). Similarly, we see the girl kill and drink the blood of a homeless man she happens upon in the street who is not shown as deserving of such a fate in the film. As a vampire, she obviously has needs and so must regularly feed on human blood. While we are never told how often or what the consequences of not doing so might be, to satiate her thirst she is obviously choosing victims that are seen as undesirable.[9] Her lack of remorse for killing the homeless street tramp indicates that her desire to change her life is unattainable, and in fact echoes a similar dilemma in *Dracula's Daughter* and *Nadja*, where both lead characters want to start anew but are eventually unable to change their respective fates.

The consequence of such uncontrollable desire is a threat to derail the girl's relationship with Arash and her dream of starting a new life elsewhere. Indeed, it hints at the inherent vampirism of the entertainment industry in the Golden State as shown in *Modern Vampires* and *Angel*. The girl kills Hossein after he forces Atti to take drugs with him. She and Atti dispose of the body by leaving it near a derelict building, but the street urchin sees this happening from his bedroom window. The following morning the boy gets Arash and takes him to the body, but because he is so petrified of the vampire, the boy refuses to tell Arash who killed his father. Arash has finally given up on his father and threw him out of their house with a handful of drugs, but seeing the dead body finally gives him the impetus to leave Bad City. Fully aware of her deed, the girl still leaves with Arash in his car but neither of them speaks as they drive away from Bad City. However, his father's cat is with the girl, which allows Arash to piece together the facts behind the murder.[10] Arash's realization becomes the decisive moment of the film. The fate of both main characters is put at stake as Arash is confronted with the girl's vampiric identity and needs to choose between its rejection—that would make both of them remain trapped together in the undead and undying simulacrum that is Bad City—or its acceptance needed to continue their escape. In an emotionally intense final scene Arash eventually chooses the latter and as the film ends he and the vampire play Iranian pop music in a cassette player as they drive off into the future.

Beyond Bad City, Beyond Simulacra

The examples examined above all speak of a loss of identity, indicating a process that separates the image, the simulacrum of a thing from its source—the utopian/ideological vision of a location over the everyday experience of actually living there—so that it loses the significance of the original, which is a quality that both Soja and Jameson see as indicative of Californian urbanization and post-modernism respectively, and which Davis sees as, potentially, continuing unabated into the future. *A Girl Walks Home* embodies the historical Hell Town, the metaphorical vampirism of Hollywood and the entertainment industry, the urbanization and loss of identity of city suburbs, as well as the inevitable stasis and decay of a city and population that appears unable to establish their own sense of self. However, in imagining a way out of Bad City the film points to a way beyond that and where what Davis calls oppositional cultures might find identity in the face of ideological anonymity. The never ending cycle of simulacra and the violent suppression of individuality is suggested in the film by the ever-mounting bodies in the ditch outside Bad City—its significance never fully explained in the film—as the ever continuing death of the real, with each body representing a move further and further away from the original. In this view there is no escape from simulation, as each attempt is inevitably killed to be replaced by another. The vampire-with-no-name embodies this vision of California, a creature of the dark who, even when delivering justice, cannot escape its own inner drives to consume, thus resembling her Spaghetti Western predecessor. The real hero, then, is Arash, the-man-with-a-name, a detail which marks him out as unique, different and oppositional to the simulated world around him, an individual that has donned the garb of the world of simulation—the Dracula costume—and yet remains himself.

Brian Massumi sees simulation as not necessarily a dead-end from which one can never escape, but a state that potentially offers a way to become more ourselves, not unlike Arash. In direct reference to what he sees as the limited viewpoint of Baudrillard, Massumi claims for the existence of "a logic capable of grasping Baudrillard's failing world of representation as an effective illusion the demise of which opens a glimmer of possibility. Against cynicism, a thin but fabulous hope—of ourselves becoming realer than real in a monstrous contagion of our own making" (97). Arash exemplifies just such hope. His acceptance of "the girl," who has killed his father and embodies the dark past of Bad City/California, is simultaneously an acceptance of the simulacrum. Rather than repeat the past once again, he drives into a new and unknown future. A future that could be anywhere or nowhere but which will always be, somehow, California.

NOTES

1. For instance see the various manifestations of Disneyland/world across the globe, such as those in Paris, Tokyo, Shanghai and Hong Kong.
2. Not unlike the imaginary quality that Baudrillard himself gives to the people of California.

3. During the Californian gold rush Los Angeles was known as Hell Town due to the murder rate there.
 4. In text quote from Allen J. Scott and Edward W. Soja, eds., *The City: Los Angeles and Urban Theory at the End of the Twentieth Century* (Berkeley: University of California Press, 1998), 1–2. Print.
 5. The vampire film *Let Me In* directed by Matt Reeves in 2010 uses a similar device for certain important characters within it, notably The Father and The Policeman, subsequently making the roles both symbolic and open so that they can be played by anyone else within the narrative.
 6. Due partly to a high unemployment rate and easy access to cheap drugs from Afghanistan, Iranian society, and particularly Tehran, has a large drugs problem (Naval n.p.).
 7. An intertextual point is made with a large poster of film icon Catherine Deneuve prominently displayed on the vampire's bedroom wall. Deneuve starred in the 1983 vampire film *The Hunger* by Tony Scott.
 8. The three films featuring Clint Eastwood as the "Man with No Name" are the "Dollars Trilogy" by Sergio Leone: *A Fistful of Dollars* (1964), *For a Few Dollars More* (1965) and *The Good, the Bad, and the Ugly* (1966).
 9. "Good" vampires feeding off bad people is a familiar solution within the genre to allow them to satiate their thirst, yet remain on the side of the just. Edward Cullen from the Twilight Saga is one recent example.
 10. Near the beginning of the film Arash goes to the pimp's house with some earrings he has stolen to pay off his father's debt. As Arash arrives at the gated property he briefly meets the girl as she leaves the pimp's house after killing him. Arash enters the house to find the pimp dead but does not seem to make anything of it until he decides to leave Bad City with the girl.

WORKS CITED

Abbott, Stacey. *Celluloid Vampires: Life After Death in the Modern World*. Austin: University of Texas Press, 2007. Print.
Almereyda, Michael, dir. *Nadja*. October Films, 1994. Film.
Amirpour, Ana Lilly, dir. *A Girl Walks Home Alone at Night*. VICE Films, 2014. Film.
Baudrillard, Jean. *Simulacra and Simulation*. Trans. Sheila Faria Glazer. Ann Arbor: University of Michigan Press, 1994. Print.
Berger, Peter L., and Thomas Luckmann. *The Social Construction of Reality: A Treatise in the Sociology of Knowledge*. London: Penguin Books, 1991 [1966]. Print.
Browning, Tod, dir. *Dracula*. Universal Pictures, 1931. Film.
Davis, Mike. *City of Quartz: Excavating the Future in Los Angeles*. London: Verso, 2006. Print.
Elfman, Richard, dir. *Modern Vampires* (a.k.a. *Revenant*). Storm Entertainment, 1998. Print.
Fisher, Austin. *Radical Frontiers in the Spaghetti Western: Politics, Violence and Popular Cinema in Italy*. London: I.B. Tauris, 2014. Print.
Frayling, Christopher. *Spaghetti Westerns: Cowboys and Europeans from Karl May to Sergio Leone*. London: I.B. Tauris, 2006. Print.
Gelder, Ken. *New Vampire Cinema*. London: Palgrave Macmillan, 2012. Print.
Gilloch, Graeme and Jane Kilby. "Trauma and Memory in the City: From Auster to Austerlitz." *Urban Memory: History and Amnesia in the Modern City*. Ed. Mark Crinson. London: Routledge, 2005, 1–22. Print.
Greenwalt, David, creator. *Angel*. 20th Century Television, 1999–2004. Television.
Hillyer, Lambert, dir. *Dracula's Daughter*. Universal Pictures, 1936. Film.
Jacob, Benjamin. "Los Angelus: The City of Angel." *Reading Angel: The TV Spin-off with a Soul*. Ed. Stacey Abbott. London: I. B. Tauris, 2005, 75–97. Print.
Jameson, Fredric. *Postmodernism: Or, the Cultural Logic of Late Capitalism*. London: Verso, 1992. Print.
Leone, Sergio, dir. *For a Few Dollars More*. United Artists, 1965. Film.
Massumi, Brian. "Realer Than Real: The Simulacrum According to Deleuze and Guattari." *Copyright* 1 (1987): 90–97. Print.

Naval, Ramita. "Breaking bad in Tehran: how Iran got a taste for crystal meth." *The Guardian*. 13 May, 2014. Web. 10 March, 2016. http://www.theguardian.com/world/2014/may/13/breaking-bad-tehran-iran-crystal-meth-methamphetamine.

Scott, Allen J., and Edward W. Soja, eds. *The City: Los Angeles and Urban Theory at the End of the Twentieth Century*. Berkeley: University of California Press, 1998. 1–2. Print.

Skal, David, *Hollywood Gothic: The Tangled Web of "Dracula" from Novel to Stage to Screen*. New York: Norton, 1990. Print.

Soja, Edward W. *Third Space: Journeys to Los Angeles and Other Real-and-Imagined Places*. London: Verso, 1989. Print.

Spadoni, Robert. *Uncanny Bodies: The Coming of Sound Film and the Origins of the Horror Genre*. Berkeley: University of California Press, 2007. Print.

Stork, Matthias. "The Ghost from the Past: The Undead Avenger in Sergio Leone's *Once Upon a Time in the West*." Ed. Cynthia J. Miller and A. Bowdoin Van Riper. *Undead in the West: Vampires, Zombies, Mummies, and Ghosts on the Cinematic Frontier*. Lanham, MD: Scarecrow Press, 2010, 207–19. Print.

True California
Vinci as Landscape of Terror
Marcin Cichocki

Television storytelling is said to be undergoing a renaissance as it bravely strides into the territory of unconventional and often complex narratives, experimenting with temporality or genre hybrids, blurring lines between series and serials, and triggering new serial formats. It is the era of what many scholars label as Quality TV (McCabe and Akass 1). One innovation that stems from the recent success story of television is the anthology series—a format that recalls the programming of the 1950s television, and in particular its landmark *The Twilight Zone*, which consisted of separate individual science fiction stories told within the constraints of a thirty-minute episode (O'Sullivan 67). As one story ended, another was born in the following episode. The format seems to have returned albeit under a different guise, as the contemporary anthology series can be characterized by stories which are reset every season rather than episodically. Shows that have employed the format successfully include *American Horror Story*, *Fargo* and *True Detective*. HBO's 2014 production *True Detective* which is the focus of this essay tells the neo-noir story of two detectives' struggle to solve a murder case as they unravel a web of corruption in a dilapidated, hurting state of Louisiana. Season two does not follow up on the lives of the two detectives, nor does it set its new story arc within the same state. Instead, the season is reset with a new independent plot that comprises its own new characters, and, most importantly for this essay, new setting. Hence, the swampy bayous of Louisiana are replaced by the dark hidden corners of California.

Season one has been greatly lauded for its gripping storyline, complex characters, as well as its powerful portrayal of the harsh and brutal realities of Louisiana, especially in the aftermath of Hurricane Katrina (Goodman, Season 1). The critical reaction in relation to season two has been less positive, with criticism leveled at the far less riveting storytelling and poor dialog (Goodman, Season 2). However, following in the footsteps of the first season, the setting of the series is once again an integral part of the show. Both seasons of *True Detective* share the tropes of noir films and hard-boiled fiction and it is through these means that the creators convey the depiction of place. In analyzing the setting, I draw on Jopi Nyman's identification of the hard-boiled narrative as stemming from dark romance and the Gothic, to establish the fictional town of Vinci, where the story takes place, as a wasteland and landscape of terror. I do so by studying the meanings of Gothic images of landscape of terror and the myth of the wasteland and how they are projected, courtesy of the creators' use of noir tropes and cinematography, onto the second season of *True Detective* to deliver an unsettling image of California.

Drawing from the Traditions of Film Noir and Hard-Boiled Fiction

Much of *True Detective*'s potency to elicit powerful and meaningful images of the setting of its stories is afforded by its engagement with a noir sensibility. The term *noir* has posed a number of problems for scholars, as some label it a genre, while others consider it to be a mood, tone, or even a movement, or in the case of Jon Tuska "a screen style... and a perspective on human existence and society" (qtd. in Neale 153). Nonetheless, there has been general agreement as to which movies fall within its canon, largely since these stand out from classic Hollywood by virtue of some of the aforementioned labels that point to noir's distinctiveness (Neale 153).

While the prime period for noirs in Hollywood can be identified as the 1940s and 1950s, the term *film noir* was not used in Hollywood during those years and its incorporation into the English language can be accredited to French critics who devised it to describe the "dark" tendency developing in Hollywood productions, which formed a strong contrast to the "traditional optimism of US cinema" (Langford 214). McDonnell notes that what makes film noir stand out from classical cinema is imbalanced lighting created through chiaroscuro-like contrasts between light and darkness (73–74). Through high-angle shots an aura of helplessness is created as we look down on the typically male private eye detective who seems lost in the space that surrounds him. Further photographic techniques include reflections shown in the mirror, tight close-ups as well as visual distortion, all working to "create iconic noir images: sultry femme fatales, a panorama of city bars, nightclubs, hotel rooms, and precinct stations" (74). Through these bleak images, people, according to McDonnell, are shown as casualties of capitalism (74–75). The intensity of the darkness adds to the sense of mystery and oddity. Hence, it can be said that the lighting and shadowing impact on the tone and mood which "can be virtually religious, hinting at a Manichaean world in which the forces of good and evil contend" (75). Darkness surrounds the characters from all sides as danger lurks around every corner.

Neo-noir revisions have drawn on these tropes and applied them to contemporary settings. These movies draw consciously on the noir style, sometimes wandering in the direction of pastiche and parody. Through its awareness of its past, neo-noir knows its rules, and accordingly, can adopt or break its standards and test its limits (Bould et al. 5). Neo-noirs often feature characters whose limitations and failings are clearly accentuated, in sharp contrast to the more heroic triumphs of Humphrey Bogart's Philip Marlowe (Neale 223). While the neo-noir draws on the noir films of the 1940s, many scholars believe that the roots of the genre can be traced back to the style of hard-boiled narratives popular in the 1920s and 1930s, in particular in light of the fact that many private-eye novels created at the time were adapted for the screen. Many of these adaptations belong to the canon of movies that established the notion of the noir in film. Similarly to the way film noir stood out from classical Hollywood optimism, hard-boiled fiction offered a contrast to classical detective fiction, as Krutnik notes: "In the 'hard-boiled' mode, ratiocination—the power of deductive reasoning—is replaced by action, and the mystery element is displaced in favour of suspense. Gunplay, illicit or exotic sexuality, the corruption of the social forces of law, and personal danger to the hero are placed to the fore ... [the] 'hard-boiled' hero—operates as a mediator between the criminal underworld and respectable society. He can move freely between these two worlds, without really being a part of either" (39). This hard-boiled style produced an imprint on the cinematic noir not only by virtue of the many film adaptations but also because writers of hard-boiled fiction were hired to write screenplays, and hence contributed to the noir "dominating the Hollywood crime film for over a decade" (Neale 165). *True Detective* itself shares its name with an American true crime magazine which published the works of authors of hard-boiled detective novels, such as Dashiell Hammett and Jim Thompson. The title therefore hints toward a connection with the hard-boiled tradition which the series screenwriter Nic Pizzolatto seems to have drawn upon.

In an analysis of hard-boiled fiction and dark romanticism, one that contributes to the understanding of space as wasteland and landscape of terror, Nyman points to the influence of romantic and Gothic traditions on American fiction and their impetus on the formation of hard-boiled narratives. He suggests that "hard-boiled fiction, despite its violent and aggressive surface and its focus on problems in contemporary society, draws extensively on romantic themes, imagery, and ideologies in order to convey a sentimentalized view of the meaning of life in modernized America. When life no longer fulfils the promise of the dream, romantic narratives become dark and threatening" (19). While the romance may suggest a glimmer of hope for the future, the Gothic influence can trigger a "world of terror and violence" in which fear and darkness are the key elements guiding the narrative (Nyman 20). Such clash of values is often evident in film noir by virtue of the light and darkness contrast that plays out in many movies. The echoes of the tradition of American Gothic, such as the explorations of evil and darkness in the writings of Charles Brockden Brown or Edgar Allan Poe where "landscapes, American and recognizable, are laden with terror, mystery and inexplicable incidents" (Nyman 21), reverberate in the hard-boiled narrative. In line with Leslie Fiedler's argument that wilderness is presented as a "symbol of evil" (qtd. in Nyman 21) in Brockden Brown's works, Nyman suggests that when it comes to hard-boiled fiction, Gothic "images of terror and doom [can be located] in everyday surroundings" (21).

The death of a protagonist or his loved one is a likely scenario of hard-boiled fiction, as the protagonist treading the landscape of terror struggles to survive in the realities of the world he finds himself in (Nyman 25). He may be searching for a better world and harmony but self-fulfillment is unlikely. Moreover, the line between hero and villain is blurred, as his actions and choices are questionable. When romantic quests fail, the protagonist acknowledges the hopelessness of his dreams, and with his inability to "construct a stable identity and to function as the center of power, his problems are foregrounded" (23). Characters struggle with the present world which is tainted by death and alienation, rendering the individual insignificant (23). In order to survive they have to adapt or else they face death. The romantic notion of self-fulfillment is a distant one in hard-boiled fiction; instead "the romanticism of hard-boiled fiction explores the darker side of the human mind in the manner of the Gothic novel and the fiction of Edgar Allen Poe" (27). Hence, human's capability of violence and murder, "dehumanization and ruthlessness" (27) are foregrounded. These aspects of hard-boiled fiction, Nyman argues, strongly resonate with the "terror-filled dark romanticism of Gothic fictions" (23).

Gothic influence is noticeable in relation to the setting of hard-boiled fiction. On the surface the setting may seem unfamiliar as it lacks the typical Gothic castle or haunted house, yet this difference, Nyman claims, is only superficial as both "hard-boiled fiction and Gothic fiction appear to share a fascination with exotic landscapes where terror reigns and characters are constantly threatened by their evil opponents" (28). Hence, just as the Gothic convention reinvents its setting over time, so does the noir, which draws from the vocabulary of Gothic haunted places tormented by evil forces, but renders them within a contemporary context. Rather than a supernatural evil, there is a social one that still maintains the role of a "Gothic landscape of terror" (29).

In his analysis of formulas that drive genres of popular literature, John Cawelti establishes the detective formula by virtue of the intricacies of the urban setting, pointing out that "the social setting of both gangster melodramas and hard-boiled detective stories was the corrupt and violent American city ruled by a hidden alliance of rich and respectable businessmen, politicians, and criminals" (61). Thus, the setting is posited as a central component of a hard-boiled detective story. What is therefore a key innovative element of American hard-boiled fiction is this prevalent evil permeating the society (Logan 91). Its roots can be traced back to the ongoing and increasing industrialization of the 1920s, which triggered a clash of values. Hence, the fiction's cultural significance can be understood by means of "the moral tension between the traditional 'western,' rural, values adopted by the detective hero amidst the corrupting influence of the modern city" (Logan 92). Logan thus claims that the urban critique which can be found at the heart of hard-boiled detective fiction "was found on the realism of the setting, and its graphic representation of the increasing, corrupting, urban influence in American society" (92), a representation of a setting pertaining to an image of wasteland and landscape of terror. This engagement with the hard-boiled tradition and its use of Gothic imagery transpires in *True Detective*.

Wasteland and Terror in Vinci

Los Angeles has been frequently used by hard-boiled writers as the setting for their corrupt worlds. Most of Raymond Chandler's novels about private eye investigator Philip Marlowe, including *The Big Sleep* and *Farewell, My Lovely*, follow the detective's missing person investigations in downtown L.A. Although, as Chandler points out, many novels portray "an exaggeration of violence and fear beyond what one normally experiences in life" (in MacShane 150), readers have largely developed their perceptions of Los Angeles through this type of literature, and, as Paul Skenazy points out, many of Chandler's books are seen as "authoritative accounts of Southern California" (33). Jason Holt, who forged the term "stylized crime realism" in relation to the noir, supports Skenazy's claim by suggesting that the noir is capable of capturing a sense of place whereby the fictionalized account of a crime-ridden and amoral world echoes the fears and psyche of American society (25).

True Detective follows the tradition of a Californian setting of hard-boiled stories by focusing on a town south of Los Angeles. Vinci is a fictional town, but it closely mirrors the real city of Vernon, which is believed to have been the inspiration for the HBO show's setting (Cohen). Vernon is a small industrial city located southeast of Downtown Los Angeles (City of Vernon). It has a population of 114, but the 1,800 businesses that can be found there employ around 50,000 people. Pointing to its corrupt history, *Vanity Fair* describes Vernon as being "home to factories of the polluting variety, slaughter houses, and chemical plants" and as being "used as a dodge and a tax haven" (Cohen). In an article in the *New York Times* Vernon has even earned the label of an industrial wasteland as it is described as "a bleak, 5.2-square-mile sprawl of warehouses, factories, toxic chemical plants and meat processors that looks like the backdrop for 'Eraserhead,' the David Lynch movie set in an industrial wasteland" (Nagourney). Although the show is set in a fictional town, perhaps to avoid controversy of linking the town to corrupt practices, the majority of the scenes were shot on location among the South Californian landscapes, including the town of Vernon. Other surrounding industrial areas were filmed, too, including the oil refineries in the city of Carson. Hence, the series does not strictly pinpoint one particular place through its criticism, but portrays the overall damage brought about by industrialization and how the fictional town of Vinci stands for these wastelands found in California.

"The dark side of romantic bleakness" (Nyman 33) transpires in hard-boiled fiction through images of the wasteland, which *True Detective* draws on to portray Southern California. Through the depiction of a wasteland we can question the advances society is making and consider the dark side of human's interactions with the natural environment. Hence in film noir and its neo-noir revisions we often see the cruel nature of industrialization and the questionable politics behind it.

In the opening credit sequence of *True Detective*'s second season a montage of images of Californian landscape and the show's characters portrays contrasting pictures that include an aerial shot of the beautiful Californian coastline stretching along the blue ocean, green mountainous areas, and a palm tree, all evoking the iconic imagery of California. Its natural beauty and reputation as a place of wealth and opportunity is also reflected in the great mansions that belong to some of the characters, including Mayor Chessani or the prosperous plastic surgeon Dr. Pitlor. Even one of the main leads of the season, Frank Semyon, seems to epitomize the American Dream. A rich and powerful businessman, he hosts great banquets and presents himself as a respectable member of society. However, viewers find out that his status and riches were gained by illegal means, as he seems to be the head of a criminal organization. Frank's journey to legitimate prosperity and toward fulfilling the Californian Dream is a corrupted one. Hence, the iconography of glamour, wealth and beauty serves as a façade behind which crime and corruption are concealed. *True Detective* focuses on a town that falls distant from the image of the land of milk and honey. It is a noir setting that transpires not only through the visual style of the show but also through the characters and the use of hard-boiled themes of violence and corruption in urban areas.

The portrayal of a fading landscape in which a character struggles for survival is an example of how "hard-boiled fiction takes recognizable everyday landscapes and turns them into locations of Gothic terror where the protagonist is in constant danger" (Nyman 80). In that fashion, the notion of California as dreamland is questioned in *True Detective*. We are shown a part of Southern California which transpires the effects of industrialization, pollution and greed of some of its inhabitants. Vinci is described by the character of state attorney Katherine Davis, who briefs her detective about the location, which, having started out as a vice haven, turned industrial in the 1920s. It is believed to be responsible for pushing out its residents to accommodate manufacturing zones and is considered "the worst polluter in the state [which] annually emits or processes 27 million pounds of toxic waste" (Night). Aerial shots of industrial plants, clouds of smoke rising above into the sky, kids playing next to a rotting factory building emitting toxic fluids all accompany this description to create a sense of doom exhibiting "a representation of the failure of the ideals of progress and industrialization ... [thereby] generat[ing] a city of terror" (Nyman 81). By night the city evokes the notion of The Golden State, but the gold we see gleaming through the darkness stems from the lit factories covering most of the landscape forming a bittersweet image of these golden riches (Zircillius). While the perpetual work of the industrial plants symbolizes productivity and wealth, the images of smoke bursting from the chimneys into the sky contribute to the ever-growing toxicity of the wasteland.

Within this industrial setting *True Detective* tells the story of the lives of different characters who are brought together by the death of Caspere. Caspere had been overlooking career criminal Frank Semyon's investment in a rail project that was to legitimize his business. His death means loss of money for Frank and triggers his own, "illegal" investigation of the circumstances of his business partner's disappearance. Meanwhile, members of different cooperating police departments gather together to initiate their own investigation. Amongst these are California Highway Patrol Paul Woodrugh, Vinci Police Department Detective Raymond "Ray" Velcoro and Ventura County Sheriff's Office Sergeant Antigone "Ani" Bezzerides. This unusual and troubled group of individuals seems far from being an ideal force to investigate the crime and unveil the web of corruption. Perhaps that is in fact the reason why they are selected. Rather than to solve the case, their incompetence is to ensure the status quo in Vinci so that the shady dealings may continue to flourish. Ray raises this doubt as he is briefed about his task: "Am I supposed to solve this or not?"—to which his supervisor's answer is nothing but a snarky smile and a comment: "Just no surprises, Detective Velcoro" (Night).

There is a reciprocity between character and setting which is similar to the representations of places found in hard-boiled novels where the appearance of a town resembles the states of minds of its inhabitants (Nyman 36). This is detectable in the title sequence. Amongst the contrasting images of the montage are the silhouettes of the main characters against the backdrop of the poisoned landscapes. This visual style of double exposure hints at how these characters are rooted within the troubles of the landscape they find themselves in. Through their silhouettes we see aerial shots of roadways. These complex webs, which repeatedly appear throughout the series, do not seem to serve purely the purpose of a cinematographic eye candy but rather to represent the complex states of mind of the characters and the web of corruption polluting the area.[1]

The Gothic and hard-boiled aesthetics of the series work to portray the setting as a wasteland. Images of California's toxic landscapes and industrial sites project the environmental decay present in the state as a backlash to its occupants' industrial abuse and neglect of the environment. Furthermore, in *True Detective*, agency is given to the setting by establishing it as a landscape of Gothic terror. California is used in the series not only as a reflection of mankind's misuse of the land but as a threat in itself. This becomes apparent through the characters' struggles with their inner demons, as well as their inability to find a place for themselves within the landscape of California.

Ray's struggles are depicted through his family life and connections with the criminal world. Although on the side of the law, he has strayed from the righteous path. Separated from his wife, he struggles to maintain a relationship with his son, as doubts appear whether he is the boy's biological father. In the tradition of hard-boiled fiction, the line between hero and villain is blurred. Ray is often seen meeting with Frank, who uses Ray's insider information for his own illegal investigation. Ray's mediation between the two worlds is noticeable toward the end of the series when Frank, despite his criminal history and illegal dealings, unites with the detectives, Ray and Ani, to escape together. Even though Ray's motives might be understandable as he wants to avenge the harm done to his wife, he becomes part of the corrupt world and thereby becomes its representative the moment he turns to Frank for help.

Ray makes peace with the fact that there is no opportunity for him to unite with his son and in a final attempt to escape he turns to the green woods of California. A place of nature and purity, where even Ray's redeeming phone message to his son cannot get through, seemingly stands in sharp contrast to the dominant urban landscapes. And yet even here nature is not beyond the grasp of civilization as the green scenery to which Ray retreats is unable to save him. It remains a place of danger for him as he is followed and, upon the realization that there is no escape for him from the landscape of terror, he desperately jumps in front of the bullets. These lands are not a wasteland

and landscape of terror yet, but their proximity to mankind's reach puts the surrounding nature constantly at danger, while at the same time the seemingly peaceful and unscathed environment refuses to provide shelter for the escaping character.

California becomes a hostile environment for the main characters of the season as a sense of claustrophobia and entrapment is created. The muddled roads are so entwined that they seem impossible to untangle, representing a maze with no escape route (Zircillius). The superimpositions between scenes contribute to this effect as we often see the faces of the characters fade out while a new scene depicting Vinci fades in to recall the effects of the double exposure found in the title sequence. One of many examples can be found in Episode Five where the image of Frank fades out and for a moment his silhouette is filled with industrial landscapes (Other). In the case of Frank, this superimposition echoes the notion of wasteland as a reflection of human behavior because Frank can be seen as a representative of the corrupt world and the greed that destroys the land. The urge to tap into California's natural resources for personal profit is irresistible to him. However, when Caspere dies, Frank loses his power and fails to push through his investment plans. His path to the American Dream is flawed and corrupted, as he can only achieve prosperity through illegitimate means. The California where Frank used to climb the social ladder and build his illegal empire becomes a threat. People he trusted and did business with have become enemies. When he realizes that escape is the only option for him and his wife, he attempts to flee with her to Mexico. The road, rather than symbolizing an opportunity for escape and freedom, here serves the role of confinement and limitation. Although aerial shots of Californian freeways appear throughout the season, they offer no escape route. The twisted entangled roads look like the claws which refuse to let Frank get away from California's clutches. In the end he is driven out into the desert by a gang and shot. It is there in the open space that he has to face his demons and past sorrows, and die with regrets. For Frank, there is no safe haven to turn to. Bleeding, without water, and far from civilization, Frank is left to die alone and without hope.

The sense of entrapment created by the superimpositions of characters' faces with landscape is also apparent through Paul's strong connection with the roads and freeways of California. "I like the bike, sir. The highway, it suits me," he claims when facing the prospect of suspension from the force (The Western). He struggles to come to terms with his sexuality, and his inability to find a place for himself transpires in the scenes depicting him aimlessly cruising down the freeway in the middle of the night. Despite the vast roads and possible destinations, Paul is unable to flee his troubled mind. His reclusiveness, solitude and sense of being lost almost drive him to suicide. In the end, despite his good intentions to solve the case and uncover the web of corruption, Paul becomes a victim of the cancerous criminal network spreading over California.

Imprisonment is also recognizable in the dialogs of the characters. Ani struggles to maintain a relationship with her estranged sister, who once says, "For a place you hate you never really got that far away" (Other). For Ani, California is not a place of fulfillment. Although she is successful at her job, her character has been shaped by past traumas which refuse to let go. Her father is the key figure at a spiritual commune at the Panticapaeum Institute, where he seems to be a preacher of peace and fulfillment through spirituality, yoga and meditation. The commune evokes an aura of a place of peace and love, and yet its sincerity is put into question as we find out that its spiritual leader, Elliot Bezzerides, a man preaching how to live, had himself significantly struggled in the past to protect and keep together his own family. Even though they had been growing up in the commune, Ani's siblings had trouble with the law, she herself had been sexually abused as a child, whereas two other siblings committed suicide. The commune might seem as a safe place for retreat but it can offer no real escape, as something is rotting at its core.

The beauty that can be found in *True Detective*'s California is often only a pretentious facade. Prospects of glamour and wealth lure young women from other parts of the world to California, but the series depicts them as ending up as sex servants to the rich. Once again, shadows are cast on the notion of a land of opportunity. When Ani goes undercover as one of the prostitutes, she is drugged and made vulnerable to the advances of the old corrupt magnates who are to be entertained and have their wishes satisfied at a grand orgy. She infiltrates the haunted, dark corridors of the house as she stumbles under the influence of drugs from one room to the next and begins to see the ghosts of her past. The men at the party recall the images of the man who had lured her into the woods and abused her when she was a child.

The lack of hope to be found in California for the characters toward the end of the series recalls the notions of dislocation and what David Fine describes as "the tension between myth and antimyth, between Southern California as the place of the fresh start and as the scene of the disastrous finish" (qtd. in Nyman 65). A search and need for a new desire is created as the characters are unable to find solace within the confines of California, signifying the closing of the frontier, whereby the only solution in the face of a limited space or land is "the construction of a new space" (Nyman 65). The final part of the series pictures the main characters' desperate attempt to escape this confined space, under the faint hope of a new life and new opportunities in the new space, Mexico. Having failed to meet the demands of Californian life, Ani, Ray, and Frank are fleeing both from the law and the criminal world. The law offers them no refuge as they know too much about the city's corrupt practices. Hence, they are rendered the enemy. This follows the tradition of the Western genre where the outlaw turns to a new, hopefully better, frontier. Richard Slotkin points out that when the original possibilities of the frontier are used up, "society lapses into habitual injustice, inequality, alienation, and hierarchy. Our only hope is to project a further frontier, a mythic space outside American space" (311). For Ray and Frank, the hope of a better frontier is crushed and as they fail to escape the clutches of California's corrupt hands.

In *True Detective* the American dreamland of California is subverted in a way that recalls the tradition of hard-boiled narratives. The California we see here is distant from the romantic depictions of wealth, success, and opportunity associated with the Golden State. Prosperity seems only attainable via corrupt means. It resonates a sense of estrangement. Hopes and promises turn to failure.

Conclusion

"What the fuck is Vinci?" asks Detective Elvis Ilinca at the end of the first episode. "A city, supposedly," is Ray's response. While Vinci does not exist, there are places which strongly resemble it. Ray's response alludes to the idea that there are cities that are almost unclassifiable. With a population of just over one hundred it is an area so industrialized that its inhabitants are kept to a minimum so as to most efficiently serve the economic interests of the industries. *True Detective* sets its crime story in such a town to unveil areas that are not often talked about but can be found in the surrounding shadows of the sunnier parts of California. In the tradition of hard-boiled fiction, these hidden areas can be described as modern wastelands that portray the fragmentation of modern society where commercial greed and urbanization have led to violence and pollution. However, the season goes beyond a representation of a wasteland, and deploys the setting as a landscape of terror by marking it as an agent of confinement. The environment's response to the harm done to it is to create "a claustrophobic sense of a closed space" (Nyman 89) within which characters are under constant threat. Through such a portrayal of the setting, the series not only aspires to tell a crime story but also engages with formal criticism of the use of land, revealing the prioritization of values of urbanization.

NOTE

1. For an interesting analysis of cinematographic techniques in *True Detective* see the online publication by Zircillius.

WORKS CITED

Bould, Mark, Kathrina Glitre, and Greg Tuck. "Parallax Views: An Introduction." Introduction. *Neo-noir*. London: Wallflower, 2009. 1–10. Print.
Cawelti, John G. *Adventure, Mystery, and Romance: Formula Stories as Art and Popular Culture*. Chicago: University of Chicago Press, 1976. Print.
City of Vernon. *Official Website of the City of Vernon, CA*. N.p., n.d. Web. 17 June 2016. http://www.cityofvernon.org/.
Cohen, Rich. "Can Nic Pizzolatto, True Detective's Uncompromising Auteur, Do It All Again?" *Vanity Fair*. Condé Nast, 11 June 2015. Web. 09 Mar. 2016.
Goodman, Tim. "True Detective Season 2: TV Review." *The Hollywood Reporter*. Lynne Segall, 11 June 2015. Web. 12 June 2016.
_____. "True Detective: TV Review." *The Hollywood Reporter*. Lynne Segall, 2 Jan. 2014. Web. 12 June 2016.
Holt, Jason. "A Darker Shade: Realism in Neo-Noir." *The Philosophy of Film Noir*. Ed. Mark T. Conard. Lexington: University of Kentucky Press, 2006. 23–40. Print.
Krutnik, Frank. *In a Lonely Street: Film Noir, Genre, Masculinity*. London: Routledge, 1991. Print.
Langford, Barry. *Film Genre: Hollywood and beyond*. Edinburgh: Edinburgh University Press, 2005. Print.
Logan, Michael F. "Detective Fiction as Urban Critique: Changing Perspectives of a Genre." *The Journal of American Culture* 15.3 (1992): 89–94. Web.
MacShane, Frank, ed. *Selected Letters of Raymond Chandler*. London: Jonathan Cape, 1981. Print.
McCabe, Janet, and Kim Akass. "Debating Quality." Introduction. Ed. Janet McCabe and Kim Akass. *Quality TV: Contemporary American Television and Beyond*. London: I.B. Tauris, 2007. 1–11. Print.
McDonnell, Brian. "Film Noir Style." *Encyclopedia of Film Noir*. Ed. Geoff Mayer and Brian McDonnell. Westport, CT: Greenwood, 2007. 70–81. Print.
Nagourney, Adam. "Plan Would Erase All-Business Town." *New York Times*. The New York Times, 1 Mar. 2011. Web. 9 Mar. 2016.
Neale, Stephen. *Genre and Hollywood*. London: Routledge, 2000. Print.
"Night Finds You." *True Detective: Season 2*. Writ. Nic Pizzolatto. Dir. Justin Lin. Home Box Office (HBO), 2015. DVD.
Nyman, Jopi. *Hard-Boiled Fiction and Dark Romanticism*. Frankfurt Am Main: Peter Lang, 1998. Print.
O'Sullivan, Sean. "The Sopranos: Episodic Storytelling." *How to Watch Television*. Ed. Ethan Thompson and Jason Mittell. New York: New York University Press, 2013. 65–73. Print.
"Other Lives." *True Detective: Season 2*. Writ. Nic Pizzolatto. Dir. Justin Lin. Home Box Office (HBO), 2015. DVD.
Skenazy, Paul. *The New Wild West: The Urban Mysteries of Dashiell Hammett and Raymond Chandler*. Boise: Boise State University Press, 1982. Print.
Slotkin, Richard. *Gunfighter Nation: The Myth of the Frontier in Twentieth-century America*. New York: Atheneum, 1992. Print.
"The Western Book of the Dead." *True Detective: Season 2*. Writ. Nic Pizzolatto. Dir. Justin Lin. Home Box Office (HBO), 2015. DVD.
Zircillius. "True Detective Season 2 Analysis: The Lost Freeway." Review. Web log post. *Zircillius: An In-depth Approach to Film Criticism*. WordPress, 24 Jan. 2015. Web. 09 Mar. 2016.

PART III: WELCOME TO DYSTOPIA

Thomas Pynchon's Hybrid California(s)
In Search of Spatial/Social Justice in Inherent Vice

DIANA BENEA

Constructing California in Thomas Pynchon's Trilogy

Thomas Pynchon's continuing preoccupation with the shifting contours of the physical and social space of America has ranged from an exploration of the role of the Mason-Dixon line in transforming the "subjunctive" space of American wilderness into the "dreamless indicative" of organized space (Pynchon, *M&D*[1] 345) in the eponymous novel,[2] to an inquiry into the changing urban scape of a pre- and post–9/11 New York in his latest work, *Bleeding Edge* (2013). The two novels serve as an *extensive* temporal arc spanning several centuries in terms of diegetic time—from the early modern, pre-revolutionary America of the 1760s, to a global, contemporary America mapped both onto the physical space of a yuppified New York, as well as onto "the still unmessed-with country" (Pynchon, *BE* 241) of Deep Archer, a virtual reality program offering "a sanctuary to escape to from the many varieties of real-world discomfort" (74). By contrast, Pynchon's other "American" novels, *The Crying of Lot 49* (1966), *Vineland* (1990), and *Inherent Vice* (2009) engage in an *intensive* investigation of the same chronotope, gravitating around the same spatial and temporal coordinates, i.e., the Golden State of California and the decade of the sixties. Often grouped together as his California trilogy, the three works offer a substantial foray into the legacy of the sixties as a "hinge decade" (Cowart 24) of contemporary American history poised between a utopian vision of social change and the anguished expectation that "everything in this dream of prerevolution was in fact doomed to end and the faithless money-driven world to reassert its control" (Pynchon, *IV* 129–130).

Providing the backdrop for a three-fold examination of the sixties spanning over forty years in Pynchon's career, California emerges in different guises in the novels, as part of three distinct inquiries nevertheless converging toward a collective statement about the fate of American land. In *The Crying of Lot 49*, Oedipa Maas' journey of initiation into the mysteries of Pierce Inverarity's legacy—which might very well be America, as she intimates at one point—unfolds against the background of a predominantly urban, homogenous, standardized Southern California of seemingly interchangeable places depicted as "a grouping of concepts—census tracts, special purpose bond-issue districts, shopping nuclei, all overlaid with access roads to its own freeway" (Pynchon, *CL49* 24). If Oedipa's California is dominated by built environments, freeways famously functioning as a "hypodermic needle" (26) keeping the cities alive, and complicated techno-scapes of various communication channels and networks, including the underground mail carrier Tristero, *Vineland* is set mostly in and around Humboldt County, in the redwoods of northern California, where Zoyd Wheeler and his daughter Prairie have taken refuge in the early 1970s, along with other former sixties radicals and fringe elements, in a "mass migration of freaks" (Pynchon, *VD* 305). Despite occasional flashbacks to scenes set in urban scapes such as "the basic L.A. business/shopping complex of high rises that stood on a piece of former movie-studio lot" (192), or other examples of functional architecture, most of the novel focuses on Vineland, imagined as a natural oasis, "where half the interior hasn't even been surveyed—plenty of redwoods to get lost in, ghost towns old and new ... a whole web of logging roads, fire roads, Indian trails" (305). Finally, *Inherent Vice* returns to the Southland, more specifically to the area in and around L.A., to offer the most substantial representation of the city in the Pynchon canon, constructing a vivid cartography which includes hundreds of references to actual places, from its various neighborhoods, to the many iconic places dominating the popular culture imaginary associated with it, all of which are infused with a typically noir atmosphere.[3]

The pretext for a third foray into the tail end of the Californian sixties is, in typical Pynchon fashion, a quest narrative recounting the trials and tribulations of the private detective Doc Sportello as his investigation of the possible kidnapping of the real estate magnate Mickey Wolfmann spirals, in a typical noir fashion, into a multi-layered story of generalized corruption, exposing an ever-expanding web of organizations and institutions with a stake in the case. Set in the early months of 1970 as the numerous references to the imminent start of the Manson trials indicate, the novel explores that specific time frame marking "the end of a certain kind of innocence" (38) about hippiedom, and a sobering acknowledgment that "the Psychedelic Sixties, this little parenthesis of light, might close after all, and all be lost, taken back into darkness" (254). Just as in the case of his other California novels, Pynchon is consistent in using the imagery pattern light-darkness to describe the promise of the sixties, and, respectively, the corruption of this promise by "those dark crews [that] had been busy all along, reclaiming the music, the resistance to power, the sexual desire from epic to everyday, all they could sweep up, for the ancient forces of greed and fear" (130). The novel thus charts Sportello's itineraries in and around a Los Angeles enmeshed in dark "tentacles of sin and desire" (91), in and out of a ubiquitous fog—an apt metaphor for the unintelligible workings of state institutions serving the interests of "invisible powers" (265)—and in and out of frequent immersions into a mythical Lemuria.

Significantly, California is represented in the trilogy as a densely layered space, grounded not only in an understanding of its spatial development and its various cultural, socio-economic, and technological scapes, from the urban Southland to the rural hinterland of the North, but also mobilizing an arsenal of broader cultural constructs reflective of its "symbolism as America's America" (McClintock and Miller 5), perpetually bridging the continuum between utopian and dystopian readings. As has been noted, Pynchon's narrative mode of representation often combines strands of realism with quite frequent irruptions of the fantastic, a strategy also visible in the ways in which his spatial configurations amalgamate a multiplicity of visions and discourses belonging to both ontological levels. Predicated on a similar two-fold approach to Pynchon's California as a hybrid of "realist," spatially specific representations on the one hand, and larger mythical constructs, on the other, this contribution sets out to analyze the ambivalent California at the core of *Inherent Vice*, a novel whose ethico-political dimension is inextricable from questions of space and spatial organization. As such, the following sections of this essay will aim to disentangle the two (conflicting? mutually enhancing?) representational strategies blending in Pynchon's latest construction of California and, in particular, of L.A.—a real/dystopian L.A.-qua-"fractal city" and a mythical/utopian L.A.-qua-Lemuria. More than a richly detailed setting for the narrative, the multi-layered L.A. of *Inherent Vice* and the broader Californian landscape—with its array of radically different spatial configurations—will be argued to function as a gateway into the deeper thematic interest of the narrative, i.e., the question of spatial/social justice.

Los Angeles-qua-Fractal-City: The Spatial/Social Mosaic of Inherent Vice

The first section of this essay aims to examine the novel in point of its articulation of various urban configurations, from Gordita Beach,[4] peopled by surfers, rock musicians, dopers, New Age enthusiasts and all manner of drifters and seekers, to ethnic neighborhoods, to suburban tract houses, to gated communities. The analysis focuses on how these different forms of spatial organization both reflect and reproduce wider social divisions and inequities, while also inquiring into whether the novel suggests any possibility of reimagining urban, and, by extension, social space.[5] The novel's epigraph, "Under the paving-stones, the beach!," a translation of the famous Situationist graffito of the May 1968 uprisings in Paris, constructs, from the very beginning, a clear horizon of expectations for the reader, suggesting the necessity of reclaiming and reconfiguring urban space in a more socially just manner. The critical framework employed to investigate this and related questions in the novel is provided by the field of contemporary critical geography/spatial theory/urban politics, in particular by Edward Soja's and David Harvey's recent studies on the relationship between the social and the spatial as two mutually informing categories. More specifically, the contribution is predicated on their similar theorizations of space as not only sustaining but also, and more importantly, producing specific social relations, including various forms of inequality, injustice and oppression. According to the two theorists, this double dynamics whereby "the social comprises the spatial, while it is also comprised by it" (Soja, *Seeking* 5) is most visible in urban spaces. As Harvey argues, the city—in its different guises as "city of God, city on a hill, ... as an object of utopian desire, as a distinctive place of belonging within a perpetually shifting spatio-temporal order" (Harvey xvi–xvii)—has always been deeply embedded within a political imaginary, representing "a major site of political, social, and class struggles" (66).

By discussing various case studies in Los Angeles, the metropolis at the center of his critical inquiries, Soja analyzes the spatiality of justice, showing how forms of (in)justice and (in)equality are embedded into the very spaces where daily lives are performed, reflecting "lasting structures of unevenly distributed advantage and disadvantage" (Soja, *Seeking* 19). Harvey, in turn, zooms in on a cluster of diverse case studies, including the post-war urban development in the United States, underscoring the ways in which the citizens' right to the city has been systematically denied by the capitalist system of unsustainable developmental drive, while suggesting strategies whereby urban dwellers can reclaim this right. While fair and equal access to the resources of the city is an important aspect of the right to the city, Harvey construes it not only as a right for that which already exists, but also, and more importantly, as a right for that which might exist, i.e., as "a right to change and reinvent the city more after our heart's desire" (25), more specifically, "a right to rebuild and recreate the city ... in a completely different image—one that eradicates poverty and social inequality, and one that heals the wounds of disastrous environmental degradation" (138). Given that the right to the city is, in Harvey's view, "not an exclusive individual right, but a focused collective right" (137), the above description amounts to a call to collective action to reconstruct urban life away from the reductive vision imposed by capitalist notions of development.

Comprising various forms of organization, the spatial puzzle of *Inherent Vice* prefigures a highly segregated urban space, not unlike the real L.A. at the beginning of the seventies, which, as Soja clarifies, was characterized by an increasing spatial and social polarization (Soja, *Seeking* 122–132). Pynchon's vision of the increasingly fractured social mosaic of L.A. in the early 1970s is thus in line with what the theorist calls, in an earlier study investigating six manifestations of L.A. as a post–Fordist "postmetropolis," a "fractal city" ruptured along the lines of widening social inequalities transcending the traditional class- and race-based schisms.

Interestingly, the first description of Gordita Beach in the novel is in terms of what that particular space no longer is or has never been. Hanging on a wall in Doc Sportello's room in Gordita Beach is a picture of "a Southern California beach that never was—palms, bikini babes, surfboards, the works" (Pynchon, *IV* 6), which functions, for Doc, as "a window to look out of when he couldn't deal with looking out of the traditional glass-type one in the other room" (6). At a symbolic level, one could argue that what is unbearable for Doc to see is the vanishing of an era. Indeed, throughout the novel, Gordita Beach is represented in sober tones, suggesting that the alternative lifestyle of the previous decade has been largely contained and the sixties ethos itself has morphed into the post–Manson atmosphere of mistrust that dominated the area at the beginning of the 1970s. However, besides such delicate nostalgia for a SoCal beach "that never was," the more immediate reason for Doc's reluctance to look out of the window of his bachelor pad is the environmental disaster unfolding before his own eyes. The physical space of Gordita Beach is recurrently represented in dystopian terms, drawing attention to the environmental effects produced by the proximity of the El Segundo oil refinery. As the narrator notes, "even when the wind here cooperated, Gordita was still like living on a houseboat anchored in a tar pit. Everything smelled like crude. Oil spilled from tankers washed up on the beach, black, thick, gooey" (104). Almost all the scenes set in Gordita Beach foreground various environmental issues—the smog blowing from downtown L.A. (98), the changes in weather caused by the high levels of pollution in the area (98–

99), the deterioration of the quality of the land on which houses are built (166), etc.—constructing a powerful environmentalist agenda, the most explicit and substantial one in the Pynchon corpus. Such descriptions of Gordita perfectly illustrate Soja's arguments about the spatiality of injustice, showing how the population of this specific area—a colorful assortment of various subcultures in this case—is more likely to suffer from environmental hazards than the residents of the more affluent spatial arrangements.[6]

Significantly, another resident of Gordita Beach, a Vietnam war veteran who developed an interest in the natural environment after seeing so much of it "napalmed, polluted, defoliated till the laterite beneath was sun-baked solid and useless" (104), has grown so obsessed with such forms of environmental abuse as the El Segundo refinery or the bulldozing of entire neighborhoods for the construction of the Channel View Estates (reminiscent of jungle clearings, in his view) that he is shooting short films on the damaged sites in an effort to raise awareness about them. His girlfriend Sortilege is skeptical that such films can make an impact and stop environmental degradation in the area, but at least hopes that "Earth has an immune system too, and sooner or later she's going to start rejecting agents of disease like the oil industry" (105). Two elements are of utmost importance here, testifying to the centrality of the environmentalist theme in the novel. Firstly, comparing the war waged on the urban landscape of Gordita Beach with the environmental impact of the Vietnam War amounts to a devastating critique of the environmental crisis of our contemporary age, the most straightforward critique of this kind in Pynchon's career. Secondly, while identifying the sources of the ecological disasters visited upon L.A. as lying in environmentally-unsustainable capitalist practices of industrial and urban development, the novel also dramatizes two contradictory modes of addressing such issues: on the one hand, the militantism of Spike's guerrilla filmmaking; on the other hand, Sortilege's quasi-mythical belief in the regenerative capacities of the Earth as a self-regulating system.

At the other end of the spectrum from Gordita Beach, the residents of the gated communities of Palos Verdes enjoy the benefits of a hyper-securitized, sterilized life in a closed-off space, far from the mean streets of Gordita Beach or "the high-density tenement scum" (347) of ethnic neighborhoods and the marginal groups that populate them. In light of Michel Foucault's concept, these gated communities might be argued to function as a "heterotopia of compensation" (Foucault 335), which aims at constructing a different and perfectly ordered space meant to serve as a counterpoint to the chaotic space of the city. Following Soja's discussion of such arrangements as amounting to a "fortressing of urban life" built on "an ecology of fear" (Soja, *Seeking* 42), one can debate whether gated communities are further examples of spatial injustice, or just an "expression of democratic individualism" (43) and the right to choose whatever spatial configuration suits one's needs. The exchange between Doc Sportello, resident of Gordita Beach, and Crocker Fenway, resident of "a gated enclave located *inside* the *already* gated high-rent community of Rolling Hills" (Pynchon, *IV* 171, original italics), suggests that Pynchon's representation of these communities is aligned with the former of these views. The signature Pynchonesque opposition between the preterite and the Elect is here reformulated in spatial terms: those "being in place" versus the endlessly displaceable "transients": "'[i]t's about *being in place*. We –' gesturing around the Visitors' Bar and its withdrawal into seemingly unbounded shadow, 'we're in place. We've been in place forever. Look around. Real estate, water rights, oil, cheap labor—all that's ours, it's always been ours. And you, at the end of the day, what are you? One more unit in this swarm of transients who come and go without pause here in the Southland'" (347, original italics).

The epitome of displacement in the novel is represented by the residents of ethnic quarters forced to relocate as their neighborhoods are being razed in order to make way for new public facilities or housing schemes for the white middle class. According to Doc's aunt Reet, the real estate agent, this series of erasures is the "long sad history of L.A. land use.... Mexican families bounced out of Chavez Ravine to build Dodger Stadium, American Indians swept out of Bunker Hill for the Music Center, Tariq's [African American] neighborhood bulldozed aside for Channel View Estates" (17).[7] This passage alludes to another widespread practice of capitalist urban development, namely urban renewal, or, as Harvey calls it, "urban restructuring through 'creative destruction'" (Harvey 16). As Harvey further clarifies, this process has always had a class dimension, since it is usually the poor (ethnic) neighborhoods that get erased in the name of urban restoration or poverty alleviation. Clearly emphasized in aunt Reet's aforementioned remark, the ethnic divide at the core of this process is further stressed by Tariq Khalil's comment on the erasure of his neighborhood as "white man's revenge ... for Watts" (Pynchon, *IV* 17).

This strand of spatial representation repeatedly calls attention to the social costs of the process leading to the destruction of entire urban communities and the networks linking their members. In one of the most poignant scenes of the novel, having just arrived on the former site of Tariq's neighborhood which now is the construction site of Channel View Estates, Doc notices, among the couples interested in buying a house there, a group of African American pedestrians apparently "looking for their old neighborhood, for rooms lived in day after day, solid as the axes of space, now taken away into commotion and ruin" (19). What they find instead are model units and almost finished homes that show no trace of the land clearance that allowed their construction, no sign of the brutal process of displacement and dispossession at the core of the new urban development. The wistful image of the ghostly presences of former residents haunting the site points to the most devastating effect of urban renewal, i.e., the erasure of an archive of the personal and communal histories unfolding in that space day after day. The wiping out of ethnic neighborhoods therefore amounts not only to a denial of the right of these urban dwellers to be part of the production of the city, but also to their brutal disconnection from the personal and communal histories constructed in that space and no longer retrievable in any other.

The aforementioned model units belong to yet another type of spatial arrangement which adds a further layer to the representation of California in the novel: a suburban housing scheme described by Doc's aunt Reet, the realtor, in unequivocal terms as "[Wolfmann's] latest assault on the environment—some chipboard horror known as Channel View Estates" (8) consisting of future homesites where "wholesome families will be gathering night after night, to gaze tubeward, gobble their nutritious snacks" (22). Named after the flood control channel it looks out on—a site of increasing environmental degradation "forgotten and cut off by miles of fill, regrading, and trash of industrial ventures that had either won or failed" (20), the housing project is therefore constructed as a parodic counterpoint to the stereotypical homebuyer expectations of riverview or mountainview panoramas. Furthermore, Channel View is also suggestive of the aforementioned activities of "gazing tubeward," pointing to the importance of television in these lives (in line with Pynchon's consistent thematization of TV consumption and addiction as a mechanism of ideological enslavement) and, in a more symbolic sense, to the channeling of vision and the social conformity promoted by this spatial arrangement.

However, the construction of Channel View Estates is abandoned as Mickey Wolfmann disappears mysteriously, thus setting in motion Sportello's, the L.A.P.D's and the FBI's parallel investigations, which reveal the cause of his disappearance to be closely linked with Wolfmann's involvement in a radically different housing project. Apparently, as a result of a recent moral epiphany urging him to give back to the community, Wolfmann decided to stop the Channel View Estates altogether and invest instead in a housing project in the desert valley between L.A. and Las Vegas, a city named *Arrepentimiento*, a Spanish word which translates as repentance. As Doc later finds out from Riggs Warbling, the architect in charge of Wolfmann's project, *Arrepentimiento* was conceived as a utopian site providing free housing in zonahedral domes, or "zomes," a specific type of construction whose unusual design makes it a great space for communal activities as well as a "space for meditation" (62). Designed by Buckminster Fuller in the late forties as an environmentally sustainable type of "better home for lower incomes"—to quote the title of one of Fuller's articles—such structures were an expression of the architect's lifelong preoccupation to improve housing by "doing more with less" (Fuller 73B) while also allowing individuals to "constantly interact within [their] many environments and at many levels of organization" (89A).

Tellingly, Mickey's disappearance entails that neither the dystopian Channel View Estates, nor the utopian *Arrepentimiento* is ever completed. What emerges nevertheless on an abandoned construction site very similar to Channel View Estates is a space hospitable to all manner of underground activities, from shooting movies to producing weapons. This alternative space clearly subverts the segregation practices that dominate the other spatial arrangements of L.A., functioning as a gathering place for all kinds of people irrespective of their ethnic or social background—Anglos and Chicanos; dopers and company executives alike (Pynchon, *IV* 143). Planned urban housing thus gives way to a spontaneous reappropriation of space. In occupying this abandoned construction site, the abovementioned diverse groups exercise their right to the city by playing an active role in the production of that particular space while subverting "the controlling forces of homogenization, fragmentation, and uneven development" (Soja 99) inherent in the capitalist vision on development illustrated, for instance, by Channel View Estates.

Los Angeles-qua-Lemuria: Bridging the Continuum between Utopia and Dystopia

As previously argued, Pynchon's California results from the interplay of various strands of representation, juxtaposing "realistic" and mythical accounts, and generally mobilizing an ambivalent imagination "perpetually situated on the brink of catastrophe, metamorphosis, or redemption" (Wilson 217). The Pynchonesque oscillation between multiple—seemingly disjointed but ultimately interdependent—layers of narrative representation is most poignantly illustrated in his second California novel, especially in the paradoxical construction of Vineland as a space encapsulating both the utopian promise of starting afresh associated with the foundational narratives projecting America as a virgin land, as well as the betrayal of that promise.[8]

"'A Harbor of Refuge,' as the 1851 survey map called it, to Vessels that may have suffered on their way North from the strong headwinds that prevail along this coast" (Pynchon, *VD* 316), Vineland serves a similar function for Zoyd Wheeler and his daughter Prairie, who are forced to leave the hippie scene of Gordita Beach and settle in northern California in order to escape from federal agent Brock Vond's various forms of harassment and abuse. Described as a largely unspoiled and uncharted land, Pynchon's Vineland is clearly reminiscent of the utopian representations of Vinland in the Norse sagas about the pre–Columbian exploration of North America, as has been noted by various critics.[9] Echoing Leif Ericson's description of "Vinland the Good" in Chapter Eight of *The Saga of Erik the Red*, Zoyd himself refers to the place as "Vineland the Good" (322), a quasi-mythical space consistently depicted through the lens of its intangibility, as permeated by "the sense … of some invisible boundary," or as summoned by "the call to attend to territories of the spirit" (317). In an ethereal place where even the stands of redwood are "too high, too red to be literal trees" (317), Prairie—a character fittingly described by Hanjo Berressem as "an allegorical figure of the young, free country and its colonization" (41)—grows up attuned to the rhythms of nature, while Zoyd himself benefits from the support of a network of friends, in a community that celebrates difference.

However, Vineland is not only a pastoral space populated by marginal figures in search of a more authentic lifestyle in closer communion with nature, but also a very tangible piece of real estate destined to one day become part of the "Eureka-Crescent City-Vineland megalopolis" (Pynchon, *VD* 317). As the narrator comments with reference to the real estate developers' recent interest in the area, it was "[a]ll born to be suburbs, in their opinion, and the sooner the better" (319). The ominous prospect of turning a still pristine natural environment into a suburban arrangement thus emerges as the latest transformation of a piece of land that has witnessed a long history of displacements and erasures, including those of the *woge*, the first humanoid inhabitants of the region, and of the Californian Native American tribe of the Yuroks.

While only intimated in *Vineland*, the intrusion of real estate developers on the Californian landscape, driven by what Oedipa Maas calls, in the earlier novel, "the need to possess, to alter the land" (Pynchon, *CL49* 178), reaches a stage of quasi-completion in *Inherent Vice*. Embedded in a scathing critique of the real estate system, the prevailingly dystopian representation of California in the 2009 novel is nonetheless similarly complicated by a utopian construct surfacing at various points in the narrative, the myth of Lemuria.

As Dora Polk notes, California has been associated with a long list of such constructs, including the aforementioned Lemuria-as-the-Atlantis-of-the-Pacific, along with "Arcadia, Avalon, the Garden of Eden, El Dorado, the Elysian Fields, the Land of Milk and Honey, the Land of Prester John, Mecca, the New Jerusalem, the Promised Land, the Terrestrial Paradise, and Treasure Island" (13). According to Sumathi Ramaswamy, the twentieth-century reinvention of Lemuria proved particularly appealing within the framework of the American occult imaginary, as it resonated in interesting ways with exceptionalist narratives projecting California as the promised Garden of Eden (76). As such, the American reappropriations of the myth proposed that the survivors of the cataclysm that destroyed the Pacific-located continent actually migrated to northern California's Mount Shasta, a space reminiscent of their own land in point of natural conditions, where they have secretly established a brotherhood of masters (73). Unsurprisingly, the cultural rediscovery of Lemuria also found particular resonance in the context of the New Age spirituality of the sixties. Imagining a new Lemurian super race that will build super cities "free of pollution and industrial waste, of crime and disease, of class warfare, greed and poverty" (85)—coincidentally, a series of "vices" plaguing the urban scape of Pynchon's novel, too—the New Age re-appropriation of the myth mobilized a prominent environmentalist agenda.

For Pynchon, Lemuria is "the Atlantis of the Pacific" (Pynchon, *IV* 101). Sortilege, the resident astrologist of Gordita Beach and one of the most colorful representatives of New Age spiritualism in the novel, believes in the imminent re-emergence of the continent, returning to us since "we can't find a way to return to Lemuria" (167). In one of the hallucinatory trips induced by Sortilege's guru Vehi Fairfield, Doc imagines himself finding safe haven "in the vividly lit ruin of an ancient city that was, and also wasn't, everyday Greater L.A." (108), as a refugee from the disaster which had submerged Lemuria thousands of years ago. Pynchon further develops his own version of the myth, recounting how three Lemurian holy men landed on the Californian shores, bringing with them the sacred stone they had rescued from their temple, which would provide the "foundation of their new life at the heart of their exile" (109). Most prominently, Lemuria resurfaces toward the end of the novel, in Doc's famous conversation with his lawyer Sauncho Smilax about maritime law and the applicability of inherent vice not only to the cargo, but also to the vessel carrying it:

> "Well," Sauncho blinked, "maybe if you wrote a marine policy on L.A., considering it, for some closely defined reason, to be a boat..."
> "Hey, how about an ark? That's a boat, right?"
> "Ark insurance?"
> "That big disaster Sortilege is always talking about, way back when Lemuria sank into the Pacific. Some of the people who escaped then are spoze to've fled here for safety. Which would make California like, a ark."
> "Oh, nice refuge. Nice, stable, reliable piece of real estate." [351–52].

If elsewhere in the novel California is a synecdoche of contemporary capitalist America and the (inherent?) vices at the heart of its practices of urban development, such excerpts reimagine a mythical California as a hospitable site reminiscent of the "Harbor of Refuge" provided by Vineland in the previous novel of the trilogy. How can one negotiate the "antiexceptionalist exceptionalism" (Dussere 147) inherent in the layering of these two radically different representations—L.A. as Fractal City, "held hostage to the future we must live in now forever," and L.A. as "some undrowned Lemuria, risen and redeemed, where the American fate, mercifully, failed to transpire" (IV 341)? Significantly, the concluding scene of the novel offers an unexpected variation of the narrative of California as a mythical ark that might point in the direction of some answers: while driving on the Santa Monica freeway, through the dense fog, Doc notices a temporary commune of drivers forming to help each other on their way home[10]; he then imagines missing the Gordita Beach exit and arriving at a border "where nobody could tell anymore in the fog who was Mexican, who was Anglo, who was anybody" (369).

While *Vineland* ends with the annual gathering of the Becker-Traverse community constructing its own trans-generational space of left-wing resistance against Reaganite America, *Inherent Vice* similarly offers a vision of a spontaneous community going against the metropolarities otherwise defining the spatial and social configurations of the novel. Located halfway on the continuum between the dystopian and utopian readings of California superimposed throughout the novel, the final scene thus calls attention to such moments of "irruption" (Harvey xvii) when disparate heterotopic groups come together to construct a radically different space, "a space of hope" (112) that reimagines the urban scape of L.A. beyond the spatial and social segregation of the fractal city. Perpetually oscillating between a sustained critique of an environmentally exhausted California and a nostalgic return to that "subjunctive" space of infinite possibility embedded in exceptionalist constructs, the novel thus strikes a moderately hopeful note in its final vision of an temporary commune, pointing to the possibility of reconstructing the social fabric of L.A. and perhaps of reimagining urban space in a more socially just manner.

NOTES

1. Quotations from Pynchon's novels will be henceforth referenced as *M&D* (*Mason & Dixon*), *BE* (*Bleeding Edge*), *IV* (*Inherent Vice*), *CL49* (*The Crying of Lot 49*), *VD* (*Vineland*).

2. For an investigation of the construction of the American West as "subjunctive space" in *Mason & Dixon*, see Brian McHale's "*Mason & Dixon* in the Zone, or, A Brief Poetics of Pynchon Space."

3. Notably, the novel was adapted into a movie of the same title in 2014 by Paul Thomas Anderson, featuring a cast that includes Joaquin Phoenix, Josh Brolin, and Owen Wilson.

4. In his article "Thomas Pynchon and the South Bay," Garrison Frost suggests that Gordita Beach, previously mentioned in *Vineland*, was modeled on Manhattan Beach, a beachfront city in southwestern Los Angeles County where Pynchon lived in the late sixties and early seventies.

5. In foregrounding the relationship between the spatial and the social, the representation of L.A. in *Inherent Vice* is reminiscent of that in Pynchon's 1966 article "A Journey into the Mind of Watts." In this rare piece of journalism, Pynchon comments upon the aftermath of the Watts riots of the previous year—constantly referenced in the novel as well (Pynchon, *IV* 17, 195, 201, 208)—and the unbridgeable divide between the white and black cultures that co-exist in L.A. In *Seeking Spatial Justice*, Edward Soja discusses the Watts riots as a critical moment when "the symbolic heart of black Los Angeles exploded" (Soja 131), calling attention for the first time to questions of spatial segregation (especially housing and school segregation), hence spatial injustice.

6. For a different reading of the trope of the beach—as a "*locus amoenus*" (Berressem 53) as well as "an inherently revolutionary site" (55) in the elemental ecology of Pynchon's fictional universe, see Hanjo Berressem's "Life on the Beach: The Natural Elements in Thomas Pynchon's California Trilogy."
7. See Mike Davis's account of the removal of 12,000 low-income residents from Chavez Ravine to pave the way for the redevelopment of Bunker Hill, and the construction of Dodger Stadium (Davis 122–23).
8. For a related reading of the construction of Vineland as a fitting setting for the annual reunion of the Becker-Traverse multi-generational community of resistance, see my article "Visions of Community in Thomas Pynchon's *Vineland*."
9. While there seems to be a general critical consensus on the utopian connotations of the Vinland reference, Erik Dussere complicates this analysis by drawing attention to another series of associations suggesting a more nuanced symbolism. As he argues, Pynchon's incorporation of the Vinland myth blends the frequently idealized interpretation of this construct as "a version of the original America" with a traumatic reference to the Norse expedition as "the first moment of European contact with and claiming of the American land—a paradise lost at the moment of origin" (Dussere 145). This interpretation is also consistent with Pynchon's brief account of the "first Act of American murder, and the collapse of Vineland the Good" in his following novel, *Mason & Dixon* (Pynchon, M&D 634).
10. For an analysis of the freeway as a spatial trope in the Pynchon canon, see Stephen Hock's article "Maybe He'd Have to Just Keep Driving, or Pynchon on the Freeway." Hock traces a shift from "the networks of modern power and capital" necessarily aligned with Pynchon's earlier representations of this space to the "network of community" (215) emerging on the Santa Monica freeway in the final scene of *Inherent Vice*, amounting, in his view, to a "repurposing of the freeway as the avenue to an alternative America" (217).

WORKS CITED

Benea, Diana. "Visions of Community in Thomas Pynchon's *Vineland*." *11th Conference on British and American Studies: Embracing Multitudes of Meaning*. Ed. Marinela Burada, Raluca Sinu, Oana Tatu. Newcastle upon-Tyne: Cambridge Scholars, 2015. 352–70. Print.
Berressem, Hanjo. "Life on the Beach: The Natural Elements in Thomas Pynchon's California Trilogy." *Pynchon's California*. Ed. Scott McClintock and John Miller. Iowa City: University of Iowa Press, 2014. 35–64. Print.
Cowart, David. *Thomas Pynchon and the Dark Passages of History*. Athens: University of Georgia Press, 2011. Print.
Davis, Mike. *City of Quartz: Excavating the Future in Los Angeles*. London: Verso, 2006. Print.
Dussere, Erik. *America Is Elsewhere: The Noir Tradition in the Age of Consumer Culture*. Oxford: Oxford University Press, 2014. Print.
Foucault, Michel. "Of Other Spaces." Trans. Jay Miskowiec. 1986. *Rethinking Architecture: A Reader in Cultural Theory*. Ed. Neil Leach. New York: Routledge, 1997. 330–336. Print.
Frost, Garrison. "Thomas Pynchon and the South Bay." *The Aesthetic*. 2003. Web. 12 May 2015.
Fuller, Buckminster R. *I Seem to Be a Verb*. New York: Bantam Books, 1970. Print.
Harvey, David. *Rebel Cities: From the Right to the City to the Urban Revolution*. London: Verso, 2012. Print.
Hock, Stephen. "Maybe He'd Have to Just Keep Driving, or Pynchon on the Freeway." *Pynchon's California*. Ed. Scott McClintock and John Miller. Iowa City: University of Iowa Press, 2014. 201–19. Print.
Inherent Vice. Directed by Paul Thomas Anderson, performances by Joaquin Phoenix, John Brolin, Owen Wilson, Katherine Waterson, Eric Roberts. Warner Bros., 2014.
McClintock, Scott, and John Miller. "Introduction: Surveying Pynchon's California." *Pynchon's California*. Ed. Scott McClintock and John Miller. Iowa City: University of Iowa Press, 2014. 1–14. Print.
McHale, Brian. "*Mason & Dixon* in the Zone, or, a Brief Poetics of Pynchon Space." *Pynchon*

and *Mason & Dixon*. Ed. Brooke Horvath and Irving Malin. Newark: University of Delaware Press, 2000. 43–62. Print.
Polk, Dora Beale. *The Island of California: A History of the Myth*. Lincoln: University of Nebraska Press, 1991. Print.
Pynchon, Thomas. *Bleeding Edge*. New York: Penguin, 2013. Print.
_____. *The Crying of Lot 49*. 1966. Cutchogue, NY: Buccaneer Books, 1997. Print.
_____. *Inherent Vice*. 2009. London: Vintage, 2010. Print.
_____. "A Journey Into The Mind of Watts." *New York Times*. 12 June 1966. 34–35, 78, 80–82, 84. Print.
_____. *Mason & Dixon*. 1997. London: Vintage, 1998. Print.
_____. *Vineland*. 1990. London: Vintage, 2000. Print.
Ramaswamy, Sumathi. *The Lost Land of Lemuria: Fabulous Geographies, Catastrophic Histories*. Berkeley: University of California Press, 2004. Print.
The Saga of Erik the Red. Trans. John Sephton. 1880. *Project Gutenberg*. Web. 12 May 2015.
Soja, Edward W. *Postmetropolis: Critical Studies of Cities and Regions*. Oxford: Blackwell, 2000. Print.
_____. *Seeking Spatial Justice*. Minneapolis: University of Minnesota Press, 2010. Print.
Wilson, Rob. "On the Pacific Edge of Catastrophe, or Redemption: California Dreaming in Thomas Pynchon's *Inherent Vice*." *Boundary 2* 37.2 (2010): 217–225. Print.

"Come to California"
The Star as a Tragic Figure of American Apocalypse in Lana Del Rey's Honeymoon (2015)

Steve Drum

The cover of Lana Del Rey's album *Honeymoon* shows the singer sitting in the back of a white open-air tour bus. Del Rey is trapped and alone. The bus stands still in the road, holding no driver or fellow travelers on board. The view beyond her is not a postcard of any identifiable landscape. Instead, Del Rey is engulfed by an empty expanse of sky, indicating no particular locale or identity. The only clue as to her whereabouts is the airbrushed Star-Line Tours logo, emblazoned in red and blue across the side of the bus, suggesting the sort of vehicle used to carry sightseers through fortified residential neighborhoods of Southern California to photograph the homes of the stars. Del Rey looks the part of both performer and consumer of celebrity, resembling a glamorous ingénue in a classic Hollywood film, playing the part of a tourist. Her expression conveys both the winsome dream of some future glory and the malaise of sated excess. Although the sun shines on her back, her sunglasses reflect the glaring flash of a camera in front of her, unsettling both the narrative of the anonymous nobody and the untouchable somebody. The album's cover image gathers several antithetical attitudes toward the Hollywood star: idolatry and alienation, nostalgia and caprice, envy and pity.

Del Rey's music composes an indiscriminate potpourri of American cultural imagery: Elvis, Pepsi, Marilyn, Hollywood and Vine, *Lolita*, James Dean, Pabst Blue Ribbon, Jim Morrison, to name only a few. Del Rey performs this sardonic pastiche of Americana without the hint of a sneer but instead with the blank stare of Andy Warhol, singing them as devotional hymns to a time-worn iconography that the world has emptied of meaning. Her frequent references to stars who died as a result of a perceived fatal flaw or unhealthy relationship to stardom follow a recognizable pattern of Hollywood fandom, in which mourners overvalue and mythologize the stars whose deaths seem to reflect the impossibility of their lives. *Honeymoon* offers several variations on the theme of the star succumbing with pious grace to her inevitable downfall, with Hollywood itself serving as metaphor for an erotic submission to her own destruction. The origin story of Del Rey's own transformative rise to fame—the meticulous re-branding of her image, name, music, and appearance to distance her celebrity from an earlier self, and the obsessive cataloguing of the project on the internet by both her admirers and detractors—alludes to a familiar Faustian narrative of the classical Hollywood era of image construction, in which a soul is bargained for an unsustainable star identity. But where the precarious line between Norma Jeane and Marilyn Monroe might be irretrievably buried by a Hollywood of the past, Del Rey's music explicitly performs celebrity mortality with a brand of cinematic glamour usually associated with a star's rise. By embodying the star's demise as a role unto itself, Del Rey adapts the figure of the star and the space of Hollywood into symbols of the relationships between individual and culture, performance and identity, glory and destruction. Using *Honeymoon*'s allusions to Hollywood as the site of the tragedy of the falling star, I hope to encounter both the projection of national anxieties onto the star figure and the imaginary space of California as an apocalyptic or pornographic setting for the death of the American individual among the ruins of celebrity culture.

The figure of the actor has always served as both a fantasy of individualism and a nightmare of alienation from self. For thousands of years, anti-theatricalists have pointed a suspicious finger at the performer's ability to double or disguise their physical and emotional realities, accusing the actor of catalyzing any number of perceived symptoms of moral degeneracy in the larger culture. Jean-Jacques Rousseau's 1758 letter imploring that Geneva be protected from the institution of the theater relies largely on an argument that a society cannot enjoy a theater without making room for the accompanying actor-laborer, whose talent is "the art of counterfeiting himself, of putting on another character than his own, of appearing different than he is, of becoming passionate in cold blood, of saying what he does not think as naturally as if he really did think it, and, finally, of forgetting his own place by dint of taking another's" (79). From Tertullian's pleas to Roman Christians in 200 CE to Jeremy Collier's call for the moral reform of the English stage in 1698, the proposed cure has remained simple and sanitary: stay out of the theater, off of the stage, and far away from actors.

Early appraisals of the cinema treat the mechanics of film production with similar shades of abject horror, a metaphor for a systemic evil pervading the culture beyond the walls of the movie palaces. The villain of the cinema is the industrial capitalist machine of image-making and artifice. The film performer—effervescent and ubiquitous in their reproducibility—comes to represent less of a moral danger than an existential breakdown in the modern relationship to self. In 1933, Walter Benjamin's alarmist reading of the cinema focused on the actor's anxiety—paralyzed by the camera, divorced from themselves, and replaced with the "phony spell of a commodity"—rather than the actor's responsibility to uphold a standard of virtue to their audience (231). Where anti-theatricalists of previous eras contain their proposed evils in the figure of the stage actor as sociopathic mercenary, the film actor is frequently painted as victim, martyr, or sacrifice to a recognizable collective disease. If the cinema is a cultural affliction, the film actor is its pitiful host-body.

In his 1916 novel *Shoot!*—written in the toddling, pre–Hollywood years of silent cinema—Luigi Pirandello observes a mechanized intimacy in the cinema that leaves its performers caught between fragmented realities. Pirandello's protagonist, cameraman Serafino Gubbio, describes the violent process of compressing the film actor into an image:

> [Film actors] are confusedly aware, with a maddening, indefinable sense of emptiness, that their bodies are so to speak subtracted, suppressed, deprived of their reality, of breath, of voice, of the sound that they make in moving about, to become only a dumb image which quivers for a moment on the screen and disappears, in silence, in an instant, like an insubstantial phantom, the play of illusion upon a dingy sheet of cloth.... And the man who strips them of their reality and offers it as food to the machine; who reduces their bodies to phantoms, who is he? It is I, Gubbio [106].

By making his narrator an operator of the cinematic machine, Pirandello implicates the film audience in the camera's violence upon the actor. At the very least, we behave as voyeurs to the depletion of the actor's humanity. Four decades later, after the peak of the studio system's authority over the film product, Edgar Morin argues that the actor's ability to yield to this cruel relationship between camera and performing body outlined by Pirandello serves as the best measure of their success. In Morin's eyes, it is the film actor's responsibility to submit to being "destroyed" by the camera, to act as "automaton and mask, object and divinity" (126, 132). The actor's most sublime and virtuosic performance is their capacity to endure their own mechanical reproduction without revealing the anxiety inherent to the transaction.

The rise of a film star from the film actor compounds these anxieties with the parallel narrative of the actor as themselves, working both to demystify the fictional performance and to invite scrutiny upon the star's performance of self. The star narrative doubles the actor with an equally illusory image. Morin argues that the star's duality between fiction and reality represents a return to the Lacanian child witnessing an exteriorized consciousness in their own image in the mirror. But where the child must internalize this duality, learning that their double and their body are synchronized in their movements, the star's twinned selves can perform independently of each other, drawing the star and the star's audience into "a dialectic of division and reunification of the personality" (54). Even the disclosure of the most rudimentary details of a star's off-camera identity (i.e., a physical form, a name, an age) enacts a gravitational pull of circumspect investigation toward some authentic center within the star persona. The star's on-camera identity serves as a body of corroborating and contrasting evidence to the star's reality. If the actor reflects to its culture a fear of supernatural access to another order of reality, the star reflects an even deeper paranoia by appearing plastic in their construction of their authentic identity or mobile between their two selves. The star's performance of stardom points to our own order of reality as performative.

The star's uncanny double-presence may be reconciled, however, by an encounter with the star's mortal body in the form of a tragic fall. The death of the star's image can be as powerful as the death of the star's body, and one death can stand in neatly for the other. Reni Celeste writes that the inorganic surface of the star already points toward death, like a waxwork: "The living star is already a ruin, a tombstone" (32). Celeste notes that Valerie Solanas sought to destroy the body of Andy Warhol "to attempt ... the closure of mediation, the collapse of the distinction between observed and observer.... The death of the star completes the image, fulfilling the *telos* of stardom" (34, original italics). Although the celebrity's audience rarely intervenes as deliberately as Solanas in bringing about the star's demise, the star's audience is always faced with the specter of their culpability. Like Sontag's photographic *memento mori*, even to be audience to the star is to participate in their "mortality, vulnerability, mutability" (Sontag 15). Because of its unavoidable mediation, the destruction of the star is likely to be as performative and artful as their auspicious rise. Perhaps more importantly, the star's fall casts a backward gaze of hindsight on the star's existing narrative, revising it into some legible (often moralistic) allegory of the star's unsustainable zenith. This epilogue can sustain the star indefinitely as both human and immortal, turning the ruin of the individual into a collective shrine of symbolic social meaning.

I would like to argue here that these three ways of seeing the film star embody their stardom—the star in narrative performance, the rise of the star's celebrity, and the fall of the star—produce a sense of voyeuristic pleasure in the star's audience. Even in mourning the star's fall or death, the audience experiences a queasy sense of gratification in the performativity of the star's destruction and in their own sense of compassion for them. It is similar to Milan Kundera's explanation of the two tears that fall from the eye in the realm of kitsch: the first moved by the drama itself, the second moved at "how nice [it feels] to be moved, together with all mankind..." (Kundera 251).

Sixteenth-century dramatic theorist Lorenzo Giacomini attempted to explain the highly contested question of why the horrors of tragedy might delight a spectator:

> Since compassion is an act of virtue, and since every operation stemming from virtue or similar to it is by nature pleasant, so in this manner can the compassion of tragedy bring delight.... Honor also brings delight, almost as a sign to the one honored, of his own virtue.... [Tragedy] makes us realize that we are free of such violent misfortunes, which cannot but bring us pleasure and joy. The last [reason] comes from learning healthy historical lessons, and principally among these, that kings and princes sometime fall into calamity and ruin [174].

Although Giacomini speaks here of dramatic performance, the highly mediated rise and fall of a film star takes on dramaturgical characteristics similar to those of a theatrical performance. In performing a life to a remote audience, the celebrity becomes a character in a highly symbolic narrative, their death acting as a sort of moralizing denouement. In *Honeymoon*, Lana Del Rey performs each of these phases of stardom for the pleasure of her audience: an actress performing a role in a closed narrative fiction, that actress' double negotiating the rise of her celebrity, and the spectral image of the fallen star from the afterlife.

Honeymoon's first track of the same name opens the album with a lush string arrangement, orchestrated with an earnest sentimentality and emotional tension, resembling the title sequence of a 1950s melodrama. Del Rey sings of a doomed love affair to a troubled (presumably male) partner with a "history of violence." She positions their desire for one another in opposition to the forces of a cruel external world, admitting it isn't "fashionable" to love her, but assuring him that the two of them can "make the rules." She whispers falsetto praise of the "guns that blaze around" her love, while reminding him of the "roses in between [her] thighs," as though her partner's brutality is of a piece with her sexual desire for him. In the chorus, Del Rey repeats that this is "Our honeymoon/Our honeymoon/Our honeymoon," revealing that her bliss is matrimonial. She rounds out the refrain with a command to validate her affections ("Say you want me too/Say you want me too"). Taken as a closed narrative, "Honeymoon" illustrates an archetypal cinematic plot: a heterosexual romance between a criminal male and a woman aroused by his danger. As the judgments and perils of the outside world close in around them, they elope as a revenge against society, growing increasingly isolated and reckless in their devotion to each other. She submits to the risks of his world in exchange for his promise of love. They will die honorably in defense of their wild passion for one another, unless someone decides they would rather live and walk away. The song casts Del Rey in a fictitious, but immediately recognizable film of the era referenced by the opening orchestration. Although it opens the album, Del Rey's performance in the song is

Honeymoon's aria. She is positioned as an actress in a stock scene of incredible dramatic tension, locked firmly in a gaze with another actor, allowing her audience ample space for voyeuristic pleasure. From this point on, however, the album's narrative falls slack, turns inward, and grows increasingly aware of the presence of the audience.

If "Honeymoon" serves as Del Rey's "on-screen" performance in a narrative fiction, "Freak" is where she invites her audience to watch her perform off-screen in a cool urban fantasy of celebrity affluence. The song's opening verse seems to look directly into the eye of the camera that she disregards in "Honeymoon," performing for her spectator as her eroto-romantic partner: "Palms reflecting in your eyes, like an endless summer/That's the way I feel for you/If time stood still, I'd take this moment/Make it last forever." Del Rey notes the direction of our gaze toward Hollywood in watching her, the reflection of California palm trees in our eyes when we look upon her image. Like with her acting partner in "Honeymoon," Del Rey is overfull with imagery both sexual and menacing, noting our "halo of fire" before squealing that she is "rising up" and "full of fire" herself. As the chorus slows into a grim electronic drone, she conflates this invitation to her body with an invitation to relocate geographically and rebrand ourselves as Hollywood stars: "Come to California/Be a freak like me, too/Screw your anonymity/Loving me is all you need to feel/Like I do." The sexual promise is folded into the promise of California, authenticity, fame, and connection. Del Rey privileges the performer (who embodies California) with a unilateral erotic pleasure in having an audience, aligning the anonymous viewer (who embodies not-California) with a stifling inhibition. The invitation to watch the star is exploded into an invitation to feel stardom course through our veins. The song performs the promise and pleasure of watching the star rise to impossible heights. "Freak" casts the star's audience as a stock character in a wild, impractical passion with the star body. Like the doomed romance of "Honeymoon," someone must either die or walk away empty-handed.

The dark narrative turn toward the star's fall is also signaled in the music video for "Freak" (directed by Del Rey). In place of the song's imagined utopic space of acceptance and liberation is a group of willowy young women (including Del Rey), hanging on an intense bearded guru, styled to resemble Charles Manson, wandering under the blanched sun of the California desert. In the decades since the Manson murders, Manson's biography has been consistently revised to portray him as a fame-seeker and a failed rock star, accounting for the carnage he orchestrated as his aspiration to glory. Filmmaker Nikolas Schreck titled his 1989 documentary on Manson's life *Charles Manson Superstar*, as though to implicate Manson's audience as culpable in creating and sustaining Manson's fame. The popular film history podcast *You Must Remember This* structured its 2015 series on the Manson murders around the various Hollywood celebrities or celebrity-adjacents to cross Manson's path, including several anecdotes of a pre-murder Manson awkwardly trying to sell his own experimental rock concepts to someone he perceived to be an insider, e.g., Dennis Wilson of The Beach Boys, or music producer and son of Doris Day, Terry Melcher (Longworth). These scenes and the bitter resentments that followed suggest a parallel history in which some form of breakthrough stardom alters the course of Manson's life to a career as a legitimate star. Furthermore, Manson's "family" of followers consisted largely of wayward youth who had arrived to California with their own fantasies of escaping bourgeois American ideals and reveling in the free-spirited counterculture of the 1960s. The dream of California was precisely what Manson preyed upon in his followers, inviting them into a warm embrace of social acceptance, spiritual exploration, and liberal sexuality, before persuading them to carry out his most violent atrocities in his name. Paired with the video's visuals, Del Rey's invitation to come to California and "be a freak" takes on notes of apocalyptic madness. The video ends with a five-minute sequence of the cult leader's female followers underwater in a slow swirl of long hair and peasant dresses to the tune of Debussy's "Clair de Lune." The camera never rises above the surface of the water, trapping the viewer with the cult followers in an environment that is both unsustainable and performative, dangerous and beautiful. The Manson figure and Del Rey, the nodal points of both the cult and the video, are noticeably absent.

On the track "Swan Song," Del Rey offers another invitation to her audience, albeit a much more vague one than that of "Freak." "Why work so hard when you could just be free?" she asks, "You got your moment now, you got your legacy." Here, toward the album's end, the audience seems to have joined the star in a position of celebrity status, having perhaps followed through on the proposition in "Freak" to join her and her star-body in California. But where "Freak" asked the listener to dance, make love, and throw caution to the wind, "Swan Song" does not package its plea in any explicitly romantic or sexual language. She asks the listener to "dive deep" into "the water where the ice meets," and to "say goodnight to the life and the world you knew." The promise made here is one of oblivion and self-immolation. In the chorus, Del Rey assures us that we "won't work another day," but also vows "never [to] sing again" herself, as though her performance has become burdensome. The seduction takes on the shades of both a suicide pact and a threat of destruction: "With just one wave it goes away/It will be our swan song." It remains unclear what Del Rey promises will disappear and whose hand will perform the disappearing. The song ends with the refrain of another indefinite command, telling her listener to "put [their] white tennis shoes on and follow [her]." The abyss into which Del Rey is leading us is no longer sexual or utopic. Our leader's purpose now is simply to escape from the performative

California that was our holy grail in "Freak." Palm trees and fire have become icy waters. The romantic ideals that framed the threat of death in "Honeymoon" have vanished and death has become an end unto itself to escape Hollywood by any means necessary.

If "Swan Song" is the star's desperate appeal for death, in "God Knows I Tried" the star seems to reflect back on life after death's release. Here, Del Rey does not direct her gaze at either another actor in her narrative or the listener in her audience. She sings outward, past her audience and into the cosmos. She wakes up to a surreal inversion of the natural world, seeing "red, blue, and yellow skies." She "[puts] on that 'Hotel California'" and "[dances] around like [she's] insane." The mention of the 1976 song by The Eagles—long debated for what is thought to be a metaphor for limbo, Hell, or satanic possession in the form of a dark and glamorous California hotel—seems apt for Del Rey's sentiment. But where the Hotel California is a battleground for a trapped soul, "God Knows I Tried" is the ballad of a soul purified and transcendent in death. Del Rey is a star who has "nothing much to live for/Ever since [she] found [her] fame." Her celebrity is killing her. From the star's outward violence of "Freak" and the star's self-inflicted violence of "Swan Song," "God Knows I Tried" shows the violence of an incessant audience pushing the star into complete isolation. She pivots between the world-weary mortal suffering of "Swan Song" and a sense of calm deliverance to the not-California she envisioned as though standing on the threshold between each realm. In the chorus, however, she offers an inventory of her life to a higher power and leaves the mortal realm completely: "God knows I lived/God knows I died/God knows I loved/God knows I lied/God knows I lived/Begged, borrowed, and cried/God knows I lost/God gave me life/God knows I tried." In death, she can admit her defeat by the celebrity machine she sought to infiltrate. Ironically, by submitting to her destruction at the hands of her audience, she fulfills Morin's prerequisite for film performance, becoming "object and divinity" to the camera's hungry eye.

In "God Knows I Tried," Del Rey performs the star's tragic fall from Hollywood royalty as a sincere melodrama. As author of her own fall, she takes on the saintly glow of the star immortalized by tragedy, closing the song in reverent refrain: "Let there be light/Let there be light/Light up my life/Light up my life." Del Rey deifies herself in a fashion resembling Morin's description of the cult surrounding the death of James Dean, projecting light upon the star's life to reconcile their mythology and its meaning: "Death fulfills the destiny of every mythological hero by fulfilling his double nature: human and divine. It fulfills his profound humanity, which is to struggle heroically against the world, to confront heroically a death that ultimately overwhelms him. At the same time, death fulfills the superhuman nature of the hero: it divinizes him by opening wide the gates of immortality. Only after his sacrifice, in which he expiates his human condition, does Jesus become a god" (107).

In *Honeymoon*, Del Rey wraps herself in this sanctified shroud of the Hollywood legend, but not merely to assure her own status as mythical heroine. Her death is ultimately a fictional performance, revealing more about the atmosphere of Hollywood's Dream Factory and the promise of California than it reveals about Lana Del Rey. Like in the album's title track, she is an actress playing a stock role in a familiar narrative for the pleasure of her audience. In allowing the narrative to "destroy" her, the music becomes a reflective surface—like the void of empty California sky caught in the dark looking glass of Del Rey's sunglasses on the album's cover. The California represented in *Honeymoon* is both a fantasy of glamour and an inhospitable ruin, showing the audience its own collective impulse to crucify that which it most desires.

WORKS CITED

Benjamin, Walter. "The Work of Art in the Age of Mechanical Reproduction." *Illuminations.* Ed. Hannah Arendt. Trans. Harry Zohn. 1936. New York: Schocken Books, 1968.
Celeste, Reni. "Screen Idols: The Tragedy of Falling Stars." *Journal of Popular Film and Television* 33:1 (2005) 29–38. Web. 3 May 2016.
Del Rey, Lana. *Honeymoon*. Interscope, 2015. MP3.
Giacomini, Lorenzo. "On Purgation in Tragedy." *Sources of Dramatic Theory: Plato to Congreve.* Ed. Michael J. Sidnell, D.J. Conacher, Barbara Kerslake, Pia Kleber, C.J. McDonough, and Damiano Pietropaolo. Trans. Bernard Weinberg. 1586. Cambridge: Cambridge University Press, 1991. 172–5. Print.
Kundera, Milan. "The Grand March." *The Unbearable Lightness of Being.* Trans. Michael Henry Heim. New York: Harper & Row, 1984.
Longworth, Karina. "Charles Manson's Hollywood, Part 3: The Beach Boys, Dennis Wilson, and Manson the Songwriter." *You Must Remember This.* Panoply, June 2015. Web. 11 June 2015.
_____. "Charles Manson's Hollywood, Part 5: Doris Day and Terry Melcher." *You Must Remember This.* Panoply, June 2015. Web. 26 June 2015.
Morin, Edgar. *The Stars.* Trans. Richard Howard. 1957. Minneapolis: University of Minnesota Press, 2005.
Pirandello, Luigi. *Shoot! (Si Gira): The Notebooks of Serafino Gubbio, Cinematograph Operator.* Trans. C.K. Scott Moncrieff. 1916. New York: E.P. Dutton, 1926. Print.
Rousseau, Jean-Jacques. "The Letter to d'Alembert on the Theatre." *Politics and the Arts.* Trans. Allan Bloom. 1758. Ithaca: Cornell University Press, 1960. Print.
Sontag, Susan. "In Plato's Cave." *On Photography.* New York: Picador, 1977. Print.

Cop Shows, Sitcoms and Oral Histories in Thomas Pynchon's *Vineland*

TOMAS POLLARD

Thomas Pynchon set three novels in California: *Crying of Lot 49* (1966), *Vineland* (1990), and *Inherent Vice* (2009), and in a recent collection titled *Pynchon's California* (2014) many critics thoroughly examine Pynchon's use of "both California's familiar cultural symbolism as 'America's America,' the leading edge of the American experiment in freedom, and the equally familiar 'noir' critique of that symbolism" (McClintock and Miller 5). Although the prevalence of television and noir echoes in *Vineland* has been noticed, my essay intends to read the novel and the characters mainly through the interplay of the image clusters of pop references to cop shows and sitcoms as well as the *real* source of counterculture in the novel, oral history. In *Vineland* pop images of cop shows capture, reproduce and recreate fantasies that delude and mostly deaden political awareness, while other pop images taken from sitcoms and TV commercials are used to represent the often frustrated urges of characters to reconnect to lost family members or domestic stability. Throughout the novel oral histories and family contacts act as a counterweight to darker implications in the police imagery in the novel. Understanding the roles of pop and oral cultures in the novel leads to a richer understanding of Salman Rushdie's and other critic's view of *Vineland* as "a major political novel about what America has been doing to itself, to its children" at the end of the twentieth century (37).

Live or on the Tube: Cop Shows and Sitcoms

The most influential culture in the novel is that of the Tubefreeks, characters whose pop preoccupations make them dysfunctional, self-destructive, or at least purblind in some way. Tubal fantasies manifest a distorted mentality that projects a cop show or sitcom framework onto the world, and many characters attempt to live out these fantasies. Television is repeatedly linked to feeling safe and in control. The narrator notices that Frenesi feels safe filming during violent protests because she does so through a "Tubeshaped frame" (202). By contrast, the time that Zoyd spends detained and beaten by the federal agents is fittingly called his "Tubeless hours" (298) as the safety evoked by TV is missing, and he feels "rectal spasms of fear" (299). In fact, television is so comforting and reaffirming that the "smartest child [that Frenesi's son] Justin ever met in kindergarten" gives him the helpful advice "to pretend his parents were characters in a television sitcom. 'Pretend there's a frame around 'em like the Tube, pretend they're a show you're watching. You can go into it if you want, or you can just watch, and *not* go into it'" (351, original italics). The advice reveals that television can teach passivity or promote engagement by making children feel safe, but in both cases there is a false sense of choice as if children get to set the terms of family interaction, as if parents like Frenesi can never choose to leave for years, and as if life were like a sitcom. For the children, the recurrent sitcom plot of solving a problem or achieving some form of resolution in the course of an episode creates the comforting impression that the genre itself can insulate them from harm and death. Taking a broader view, an adult character named Takeshi comes to believe that TV "with its history of picking away at the topic [of death] with doctor shows, war shows, cop shows, murder shows, had trivialized the Big D itself" (218). To be "Tubed" in the novel is to base one's construction of reality on televised images instead of relying on the social construction of reality. At the very least the Tube confirms characters' worldviews, and the characters prefer sitcoms and cop shows to all other TV genres in the novel. Police dramas are more popular with the government employees Frenesi Gates and Hector Zuñiga.

A fan of cop shows, Frenesi chooses to become a state agent in the novel after betraying her friends who are peace protesters and plotting the murder of Weed Atman, her activist lover. Although raised by labor union activist parents and rescued from government detention by another activist DL, Frenesi cooperates with federal investigators as an informant and opens up an avenue of freedom for her own "Woodstock" and "Revolution": "[Frenesi] understood her particular servitude as the freedom, granted to a few, to act outside warrants and charters, to ignore history and the dead, to imagine no future, no yet-to-be-born, to be able simply to go on defining moments only, purely, by the action that filled them" (71–72). Living in the moment and ignoring her own culpability in the murder of her lover, she acts out an identity and memorizes fabricated life stories for each assignment. However, within those perimeters she can live out a pop fantasy of "freedom" derived from state obedience.

Cop shows become intertwined with her sexual fantasies in the novel. Like her mother, who marries a World War II veteran, Frenesi feels "crazy about uniforms on men" and "a helpless turn toward images of authority ... live or on the Tube." Her lifelong preoccupation with any man in uniform extends from bellboys to athletes to policemen. Frenesi visualizes herself as one of many women who have had "fantasies while on the freeway about the Highway Patrol and ... enjoyed masturbating to Ponch and Jon reruns [in the motorcycle cop show *ChiPs*] on the Tube." While having an affair with federal agent Brock Vond, she imagines her life as a video game that she plays as an anonymous actor for the state in a "falsely deathless perimeter" (292–93). Her longing for men in uniform, and pop fantasy initiate her into "the dark joys of social control" (83), which makes her betrayals possible. The triumph of the law in cop shows tends to suggest that law enforcement will only violate the civil rights of criminals, so civil resistance, alarm, and paranoia among the more law-abiding folk seem completely unwarranted. Although Frenesi is deeply invested in protest and knows how often law officers neglect civil rights when maintaining order, cop shows make it easier for her to find social order irresistible and become a turncoat, a government informant.

Police dramas also generate a copycat cop star in the novel who becomes so dysfunctional that, ironically, his fantasies end his policing career. Hector, a DEA (Drug Enforcement Agency) field agent, undergoes Tubaldetox, a rehabilitative treatment for those suffering from Tubal abuse. The treatment starts off treating TV addicts by denying them TV access but ends up using a homeopathic treatment of watching TV to cure the addiction (335). Slade explains that the "real narcotic in the Vineland is television" (78), and Hector is the best example of an addict, humming theme tunes and watching TV while driving. Ironically, he finds a new life by planning to make a TV drama based on his life as a drug cop. As a cop, he reenacts TV cop iconography with a slight difference. Unlike an action cop in 1980s films like *Beverly Hills Cop* (1984) and *First Blood* (1982) who "is able to make things 'right' again, a hero who, in fiction, can reestablish the communal ideals of a nation obsessed with wealth and suppressed by government and big business" (Brown 79), Hector is a corrupt cop: his Hollywood dreams lead him to be a model cop confiscating property and holding detainees. Hector imitates action cop icon Clint Eastwood (28) and, fittingly, Ricardo Montalban (28) known most for his role in TV sitcom *Fantasy Island*, a confirmation that Hector's Tubal fantasies separate him from real life as his delusions lead to the loss of his job and family. When he approaches Frenesi about starring in his movie, Frenesi explains to Hector that he is "so Tubed out [he] can't even think straight" (345). His behavior triggers her to reflect on his reliance on television shows for his self-image: "he depended on these Tubal fantasies about his profession, relentlessly pushing their propaganda message of cops-are-only-human-got-to-do-their-job, turning agents of government repression into sympathetic heroes" (345). Cop shows give Hector a model for being a policeman, and he also adopts Hollywood dreams to create a new film to support the repressive War on Drugs, one of the plot elements that connects 1984 in the novel to George Orwell's *1984*. Both books use simulated wars and make-believe victories as a way to deepen their grip on an ill-informed public. The irony is that in Pynchon the American public in 1984 is not fooled by state propaganda but seems too distracted by pop culture to care about being fooled.

Although pop culture deepens and darkens the fantasies of federal agents, sitcoms offer pipe dreams for Zoyd and Prairie who are abandoned by Frenesi until their anti-climactic reunions at the end. In a broader sense, television shapes Zoyd's expectations about his ability to overcome obstacles. In one of most quoted and touching passages, Zoyd expects to love baby Prairie as much and as conveniently as he loves his television, and their escape is like the end of a sitcom episode after all the problems have been sorted. Fittingly, her presence becomes a "night-light" like that of a TV left on all night: "he understood that like all suffering Tubeheads he must have really thought, as he and the baby were making their getaway, that that was it, all over, time to go to commercials and clips of next week's episode.... Frenesi might be gone, but there would always be his love of Prairie, burning like a night-light, always nearby, cool and low, but all night long" (Pynchon 42, original ellipsis). Even the narrative voice undercuts the absurdity of this peaceful tranquility, pointing to an open ending, that they would have to go "living years" beyond the escape. Zoyd's affection for his ex-wife also finds its expression in a wistful commercial imagined for television. Zoyd fantasizes that Frenesi would hear his "dream album," full of tender oldies about true love, advertised on television, and know that every song was about her (36). TV provides the content of his views of the future and many unfulfilled fantasies.

For all the expectations that television generates for Zoyd, those related to cop shows are more morbid and dark, lacking any sentimentality. In a moment of despair Zoyd actually decides not to commit suicide in Hawaii after losing Frenesi due to the line that Jack Lord always uses in scenes when suicide victims' bodies are found in the cop show *Hawaii Five–O*: "Book him, Danno—Suicide One" (60). Ironically, Zoyd loses his autonomy when the drug cops "frame" him in the role of a trafficker and confiscate his home, revealing that law enforcement can wreak havoc using the same cop show plots that create a sense of public safety in most shows.

In rare cases characters can use TV iconography for their own ends, but a sense of desperation is often inherent in their actions. Inspired by move seen in a *Three Stooges* episode, Justin sits between his parents, Frenesi and Flash, to keep an argument from escalating on an airplane (352). Justin's move works, showing undoubtedly a positive influence of pop culture in the novel, as the sitcom genre shapes this and similar redemptive moments. Opting for the moves from cop shows points to a more pathetic set of circumstances, even if some autonomy can be achieved. In the opening chapter Zoyd crashes through a store window dressed like a woman so that he can prove his unstable mental state and qualify for his mental health disability check for another year. TV news crews film the annual event, which is then analyzed by a panel of experts (15). Zoyd uses the media for his own ends, although he appears on TV as a comic victim and his nemesis Vond as a charming prosecutor, both playing roles scripted in cop shows.

Girls and Media Images

Media images generate most anxiety for Zoyd's daughter Prairie, as she is a sensitive adolescent searching for a sense of identity and belonging. Her longing to be reunited with her mother also has her "Tubed out worse than Hector," according to Zoyd (51). Prairie compares her desperate use of every possible clue about Frenesi's whereabouts to the cartoon elephant Dumbo who breaks his fall by waving a feather (100). When she sees her mother's film of the murder of Weed Atman that she instigated, Prairie still imagines that Frenesi is like the Statue of Liberty holding the "hard frightening lights" while filming (261). Knowing her as a cold-blooded murderer and double crosser, Prairie comes to see Frenesi as a "celebrity" when they are reunited, more a projected fantasy than a mother (375).

Prairie's earlier search for her inner mother's daughter collides with mediated images of girlhood, a theme that Pynchon treats comically before revealing its tragic implications. As a teenager, Prairie teams up with two-dozen teenage girls on roller skates to stage the Great South Coast Plaza Eyeshadow Raid, stealing makeup and accessories from a mall shop and rescuing her friend Che like the bionic woman on skates (328). The raid is a form of teenage resistance to the power of malls, as well as a desperate attempt to live up to a media image of pretty girls and, more importantly for Prairie, good daughters, as can be seen in the comparison between the roller skaters and ice skaters. The roller skaters contrast with the ice skaters seen in the Noir Center a few pages earlier when Prairie "liked to imagine herself as just such a figure of luck and grace, no matter what hair, zit, or weight problems might be accumulating in the nonfantasy world." The ice skaters look "perfect" like girls on television, "teenagers in sitcoms, girls in commercials learning from their moms about how to cook and dress" (327). By stealing makeup and learning to cook, she lives up to the glossy image of a pretty model and a good daughter. With the help of a "recipe out of the TV section" (111) Prairie proves her cooking skills during a sort of rite of initiation for the Sisterhood of Kunoichi Attentives who are led by Sister Rochelle, "mother superior of the place" (108). The media creates the expectations that she meets to please an ever absent or a substitute mother, and Prairie becomes increasingly similar to women in well-lit studios and glossy magazines.

However, media images of women tend to cause problems for characters when they feel compelled to project highly eroticized versions of themselves. On their last day in the mall together, during a "nostalgic" farewell, Prairie and her friend Che shoplift lingerie together following a routine used earlier. Due to a dysfunctional home situation caused by her mother's boyfriend being a sexual predator, Che decides to leave home and become a prostitute (329–31). Prairie watches Che and her roommate Fleur with the stolen underwear "playing centerfold" (332) before trying it on herself to please them. Prairie copies their imitation of a sexual fantasy, briefly pleasing her esteemed older friend and affirming a sense of belonging before their farewell. For Frenesi, who had imagined that her abandoned daughter would be "wearing centerfold attire" for her boyfriend at this age, the teenage girls seen at another mall feed her curiosity as she is "desperate for any detail" about her daughter's generation (68). The girls represent her daughter for Frenesi as other mall girls represent teens with a mother for Prairie. Media-created images of other women and the consumer desires created by these images projected onto mothers and daughters in their surroundings become a main commodity and preoccupation for these two estranged women to imagine themselves as a mother and daughter. The prominence of pornography in their conceptualization as parent and child shows not only the eroticization of girls, but also the consumerization arising out of dysfunctional families and the subsequent circulation of expectations for family ties based on advertising and media fantasies. Filling an emotional void, these expectations are strongly associated with sexual exploitation, feelings of alienation, abandonment, and betrayal; subjects more appropriate for a cop show than the sitcom format, as the former lays "emphasis on the inevitable victory of good over evil when disparate individuals learn to work as a team" (Brown 84). The team of Takeshi, DL, and Prairie work together to outwit and outrun the federal officials led by Brock Vond, and, after one escape, Prairie longs to wake into a sitcom setting, "something more benevolent," a family "with no problems that couldn't be solved in half an hour of wisecracks and commercials, on their way to a fun weekend at some beach" (191), but her experiences and family history belong in a cop-action genre.

Cop shows and the cop-action genre with malevolent government officials are irretrievably linked to the back-story of the chief executive in 1984, Ronald Reagan, and Prairie's family. Although political repression is most often associated with the backlash to the 1960s Revolution (when Reagan was the California Governor), labor disputes also become connected to pop culture and Prairie's family through Reagan. As an actor and anti-union organizer in Hollywood, Reagan played a role in the Screen Actors Guild, a fact that angers Prairie's grandmother Sasha. Sasha reflects on the influence of the film industry on politics during the 1950s: "the blacklist period, with its complex court dances of fuckers and fuckees, thick with betrayal, destructiveness, cowardice, and lying, seemed only a continuation of the picture business as it had always been carried on, only now in political form" (81). Later, Sasha explains that in the 1950s, Reagan was a part of the "dark recrudescence of that hard-cased antiunion tradition of Hollywood" (289). Asked to work as a strikebreaker, a scab, Sasha's husband Hub joins the strike before he even gets hired and is hit in the head with a bolt by a company thug. Although Reagan and others claimed that the union was a group of Communists, the dispute revolves around cheap labor, but the newspapers present it as a strife between two unions instead of a conflict between labor and management over wages.[1] Cold War politics merges with business opposition to union demands, and the betrayal of trust and fair representation infuriates Sasha and her husband Hub. The behind-the-scenes look at Hollywood's labor issues is similar to the novel's exposé of the status quo muffling political dissent in the 1960s. The similarity points to the fact that the news can create a false sense of safety when it neglects to report the real political maneuverings of movie corporations in Hollywood and the government in the 1960s protests. During both moments, restoring order realigns business interests with the state in the novel.

Pop and political culture merge when drugs become a part of the culture wars during the 1984 presidential campaign. The anti-drug leanings of a few bureaucrats and politicians need popular support, and Pynchon's Hollywood acts as a conduit to find it, mainly because it is under political pressure to do so. As Hollywood is coming under growingly intense scrutiny due to its own drug users, the media and the public react positively to Hector's idea for an anti-drug film. The fictional Ronald Reagan praises the film in one of his campaign speeches in 1984 (342). Through comic excess Pynchon highlights the fact that the anti-drug film and movement are self-conscious moments of moral posing for Hollywood and Washington that disguise their darker ulterior motives. Although the music industry outwardly supports the 1960s peace movement, pop music trivializes and undercuts its goals "as revolution went blending into commerce" (308). The teenager Isaiah argues that the Revolution failed because the "Minute the Tube got hold of you folks that was it, the whole alternative America ... sold it all to its enemies" (373). The film, music, and television industries counteract the labor and protest movement in the novel. What Pynchon actually suggests is that any entertainment-oriented act of breaking the labor and peace movement down into consumable images or lyrics robs them of the nuance and logical justification that give them their energy.

By contrast, Frenesi's favorite cop show *CHiPs* (1977–1983) was also a feel-good series humanizing the California Highway Patrol (CHiPs). In a more devious example not alluded to in the novel, a cop show set in California in the 1960s like *Dragnet* used "a full array of 'others' who serve as raw meat for [its] angry, voracious ideological appetite: hippies, protestors, pot smokers, black militants, liberal intellectuals, and a gaggle of miscellaneous social misfits" portrayed as a "fantasy of the Right" (Sharrett 167) that "today seems little more than propaganda for the Los Angeles Police Department" (165). The catalogue of "others" mentioned above sound like most of the non-governmental characters in *Vineland*. Although pop culture is not inherently reactionary, cop shows and police dramas can be striking examples of unqualified law enforcement boosterism, and this aspect of pop culture encourages such characters as Hector and Frenesi, who are involved in murder, family betrayal, and illegal drug entrapment for the state.

Oral History and Allegories of Activism

Pop culture finds its counterweight in oral histories and family ties, although they are not depicted as perfect media, either. Although the families of DL and Che are clearly not nurturing, Hayles points out that families are still "the best chances for connection and bonding" in *Vineland* (27). For instance, the oral histories of Sacha offer her granddaughter Prairie a meaningful set of terms to create a sense of self. Through Sasha's stories, Prairie uncovers the political manipulations of her corrupted mother, and darker moments of California labor violence such as Hollywood black lists, intimidation, and outright murder. With her insights, she sees through the false facade of the Noir Center in Hollywood: "she personally resented this increasingly dumb attempt to cash in on the pseudoromantic mystique of those particular olden days in this town, having heard enough stories from Hub and Sasha, and Dotty and Wade, to know better than most how corrupted everything had really been from top to bottom, as if the town had been a toxic dump for everything those handsome pictures had left out" (326). Seeing through the veneer of California as a dream, Prairie adopts a view similar to that of Liahna Babener who describes it "as empire built on spurious foundation decked in tinsel, and beguiled by its own illusory promises" (127). Oral history helps the character spot the false images of the past, but she finds it more difficult to see through the media-generated images of mothers and perfect sportswomen, especially the ice skaters that Che and she see in the Noir Center. Frenesi remembers her mother reading, reviewing, and writing innumerable scripts that will never become films: "Sasha had finally wised her up, likening [the chances for a script to become 'real' on screen] to one sperm cell out of millions reaching and fertilizing the egg" (346). Sasha's oral histories debunk Hollywood's mythic past and the mirage of easy employment and wealth to be acquired by filmmaking in the union-breaking California.

Those who live by oral histories in the novel rarely watch television, and when Prairie's Traverse family watches TV, they often "bootleg[g]" it instead of paying for cable (324). Ninja and rebel chick Darryl Louise Chastain, known as "DL," is only seen watching television once, with the sound off, while she waits to assassinate her future partner Takeshi, the man she believes to be the nemesis and federal agent Brock Vond (141). Storytellers and their listeners tend to get entangled in labor politics in *Vineland*. The matrilineal line of Eula Becher, Sasha Traverse, Frenesi Gates, and Prairie Wheeler are inextricably linked to political violence and turbulence. At the time of the great-grandmother's birth, signs of political violence are mentioned: "family friends [were] known to have shot at as well as personally dropped company finks, styled 'inspectors,' down mine shafts so deep you might as well say they ran all the way to Hell" (76). Her husband Jess Traverse is crippled when a company thug releases the wedges on a pre-cut tree that falls on him during a baseball game (75). Before his injury they live on the road as labor organizers "getting arrested" and "shot at, by Pinkertons," strikebreakers hired by companies and farming organizations (76). Before World War II Sasha also joins the labor movement "standing midwatch guard against vigilante squads and hired guns from the Associated Farmers, getting herself shot at more than once" (77). Eula and Sasha are closely involved as storytellers as well, and the novel focuses on Sasha finding her political voice when her husband listens to her thoughts about injustice (80), linking labor politics to family experience. Families provide political education in the novel, as seen in Sasha's teaching, although Frenesi decides to turn against her mother's teaching and Prairie seeks additional teachers as well.

Other characters, like DL, Rochelle, and Weed, also provide important political lessons for Prairie and the reader. The last section of the novel contains two political allegories relevant to pop culture. The first is the story of why activism failed in the 1960s, and the second aims to rejuvenate activism for the future. In the first allegory Weed Atman, a mathematician and political activist, becomes a Thanatoid after he is murdered with Frenesi's help. Meaning "death, only different in Greek," Thanatoids appear most regularly after the Vietnam War (320) and watch a lot of television (170). They represent the disillusioned political activists who have given up their hopes of making a difference, and have relocated to rural areas such as the countryside outside of Vineland. Although murdered, Weed is never described as a ghost; he is an amiable living dead symbol. The Thanatoids can be interpreted as an updated version of the Tralfamadorians in *Slaughterhouse-Five* by Kurt Vonnegut; however, their passivity derives not from seeing the past and future, but from their disillusionment with failed political activism.

The first allegory occurs in one of Weed's dreams about guilt-ridden men who prevent his murder from being solved. His death is symbolic of the lethargic termination of the revolutionary energy released in the 1960s. The men in the dream are opposed to political activism and wish to conceal its disappearance, and thus Weed's murder. Although the allies of the murdered man in the dream wish to seek a coroner to find the murderer, "every jurisdiction [the men with Weed's cadaver] come rolling into was notified in advance, each time men in hats, carrying weapons, standing on the platform, waving us on, who only want to swear they never saw us." Weed reveals his dream to Prairie at the moment that she, knowing her mother set up Weed's murder, asks what he plans for revenge. Weed immediately replies, "It depends a lot on who you've turned out to be" (365), and he confesses that he does not wish any vengeance as the instigators of the murder who gave orders to Frenesi and Brock are now out of power (366). The dream is a comment on the 1960s, as the countercultural dreams have been co-opted by those in power and by the mass of disaffected voters and activists who stop pushing for changes and tune out by watching TV.

By contrast, the second allegory, calling for a political reawakening, is told by Sister Rochelle to the Japanese counteragent Takeshi when she worries that his new love life may lead him to retreat from fighting against the corrupt federal agents, the "unrelenting forces" (383). This allegory, a coda placed in the third-to-last paragraph in the novel, can be read as a veiled message to the reader as well. In the allegory a paradise Earth is fought over by Heaven and Hell. After Hell's victory, its people occupy, rule, and visit Earth as tourists. Still, when "the novelty wore off," the people of Hell stop visiting, and the administrators and troops leave. The tunnels and "gateways to Hell were finally lost to sight" and what remains for earthlings is "sad recitals that ask why the visitors never came anymore." Rochelle concludes, "So, over time Hell became a storied place of sin and penitence, and we forgot that its original promise was never punishment but reunion, with the true, long-forgotten metropolis of Earth Unredeemed" (382–83). Taken literally, Rochelle's allegory is a plea to Takeshi not to forget others now that he has found true love. As a political allegory, the people of Hell represent Coach Potatoes too obsessed with watching television to care about politics anymore. In a *New York Times* article "Near, My Couch, to Thee" Pynchon links the sin of Sloth with Couch Potatoes: "Any discussion of Sloth in the present day is of course incomplete without considering television, with its gifts of paralysis, along with its creature and symbiont, the notorious Couch Potato. Tales spun in idleness find us Tubeside, supine, chiropractic fodder, sucking it all in...." (n.p.). The world-weary people of Hell are like Couch Potatoes preferring mediated images to the "true, long-forgotten metropolis of Earth Unredeemed." Narratives based on a "storied place of sin and penitence" are similar to the plots of crime and punishment in police drama. By contrast, stories of reunion fit the sitcom genre, and the literary tradition of comedy and satire that can provide these stories with their "edge," "imitations of defiance" and a sense of redemption for listeners (382, 384). Dreams, allegories and oral stories present resistive narratives that reawaken hibernating and repressed political dreams in a novel dominated by the images taken from pop culture that lull its audience into a sense of security and political apathy.

In conclusion, cop shows repeatedly inspire characters to serve some state function that undermines or thins out political will and family contacts. *Vineland* can almost be placed next to *The Crying of Lot 49* and *Inherent Vice* in Scott Macleod's reading of their striking "a delicate balance between instilling readerly familiarity while introducing elements of genre subversion" (117), although *Vineland* never aims to subvert a genre but to expose a political state. After understanding the "pseudoromantic mystique" created by pop culture and used to market a nostalgia for a completely fabricated California, attentive readers can consider what to think and do about the "toxic dump" (326) created by labor violence, sexual exploitation, corrupt government, and political manipulation. While *Vineland* does not provide political answers and its affirmations are usually limited in scope, its stories of family reunion and allegories provide narratives to inspire a cultural Tubaldetox and a return to meaningful human connections including family ties and political action. A closed sitcom ending with an unqualified triumph of a new Revolution may meet TV viewing expectations, but Pynchon views counter-narratives that stimulate participation and political awareness as only a starting move to revive a California deteriorating due to neglect, greed, and apathy. If fiction and even pop culture can serve as forms or oral history, Pynchon seems to suggest, perhaps there is a way out of the maze created by political and commercial manipulation.

NOTE

1. To verify Pynchon's version of the strike and representation of Reagan's role, see Horne vii–ix and Clune 23–24.

Works Cited

Babener, Liahna K. "Raymond Chandler's City of Lies." *Los Angeles in Fiction: A Collection of Essays*. Ed. David Fine. Albuquerque: University of New Mexico Press, 1995. 127–49.
Brown, Jeffrey A. "Bullets, Buddies, and Bad Guys." *Journal of Popular Film & Television* 21.2 (1993): 79–88.
Clune, Lori. "Political Ideology and Activism to 1966." *A Companion to Ronald Reagan*. Ed. Andrew L. Johns. Malden, MA: Wiley Blackwell, 2015. 22–39.
Hayley, N. Katherine. "'Who Was Saved?' Families, Snitches, and Recuperation in Pynchon's Vineland." *The Vineland Papers: Critical Takes on Pynchon's Novel*. Ed. Donald J. Greiner and Larry McCaffery. Normal, IL: Dalkey Archive Press, 1994. 14–30.
Horne, Gerald. *Class Struggle in Hollywood*. Austin: University of Texas Press, 2001.
Macleod, Scott. "The Origins of the Family, Private Property, and the State of California in Pynchon's Fiction." *Pynchon's California*. Ed. Scott McClintock and John Miller. Iowa City: University of Iowa Press, 2014. 91–111.
McClintock, Scott, and John Miller. "Introduction: Surveying Pynchon's California." *Pynchon's California*. Ed. Scott McClintock and John Miller. Iowa City: University of Iowa Press, 2014. 1–14.
Pynchon, Thomas. "The Deadly Sins/Sloth; Nearer, My Couch, to Thee." *New York Times Book Review*, 6 June 1993. Print.
_____. *Vineland*. London: Secker & Warburg, 1992.
Rushdie, Salman. "Still Crazy After All These Years: *Vineland* by Thomas Pynchon." Rev. of *Vineland*, by Thomas Pynchon. *The New York Time Book Review* 14 Jan. 1990: 1, 36–37. Print.
Sharrett, Christopher. "Jack Webb and the Vagaries of Right-Wing TV Entertainment." *Cinema Journal* 51.4 (2012): 165–71.
Slade, Joseph W. "Communication, Group Theory, and Perception in Vineland." *The Vineland Papers*. Above, 68–88.

These Kind of Dreams
Dystopian Depictions of California in the Music Video "Californication"

Daniel Klug

The Red Hot Chili Peppers are probably associated with Los Angeles more than any other American rock band (Apter 10-44). Many of their songs—such as "Out in L.A." (1984), "Deep Kick" (1995), "Desecration Smile" (2006), or "Happiness Loves Company" (2011)—evidence a strong emotional and personal connection to the complex and erratic culture of Los Angeles, its people and lifestyle. And many of their music videos include visual references to the city and Southern California. Most prominently, their song "Californication" deals with living in Southern California and the darker sides of the so-called American dream. This essay focuses on the depiction of California, Los Angeles, and Hollywood in the music video "Californication." It analyses how the lyrics and images together present the subtle realities, attitudes, lifestyles, and culture of Southern California.

Music videos are short audiovisual media artifacts that add various moving or still images to a pre-existing pop song (Vernallis, *Unruly* 208-10). They present artists and bands as performers and stars, establish music-based visual styles, and elucidate the lyrics of songs visually. In general, music videos are variously classified as musical performances, narratives, loosely connected situations, or illustrative elements, but they usually combine or alternate between two or more of these types of visualization (Altrogge 37-40). Music videos are based on the linearity of the underlying song (Chion 165-68), but there is no spatial, temporal, or causal relationship between the music and the visually depicted actions (Keazor and Wübbena 56). The music and lyrics are never generated by the actions in the images (Klug 206-12). Instead, sound and video are more often connected by rhythmical arrangements (for example, in a montage to the beat of the song), visual interpretations of the lyrics (such as filmic sequences or narratives), and illustrations of its musical atmosphere (Goodwin 85–90). Most often the analysis of music videos therefore focuses on the coherence of image, text, and tone and on the surplus that is created when they are synced together (Vernallis, *Experiencing* 175–83).

The song "Californication" was released in 2000 as the fourth single of the album *Californication* (1999), which marks the culmination of the Red Hot Chili Peppers' artistic engagement with Southern California. Several other songs on the album—like "Around the World," "Emit Remmus," "Purple Stain," and "Parallel Universe"—combine descriptions of California and references to Los Angeles with catchphrases of pop culture to create negative metaphors for the American dream (Jost et al. 118).[1]

"Californication" is the album's most distinct song about the dark side of Californian culture and its propagation through Hollywood and its movie industry—and maybe the most critical Red Hot Chili Peppers song on this subject altogether. The term *Californication* is a portmanteau of *California* and *fornication*. It was popularized in 1972 by *Time* reporter Sandra Burton in reference to "the haphazard, mindless development [of land] that has already gobbled up most of Southern California" (17). According to Burton, Californication was spurred by the increasing numbers of people moving to the arid lands of Southern California. But Californication also transcends the borders of the state: as a verb, *californicate* describes the spread of negative aspects of the Californian lifestyle, such as pollution and consumerism, especially to Oregon and Colorado (Pryde 13–14). Since Burton's introduction of the term, *Californication* has been used as a derogatory term for stereotypes connected to the Californian lifestyle, for instance beauty standards (van Wolputte 264). It has thus become a pejorative for cultural attitudes that contrast with the stereotypical image of the "Golden State" as synonymous with a carefree and paradisiacal life.

"Californication" is characterized by a raw, down-to-earth sound and a slightly varied main-guitar motif that connects the verse and the bridge. A harder bass touch, a distorted guitar sound, and chanted singing define the chorus (Jost et al. 105–10). The verses of "Californication" consist of metaphorical and sometimes cryptic statements that unveil life in California as a paradox of self-determination and heteronomy. The equal coexistence of superficiality and fornication is most apparent in the lyrical contrast of the bridge that reframes the statements of each verse. The first line of the bridge uses "firstborn" and "unicorn" as metaphors for leadership, exclusiveness, innocence, and Disneyesque magic. But the second line describes humiliation, filthiness, and the existence of hidden opposing realities by directly mentioning pornography as aspects of fornication. Given this contrast, the repetitive imperative of the subsequent chorus line to make Californication the goal of one's dreams oscillates between firm demand, desperate warning, and sarcasm. In general, the lyrics offer some kind of advice or warning. The verses, in particular, deal with the fact that the individual human is constantly threatened by the predominant and uncontrollable culture of Californication (cf. Jost et al. 103–05).

In contrast to "Californication," most other Red Hot Chili Peppers songs simply mention California or Los Angeles to refer to the band's origin and their musical background in the city's 1980s punk scene. Only "Dani California" (2006) from the album *Stadium Arcadium* contains a noticeable criticism of the difference between the American dream as a desired goal in life and actual Californian reality. The lyrics describe the short, unsteady, and poor life of a fictional girl named Dani California from the Deep South and her struggle to make it in Hollywood.[2]

All genres of pop music have addressed the culture and lifestyle of California and Los Angeles, reflecting the ways the image of Southern California has been changing throughout the decades. For example, songs from the 1960s, like "California Dreamin'" (1965) by The Mamas & the Papas or the works of The Beach Boys, express escapism and Summer of Love romance. In contrast, early 1990s gangsta rap, such as "Nuthin' but a 'G' Thang" (1992) by Dr. Dre feat. Snoop Doggy Dogg or the music of rapper Ice-T, describes the darker sides of Los Angeles's multifaceted culture (Romig 109–19). In general, numerous songs, such as "Hotel California" (1977) by The Eagles, "Welcome to the Jungle" (1988) by Guns N' Roses, "Into the Great Wide Open" (1991) by Tom Petty and the Heartbreakers, "California Love" (1995) by 2Pac feat. Dr. Dre and Roger Troutman, and "Hollywood" (2003) by Madonna, include subliminal messages about dark and rough experiences of living in California. Especially Los Angeles and Hollywood are perceived as "a sad reality that has made [them] the subject of both fascination and scorn" (Hayes 89).

This critical engagement transfers into the music videos. For example, in two scenes of the music video for "Hollywood," Madonna presents herself on a medical stretcher receiving Botox injections. Together with the lyrics, these scenes criticize Hollywood beauty standards, which, ironically, Madonna also embodies (Peverini 138). "Welcome to the Jungle" shows a different dark side in the beginning of the music video, when Axl Rose walks through Los Angeles at night and stops in front of a wall of television screens that display acts of violence and destruction (Austerlitz 89). The music video then cuts between these televised images and a live performance of the band to specify the jungle metaphor of the lyrics and to create a subtle apocalyptic atmosphere. "California Love" sets the performance of the song in a dystopian, *Mad Max*-like setting to present an even more radical interpretation of the song's cultural criticism (Austerlitz 104). The music video for "Into the Great

Wide Open" focuses on the dark side of Hollywood's music business rather than on an apocalyptic society. The song and the music video both tell the story of an ordinary boy who becomes a rock star in Hollywood but cannot handle success and in the end loses his love and his career.

Many Red Hot Chili Peppers songs also deal with the above subjects. They most frequently combine references to Los Angeles with descriptions of the (former) band members' histories of drug abuse—especially that of singer Anthony Kiedis. "Under the Bridge" (1992), the band's emotional tribute to their hometown, is maybe the most iconic example (see Apter 227–33). The song is based on Kiedis's experience of coming to terms with his drug-related isolation (see Kiedis and Sloman 264–66). It describes Los Angeles as a shelter in hard times and, metaphorically, as the only person who can understand his suffering (Jost and Klug 202).[3] The music video adds a simple but meaningful layer to the lyrics and musical structure of the song. Instead of the usual landmarks and Hollywood splendor, it shows the diversity of regular people living in the city (Austerlitz 141–42). Kiedis walks through downtown Los Angeles, greeting people in the streets, and reconnecting with his past struggles and addiction, which, together with the lyrics, creates an emotional and personal message (Pesses 152).

Visual references to Los Angeles and/or California are almost always present in Red Hot Chili Peppers music videos regardless of the lyrics of the song. For example, "Suck My Kiss" (1992) cuts between the band in the recording studio and what appears as found footage of a military parade in Los Angeles (Pesses 152–53). The music video for "The Adventures of Rain Dance Maggie" (2011) shows the band performing on a rooftop in Venice Beach for people dancing in the streets. In "Charlie" (2007), child versions of the Red Hot Chili Peppers drive around rural California in a van. They pick up random people and party on Venice Beach at the end. The balladic "Road Trippin'" (2000) again uses images of the beach and surfers, which cut to the band sitting in a beach house at night playing the song, while in "By the Way" (2002), Kiedis is kidnapped by a crazy cab driver who drives him around Los Angeles before his bandmates finally save him (Austerlitz 155).

These music videos mostly present a positive and easy-living atmosphere that is based on the stereotypical Californian lifestyle. But the band's collaboration with directors Jonathan Dayton and Valerie Faris—who also directed "Road Trippin'" and "By the Way"—produced some rather dark, subtle, and more critical music videos. The video for "Otherside" (2000), which again deals with Kiedis's history of fighting drug addiction (Kiedis and Sloman 461), uses surrealistic dark and cubist images inspired by German expressionist films (Austerlitz 154–55). In contrast, the music video for "Tell Me Baby" (2006) seems to be a simple performance video, but the band performs with people who are shown to have moved to Los Angeles to become rock stars and failed (Pesses 154).

Dayton and Faris also directed the music video for "Californication," which is a combination of clips from a fictional platform video game of the same name and sequences of the band performing the song. Each band member of the Red Hot Chili Peppers has an avatar in individual levels of the video game (Jost et al. 93), and each game level is linked to either a landscape (the Sierra Nevada and Yosemite National Park), a city (Los Angeles and San Francisco), a lifestyle (such as surfing), or a cultural industry (Hollywood) of California. In the last level, the effects of Californication inevitably lead to disaster when an earthquake destroys a part of the downtown. Control icons, the third-person point of view on the avatars, and the changing of levels and players suggest actual interactive game flow or control over the avatars (Keazor and Wübbena 391). But the avatars do not perform any typical game-play actions apart from navigating through particular settings. In fact, they lead the viewer through the different levels so as to present landscapes, locations, and events matching the descriptions of California or fornication in the lyrics. In this way, the computer-animated depictions of Californication illustrate the dense and cryptic lyrics of the song (Jost et al. 118).[4] At certain points in a level, the avatars discover a floating red double cross, the band symbol of the Red Hot Chili Peppers, and jump onto it. Subsequently, the video-game icon, which usually shows the band performing in a small picture-in-picture, expands into a full-screen window showing the Red Hot Chili Peppers performing the song in a desert setting with blue cloudy skies (Jost et al. 99–102).

The lyrics for "Californication" contrast with the bright colored aesthetics of the music video. The verses describe singer Anthony Kiedis's love-hate relationship with the commercialized culture of Los Angeles and California (Fitzpatrick 102). The first verse of "Californication" deals with the dream of a successful movie career whereas the first video-game level emphasizes negative aspects of Hollywood. The lyrics refer to how the naïve dream of effortlessly becoming a movie star draws young women from all over the world to Hollywood. The lyrics specifically mention aspiring starlets from Sweden to underline their cultural distance, which reinforces the naïvety of the dream and possibly refers to Hollywood's demand for exotic beauty. In the video-game simulation, the avatar "John" (John Frusciante) is running down the Hollywood Walk of Fame.[5] He passes a young blonde woman who gets off a bus and walks to a rundown casting agency. This short scene shows how the video-game sequences specify the lyrics of "Californication." The visualizations offer alternate interpretations, and, together with the lyrics, lead to an audiovisual surplus in the depiction of Californication. Several similar looking blonde women in short skirts line up in front of a filthy casting agency with a broken billboard that says "LOO ING FOR HOT TALENT"; they are waiting to be exploited by the adult-entertainment industry (Keazor and Wübbena 388). The images thus specify the rather vague lyrics, which describe the naïve willingness of young, beautiful women to follow their illusion of the American dream as an effect of Californication.

The subject of beauty is furthermore explored in the first bridge of "Californication" and the corresponding video-game level. The avatar "Anthony" (Anthony Kiedis) dives through an underwater setting with women in bikinis, which refers to television shows about the Californian lifestyle like *Baywatch* (1989–2001) or the *Beverly Hills, 90210* franchise (1990–) and the ideal Californian body image they present. At the same time, the lyrics in the bridge describe everlasting youth and beauty standards as Hollywood's greatest goods. Both can only be achieved with expensive medical interventions.

The critique of the Hollywood entertainment industry is picked up again in the visualization of the fourth verse. In this video-game level, "John" leads the viewer through three settings of a movie-studio complex. First, he passes through a science-fiction movie set resembling *Star Wars*, which creates a sharp audiovisual coherence with the lyrics that refer to the cinematic achievements of Hollywood (Keazor and Wübbena 388). "Space may be the final frontier"—a quote from *Star Trek: The Original Series* (1966–69; Season 1, episode 3) in the lyrics—symbolizes humankind's quest to unravel the mysteries of the universe, but may also be interpreted as referring to the hypothetical infinite sprawl of Californian culture even beyond Earth. The lyrics pursue this threat further in a reference to the fictional *Star Wars* planet Alderaan, "a world of unspoiled beauty and a center of art, culture, and education" (McKinney et al. 6), which is destroyed for no reason. This reference offers a metaphor for the social and cultural consequences of Californication. "John" then runs into a porn-movie set while the lyrics mention movie productions taking place in a basement rather than a film studio. The visualizations thus immediately contrast blockbuster movies with Hollywood's equally successful adult-entertainment industry. While science-fiction movies are one common image of Hollywood, the hidden, amateurish, and filthy character of porn films suggests an arbitrary coexistence of these different cultural outputs. In this way, both the lyrics and the images create a direct confrontation of California and fornication. Finally, "John" stops in a third movie set where one sees paintings and inventions by Leonardo da Vinci, which suggest an artistic perspective on popular culture. The corresponding lyrics similarly hint at pop-cultural figures when they refer to David Bowie's album *Station to Station* and describe Kurt Cobain as an example of a misguided and tragic American music career that falls to the false temptations of the Hollywood music industry (Keazor and Wübbena 389).

Overall, the video points to popular mass media, especially radio and television, as the primary propagators of Californication. In the third verse, their importance is addressed in the video-game level of the avatar "Flea" (Flea). The level links the image of Californication as a monopolized culture to the rural areas of California. "Flea" is running through a forest where he stops at a cabin with a satellite receiver and a pregnant woman standing outside. Signs in front of the cabin read "Aliens Welcome" and "This Is ARE Land." The scene invokes the credulity of a rural population that is subjected to a manipulative media system and conservative nationalist politics. The lyrics of this third verse can be interpreted in a similar way. They describe a young pregnant girl who lives sealed-off from the real world. She is easily deceived by the news and obsessed with televised images of Hollywood fame. This theme is later picked up and further developed in the song "Dani California."

In addition to describing and picturing the Hollywood media industry and its cultural artifacts as the creators and circulators of Californication, the lyrics and video-game sequences also tie the origin of Californication to well-known places in California. It is suggested that California is hiding its deviousness behind decals of graceful nature. But the video-game world of "Flea" also refers to how the gluttony of Californication endangers California's natural landscapes, such as Yosemite National Park. At the end of the level, "Flea" encounters a group of loggers that surround and threaten him. The avatar escapes by floating up into the top of a tree from where he witnesses the forest being cut down.

In the final level of the video game, the forces of nature become the crucial element. All four avatars meet in the downtown of a city, presumably Los Angeles, during an earthquake. Buildings are collapsing around them. This devastation is predicted in the lyrics of the preceding fifth verse. There, Californication is described as a destructive force that, on the one hand, makes life rough for those who experience it, but, on the other, can inspire creative ways of coping. This combination can furthermore be interpreted as a suggestion that people become so used to Californication that they ignore its destructive power. In the fifth verse, however, the music video shows the performance of the actual band instead of the video game. In this way, the lyrics are transformed into a direct statement by the band on the effects of Californication on people's lives.

After the earthquake destroys Los Angeles in the final scenes of the video game, all four avatars fall one by one into a fissure in the ground, and then come together on a rock. The performance icon of the video-game control bar is floating between them. They touch it at the same time and transform into the real musicians. The text "Game Over" appears, but then the music video ends with a blue screen, the white text "Next Game?" and a blinking "Yes."

The music video for "Californication" does not primarily deal with the issue of Californication in its general understanding. Instead of addressing the effects of Californian culture on other states, the video game shows aspects of Californication within California, which could then spread into other places and cultures. The overall concept of "Californication" is thus not to present a coherent story but to highlight the fornication in each of the video-game levels. The video-game visuals are only a simulation and lack any actual gameplay activity on the part of a hypothetical player; neither do the avatars perform any actions that would counterbalance the depicted origins or effects of Californication. In this way, the video-game events offer a playful warning by showing the consequences of carelessly choosing California without considering the inevitable and always immanent fornication. Los Angeles is depicted as the geographical culmination of Californication, and Hollywood is understood as the center of a global entertainment industry that reproduces, maintains, and spreads Californication across the world. In the music video, Californication is thus more than just the spread of a cultural attitude because it creates numerous pop-cultural products that are preserved and passed on. Consequently, the video-game aesthetics of the music video primarily focus on revealing stereotypes that are commonly connected with California as superficial and fake (Keazor and Wübbena 391–92). From this perspective, the video game may be interpreted as a reminder to stand together and fight against the cultural spread of Californication, but it does not give any advice about how to do so.

The bright-colored action of the video game makes the quite vague descriptions of Californication in the lyrics more concrete. The music video can be interpreted as an audiovisual metaphor for a lifelong struggle with Californication, which is marked by wanting, choosing, admitting, and resisting its dubious cultural effects. But it also creates a playful distance to dystopian views on Southern California, Los Angeles, and Hollywood, instead of expressing cultural criticism.

The final scene of "Californication" also emphasizes the biographical background of the Red Hot Chili Peppers. Every band member has gone through battles with drug abuse and can therefore be understood as a survivor of Californication, which has led the band to deal with California's hypocrisy creatively (MacPhail-Fausey 14–15). At the end of the fictional video game, the Red Hot Chili Peppers escape Californication when they are transformed into live-action musicians. But the avatars do not overcome Californication over the course of the game plot, and the possibility of playing again ultimately shows the invincibility of Californication. Even if one can temporarily escape it, the temptation to play through Californication again and again remains.

Part III: Welcome to Dystopia

Notes

1. For the lyrics of these songs, see Red Hot Chili Peppers, *Californication*.
2. For the lyrics of "Dani California," see Red Hot Chili Peppers, *Stadium Arcadium*.
3. For the lyrics of "Under the Bridge," see Kiedis and Sloman 265.
4. For the lyrics of "Californication," see Kiedis and Sloman 418–20.
5. I use quotation marks around "John" to distinguish the avatar from the actual person.

Works Cited

Altrogge, Michael. *Tönende Bilder: Interdisziplinäre Studie zu Musik und Bildern in Videoclips und ihrer Bedeutung für Jugendliche*. Vol. 2, *Das Material: Die Musikvideos*. Berlin: Vistas, 2001.
Apter, Jeff. *Fornication: The Red Hot Chili Peppers Story*. London: Omnibus, 2004.
Austerlitz, Saul. *Money for Nothing: A History of the Music Video from the Beatles to the White Stripes*. London: Continuum, 2007.
Burton, Sandra. "The Great Wild Californicated West." *Time* 100, no. 8, 21 Aug. 1972, 17.
Chion, Michel. *Audio-vision: Sound on Screen*. New York: Columbia University Press, 1994.
Fitzpatrick, Rob. *Red Hot Chili Peppers: Give It Away; The Stories Behind Every Song*. London: Carlton Books, 2004.
Goodwin, Andrew. *Dancing in the Distraction Factory: Music Television and Popular Culture*. Minneapolis: University of Minnesota Press, 1992.
Hayes, David. "From New York to L.A.: US Geography in Popular Music." *Popular Music and Society* 32, no. 1 (2009): 87–106.
Jost, Christofer, and Daniel Klug. "Integrierte Bild-Text-Ton-Analyse: Am Beispiel des Musikclips Californication." *Die Bedeutung populärer Musik in audiovisuellen Formaten*. Ed. Christofer Jost, Klaus Neumann-Braun, Daniel Klug, and Axel Schmidt. Baden Baden: Nomos, 2009, 197–242.
Jost, Christofer, et al. *Computergestützte Analyse von audiovisuellen Medienprodukten*. Wiesbaden: Springer VS, 2013.
Keazor, Henry, and Thorsten Wübbena. *Video Thrills the Radio Star: Musikvideos; Geschichte, Themen, Analysen*. transcript, 2005.
Kiedis, Anthony, and Larry Sloman. *Scar Tissue*. New York: Hyperion Books, 2004.
Klug, Daniel. *Lip Synching in Musikclips: Zur Konstruktion von Audio-Vision durch musikbezogene Darstellungshandlungen*. Baden Baden: Nomos, 2013.
MacPhail-Fausey, Alexander. "I Am with You: The Red Hot Chili Peppers, the Fans, and the Harmful Effects of Californication." *English Seminar Capstone Research Papers*, paper 31, 2015, http://digitalcommons.cedarville.edu/english_seminar_capstone/31.
McKinney, Brandon, et al. *The Essential Guide to Planets and Moons (Star Wars)*. New York: Random House, 1998.
Pesses, Michael W. "The City She Loves Me: The Los Angeles of the Red Hot Chili Peppers." *Sound, Society and the Geography of Popular Music*, edited by Ola Johansson and Thomas Bell. Burlington, VT: Ashgate, 2009, 145–60.
Peverini, Paolo. "The Aesthetics of Music Videos: An Open Debate." *Rewind, Play, Fast Forward: The Past, Present and Future of the Music Video*, edited by Henry Keazor and Thorsten Wübbena. transcript, 2010, 135–54.
Pryde, Philip R. "Thirty Million Californians Can't Be Wrong: Reflections on Reaching a Dubious Milestone." *Yearbook of the Association of Pacific Coast Geographers* 54, 7–22.
Red Hot Chili Peppers. *Californication*. Warner Bros. Records, 1999. Liner notes.
Red Hot Chili Peppers. *Stadium Arcadium*. Warner Bros. Records, 2006. Liner notes.
Romig, Kevin. "A Listener's Mental Map of California." *Sound, Society and the Geography of Popular Music*, edited by Ola Johansson and Thomas Bell. Burlington, VT: Ashgate, 2009, 107–21.
van Wolputte, Steven. "Hang on to Your Self: Of Bodies, Embodiment, and Selves." *Annual Review of Anthropology* 33, no. 1 (2004): 251–69.

Vernallis, Carol. *Experiencing Music Video: Aesthetics and Cultural Contexts.* New York: Columbia University Press, 2004.
_____. *Unruly Media: YouTube, Music Video, and the New Digital Cinema.* Oxford: Oxford University Press, 2013.

Conclusion
Californias Everywhere
KATARZYNA NOWAK-MCNEICE
and AGATA ZARZYCKA

As illustrated by the essays in this collection, Californian iconography is a patchwork in which shreds of hope mingle with eruptions of disappointment, cynicism, outrage or fear in the face of the Golden State's myth being warped, undermined or mocked in confrontation with the complexities of the region. The tensions between the different facets of California are most spectacular when captured in binaries—good and evil, beauty and ugliness, strength and weakness, reality and illusion, light and darkness—to the extent where challenging them or revealing their lability is as likely to bring about a sense of confusion or crisis as a productive release from limitations.

The uniqueness of such an effect is captured in Jean Baudrillard's comment encapsulating the ambiguity of culture in the geo-historical context: "The myths migrated. Today, all the myths of modernity are American. It will do us no good to worry our poor heads over it. In Los Angeles, Europe has disappeared" (81). The disappearance of Europe in Los Angeles—and more widely in California—might be understood in the light of the region's infamous anti-intellectualism—a reciprocated sentiment, since Mike Davis calls Los Angeles "the city that American intellectuals love to hate" (21)—which Baudrillard speaks against, but going a little further, it might also signal the necessity for the categories of otherness and alienation, which opens up many critical avenues to pursue in an effort to understand California.

Thus, the overall significance of polarities manifesting throughout this collection may put into question the status of a nomadic subject that, as argued in the Introduction, has guided our attempt at an approximation of California's presence in culture. The opening section of this volume has explored the potential of liminality, but also scrutinized its shifts into more fixed categories of center and margin, thus acknowledging the volatility of non-binary conceptualization. The middle section turned to—interpretatively productive but generically ambivalent—Gothic ways of processing emotional, aesthetic and political consequences of both a destabilization of categories and a clashing of the opposites. Finally, the third part of the collection has faced the most explicit and predominantly pessimistic approach to Californian ambiguities in the form of dystopian tropes that tend to rely on contrasts accentuating the unreachability of perfection. As Kevin Starr notes, "there has always been something slightly bipolar about California. It was either utopia or dystopia, a dream or a nightmare, a hope or a broken promise—and too infrequently anything in between" (343).

However, the nomadic qualities that we strive to locate in cultural appropriations of California imply not so much an avoidance of polarizations as their incorporation into a multidirectional network providing them with a contextual diversity in which they tend to swap fixedness for resonance with other concepts, sometimes in an unexpected web of meanings. In order to visualize the presence of such a network in the survey of Californian icons offered by the essays comprising this book, let us, by way of conclusion, reverse the volume's internal logic and consider a conceptual arc drawn from the sharp realization of the myth's faultiness in metonymic dystopia to the cultural echoes of California as a liminal category detached from its specific geographic location. The nomadism we seek is evoked not only by the very reversibility of thinking about the Golden State, but also the inconspicuous harmonies at the crossing points of the three axes of this volume.

It would be understandable to search for the roots of the dystopian undercurrent in California's history of discrimination, abuse and maltreatment of many communities, starting with Native Americans, Californios, the Chinese, continuing with the Dust Bowl refugees, the Okies, up to the more recent examples of injustice evidenced by the Rodney King riots or the battle for Proposition 8. They all introduce uneasiness into the Californian heritage, yet when it comes to the narration that illustrates the beginnings of the region's entanglement in the binary dialectics of pursued ideal versus harsh reality, one story stands out.

Among the most pervasive symbols of California's dubious character is the story of the Donner-Reed party. Every Californian knows it and would recite it, if called upon; not all are so sure of the ultimate meaning of the story, though. The facts are rather clear: a group of immigrants got together in the spring of 1846 with the intention of reaching California, settling there, and partaking in its riches. They set off from Independence, Missouri, where the California Oregon Trail began, in May, hoping to reach the Promised Land before the winter snowstorms closed the passes through the last and the most perilous part of their journey: the passage through the Sierra

186   Conclusion

Nevada. Yet the lack of experience, a series of errors in judgment and various mishaps accumulated and their results were tragic. They ended up stranded in the snow-covered mountains for five months, with hardly any food or shelter. They resorted to cannibalism and murder. Upon learning of the harsh fate that befell the Donners and their companions, the citizens of California organized several rescue parties, yet because of the weather and geographical conditions, not even half of the original group of the fated Donner–Reed party endured. When the news of their predicament spread, the allure of California was tarnished forever: it would no longer be the land of sunshine and happiness, but also a land of darker elements that govern the logic of the story of California immigration. Their story, as Kevin Starr ascertains, "remains to this day a fixed and recurring statement of California as betrayed hope and dystopian tragedy" (63).

Simultaneously, however, Joan Didion stresses the need to recognize "the moral ambiguity of the California settlement" (75). She quotes the moral lesson drawn from the Donner party ordeal by one of its survivors: "Remember, never take no cutoffs and hurry along as fast as you can" and assesses it as a sign of "the artless horror and constricted moral horizon" (75). Didion further states, "The redemptive power of the crossing was, nonetheless, the fixed idea of the California settlement, and one that raised a further question: for what exactly, and at what cost, had one been redeemed?" (36–37). With these questions, Didion puts the story of California's darkness within the context of ethical deliberations. How do we reconcile the two sides of the Golden State, its sunny and its dark face, and is it even possible? Within what parameters of ethical obligation, empathy, and responsibility can we situate California history and the scenarios of its culture? How can we talk of the various traumas of California history without silencing ourselves to oblivion? What ethical response—in the sense of an ethical call that both Emmanuel Levinas and Judith Butler speak of—does California's darkness elicit? While such questions remain open, as confirmed by the subjects raised in this book, their close connection with the very origins of Californian mythology makes them part and parcel of the dystopian trope. Thus, the self-conscious, and predominantly disappointing clash of the opposites implied by dystopia enters early twenty-first-century culture together with an implied metareflection, pushing subsequent perpetuations of the trope outside the comfort zone of a simple demythicization of the Golden State and into the search for ways of dealing with its myth that, debunked by default, does not cease to inspire new stories.

A further relevant context and direction for such musings may be found in their Gothicized renderings, even though one might be tempted to interpret it as fueled by resignation in the face of California's paradoxes, or their excessive anesthetization, rather than an urge to step beyond them. As put by David Punter, "Gothic speaks of phantoms…. The Gothic speaks of …

specters.... Gothic has to do with the uncanny.... And Gothic speaks, incessantly, of bodily harm and the wound" (2). If we think of the phantoms of the abused and the specters of the victimized that populate California's history; if we think of the category of the uncanny, which makes problematic the very category of home that certain groups of people claim for themselves while denying the same right to others; if we think of the bodily harm systematically inflicted on numerous Californians throughout its history, then the Gothic emerges as a highly adequate context for the story of California and the Donner–Reed party.

And yet, the trademark Gothic attributes of terror, horror, and overall discomfort caused by the transgression or erasure of boundaries may direct Californian iconography toward new territories of meaning. In his 2005 commentary on the socio-political consequences of the WTC attacks, Brian Massumi argues that "fear itself will continue becoming—the way of life" (47); a claim rooted in the understanding of "threat" as something which "is only a threat if it retains an indeterminacy. If it has a form, it is not a substantial form, but a time form: a futurity. The threat as such is nothing yet—just a looming. It is a form of futurity yet has the capacity to fill the present without presenting itself. Its future looming casts a present shadow, and that shadow is fear. Threat is the future cause of a change in the present" (35).

Indeed, various anxieties fueled by tensions between the present and future find their reflections in the spectrum of the aesthetic approaches to California discussed in this volume—from the Gothic and horror, to noir, to psychedelic, to apocalyptic and post-apocalyptic. Still, what makes those employments of popular, and more or less generic conventions unique is their reference to one specific region, whose historical constitution as well as cultural renderings turn it into a space predisposed to confront the unknown. As put by Kevin Starr, California is "one of the prisms through which the American people, for better and for worse, could glimpse their future.... It had also become not the exclusive, but a compelling way for this future to be brought into existence" (xiv). Thus, what is terrifying about California—for its conflicted conceptualizations, or its liminality—may simultaneously stimulate the anticipation of challenges that will, sooner or later, gain a broader significance.

As Starr comments, "California is an American story that from the beginning has been a global story as well" (xiii), which is one of the reasons why we have chosen to consider the incorporation of a Californian imagery, together with its tensions, dystopianism and horrors, into the liminal sphere of cultural appropriations with reference to a seemingly detached perspective of Polish culture.

In Poland there is a long tradition of writing about California: the cherished Polish writer Henryk Sienkiewicz wrote his *Letters from the Jour-*

neys in America between 1876 and 1878, a series of journalistic impressions serialized in a Polish magazine; there, he wrote about California extensively. In fact, he went to California with Helena Modrzejewska (who would change her name to Modjeska, a gesture toward American audiences), an internationally acclaimed Shakespearian actress, and other friends. There, they established a utopian community—a project that failed fairly quickly, yet one that is commemorated in California's history through place names, such as Modjeska Canyon. Modrzejewska's memoirs sketch a clear picture of this failure: responding to the promotion of California's image as an earthly paradise (perpetuated by the state's agents in whose best interest it was to attract new inhabitants to the region), the settlers imagined a sentimental world of hardly any labor and ample rewards, with benevolent nature and friendly natives. The Polish colony in California made up of artists and aristocrats not used to menial labor in an unknown climate was bound to fail, yet it remains a colorful illustration of the many unexpected connections between the two vastly distant regions.

Sienkiewicz, in turn, was a writer famous in Poland not only for his explorations of American themes but also for fast-paced historical novels appealing to patriotic sentiments at a time when Poland's national identity was being tested by the impact of the Partitions. He combined those two sets of subjects in a 1889 short story "Sachem": the eponymous character is the sole survivor of a massacre in which German settlers brought an end to a Native American village, and the son of the exterminated tribe's chief. Having been adopted and brought up by a group of circus artists, he currently acts out his tragic tale as a part of the show and humbly accepts money from the audience. The story can easily be inscribed into a broader tendency on the part of Polish authors referencing the American West, who, according to Ray Allen Billington, quite often drew comparisons between Native Americans and Poles, as both groups were deemed the subjects of oppression from their conquerors and likely doomed (146–47).

While such analogies should undoubtedly be approached with caution due to all the historical and cultural factors informing the respective identities and experiences of the nations involved, references to Native Americans testify to the complexity of the ways in which Polish cultural practices have been appropriating the ideal of freedom in general, and its American conceptualizations in particular. That inspirations with the most American, the most Western, and perhaps also the most utopian of all virtues: freedom, have been visible in a variety of Polish contexts does not come as a surprise. What, however, proves more significant in terms of this book is that the combination of American liberty, Western spirit and utopia frequently finds expression in the localized icon of California that resonates with Polish texts of culture in strikingly diverse ways.

For instance, selected depictions of California in Polish mainstream as well as underground music from the period between the 1970s and 2010s seem to draw an arc from predictable affirmations of universal utopia through dystopian contrasts with conceptualizations of Poland, to highly localized contexts in which the imagery of the American state is used to construct the identities of specific places. In their 1978 song "California Mon Amour," the Polish folk-rock band 2+1 renders California in terms of dreamy and surreal perfection. The dystopian potential of Californian imagery, in turn, has proved attractive for Polish punk, as confirmed not only by Kazik Staszewski's 1994 cover of "California Über Alles" by the Dead Kennedys, but also a domestication of the American referent in "Kalifornia"—a 2002 song by punk rock band Hartal—that juxtaposes Polish mundanity with the Golden State that seems to signify, first of all, a state of mind. California as a counterpoint for identifications of Polish localities proves relevant also in the realm of Polish hip-hop music. "Moja Kalifornia" [My California] by Vixen (2009) describes Poland as California in order to highlight the rapper's dedication and attachment to his home community and country despite its difficult realities. In "Brudna Kalifornia" [Dirty California] Wale Grubo (2012) employs the Californian reference in a similar manner to illustrate their more specific identification with the most prominent mining region in Poland, Upper Silesia. An even more focused appropriation of California is connected with a campsite in Mielno, a seaside tourist resort. The campsite, called California Camp, appears on a regular basis in Polish hip-hop songs,[1] with the America-related part of the name as an icon of consumerist happiness and freedom with which the localized Polish experience can compete or polemicize, affirming the spark of Californian paradise in the accessible milieu.

The above brief and fragmentary insight into the presence of California in Polish music is hardly representative of the impact of the Golden State on popular culture in Poland, yet it does seem sufficient to signal its surprisingly diverse forms and overall complexity. When one sees Modjeska's statue in one of Anaheim's public parks or when one visits Modjeska's California home, Arden, one is transported into the world of a nineteenth-century Cracow, and suddenly California becomes more Polish, just as Poland becomes more Californian in Sienkiewicz's writing or in Polish popular music today.

While the paradisiac layer of Californian imagery prevails, its darker facets—laid bare and explored throughout this volume—do not seem to negate the appropriations of California in the examples mentioned above, or dismiss them as superficial. Instead, the unacknowledged Californian "darkness" seems to resonate with the bittersweet depictions of Polish reality that emerge from such endeavors. Thus, the liminality of California's iconization makes it relatable even for these distant cultural discourses that in turn expand the network and renegotiate the map of California's overall cultural "identity" as a sign and construct.

The inconspicuous semiotic bridge between the Golden State and Poland, that is surely bound to have equivalents in other localized cultures around the world, can be seen as a testimony to California's nomadism. Given the iconographic cornucopia formed by the sheer diversity of contexts in which California proves relevant for texts of culture, be it as a site of their production, a provider of settings or tropes, a theme, or a character, we had expected it to emerge as a nomadic subject that crosses the boundaries of media and genres, evades clean-cut interpretations and refuses to be anchored in any dominant cultural discourse. Striving to provide an environment for such a construct to form in, we had pictured this collection as an inclusive cross-section of source materials and interpretative approaches, rather than a strongly controlled realization of a predesigned structure. That is why, as mentioned in the Introduction, some themes that have, in the course of time, become fundamental in the explorations of California's cultural history and impact, may have remained out of the spotlight in the discussion spectrum of *A Dark California*, in favor of apparently less characteristic phenomena and perspectives.

Simultaneously, however, as the essays in this book signify, connectivity does not mean an erasure of paradox from the Californian subject. Indeed, the appearances and readings of California offered by the authors of particular essays are diverse, yet they seem to share a depiction of the Golden State as a site of discrepancy that either polarizes and sharply divides its territory or swallows it and turns it into a suspended zone. The discrepancy itself may be located between ideals and reality; reality and constructedness; constructedness imposed and intentional.... This regularity, subtle as it may be when applied to particular analyses, induces the collection as a whole with a sense of interpretative symmetry that may work against the decentralized, and decentralizing nomadism, that this book seeks in California. Simultaneously, however, the diversity of positions and manifestations of the Californian subject in confrontation with discrepancy is made all the more prominent by that common axis of reference. In the face of both ontological and epistemological crises explored in particular essays of this volume, the locale that brings them all together plays different roles—from a passive background, to an ultimate source of or testimony to the problem, to an active opponent, to a promise of a way out.

Commenting on the fluidity of the boundaries between the rhizome and the "tree or root structur[e]," Deleuze and Guattari emphasize that "The coordinates are determined not by theoretical analyses implying universals but by a pragmatics composing multiplicities or aggregates of intensities" (15). Thus, the California that emerges from this collection replicates as well as reflects upon the paradox of its own cultural construction that struggles to combine horizontal spread with vertical growth. It is the straightforward acknowledgment of and confrontation with Californian darkness that we see as the most relevant effort collectively performed in this book, as we believe that in the dark, conflicted hopes and longings breed until they are ready to see the light as fully formed ideas.

NOTE

1. For instance "Kalifornia Camp" by Fu & Spalto (2012) or "Kalifornia Camp" by HCR ft. Golab, Fu and Aleksandra Krupa (2014).

WORKS CITED

Baudrillard, Jean. *America*. Trans. Chris Turner. London: Verso, 1988.
Billington, Ray Allen. *Land of Savagery, Land of Promise: The European Image of the American Frontier*. New York: Norton, 1981.
Butler, Judith. *Precarious Life: The Power of Mourning and Violence*. London: Verso, 2004.
Davis, Mike. *City of Quartz: Excavating the Future in Los Angeles*. London: Verso, 2006 [1990].
Deleuze, Gilles, and Félix Guattari. *A Thousand Plateaus*. Trans. Brian Massumi. Minneapolis: University of Minnesota Press, 1987.
Didion, Joan. *Where I Was From*. London: Harper Perennial, 2003.
Fu & Spalto. "Kalifornia Camp." YouTube. 18 May 2012. 30 June 2016. https://www.youtube.com/watch?v=iOXpsZdy6uM.
Hartal. "Kalifornia." Demo, 2002.
HCR, ft. Golab, Fu and Aleksandra Krupa (perf.). "Kalifornia Camp." *Lepszym człowiekiem*. Sony Music Entertainment Poland, 2016.
KNŻ. "Kalifornia ponad wszystko." *Na żywo ale w studio*. S.P. Records, 1994.
Levinas, Emmanuel. *Otherwise Than Being Or Beyond Essence*. Trans. Alphonso Lingis. Dordrecht: Kluwer Academic, 1992.
Massumi, Brian. "Fear (The Spectrum Said)." *Positions* 13:1 (2005): 31–48.
Modrzejewska, Helena. *Memories and Impressions*. New York: Macmillan, 1910.
Punter, David. "Introduction: The Ghost of a History." *A New Companion to the Gothic*. David Punter, ed. Chichester: Wiley-Blackwell, 2012. 1–9.
Sienkiewicz, Henryk. *Portrait of America: Letters*. Charles Morley, trans. New York: Columbia University Press, 1959.
_____. "Sachem." *Lillian Morris and Other Stories*. Jeremiah Curtin, trans. Boston: Little, Brown, 1894. 155–76. The Project Gutenberg. 4 December 2014. 30 June 2016. https://www.gutenberg.org/files/47527/47527-h/47527-h.htm#Page_155.
Starr, Kevin. *California: A History*. New York: The Modern Library, 2005.
2 Plus 1. "California Mon Amour." *Teatr na drodze*. Polskie Nagrania Muza, 1978.
Vixen. "Moja Kalifornia." YouTube. 17 November 2009. 30 June 2016. https://www.youtube.com/watch?v=CpZsQcGRlAs.
Wale Grubo. "Brudna Kalifornia." *Ewidentnie*. 5 February 2012. 16 June 2016. https://www.youtube.com/watch?v=7YLI9sluUDk.

About the Contributors

Simon **Bacon** is an independent scholar based in Poznan, Poland. He has contributed essays to publications on vampires, monstrosity, science fiction, and media studies. He is the coeditor of *Undead Memory* (2014), *Seductive Concepts* (2014), and *Little Horrors* (2016).

Diana **Benea** is a junior lecturer in the Department of English at the University of Bucharest, where she teaches twentieth- and twenty-first-century American literature and cultural studies methodologies. Her research interests focus on various aspects of American studies.

Rose **Butler** is an associate lecturer and doctoral candidate in film studies at Sheffield Hallam University. Her dissertation explores the German crime film and cultural trauma. Her broader research interests include American cinema and television and popular European film cycles.

Marcin **Cichocki** is a research assistant in the Department of English and American Studies at Paderborn University. His teaching and research interests include American culture, film studies with a focus on the road movie and the noir, seriality and television. His dissertation is on the revival of the anthology series.

Christopher K. **Coffman** is a senior lecturer in humanities at Boston University. He is the coeditor of *Framing Films* (2009) and *William T. Vollmann* (2015). Among his other publications are articles and essays devoted to a variety of topics in rhetoric and literature.

Carys **Crossen** has a Ph.D. from the University of Manchester and studies gender and sexuality in werewolf fiction and film. She is also interested in monster theory in general, the horror film, the Gothic, feminist theory, and the graphic novel.

Steve **Drum** is a doctoral candidate in the Department of Drama and Dance at Tufts University. His research interests include celebrity performance, film history, and the history of Hollywood. His dissertation is on local theatrical culture in Los Angeles from 1914 to 1945.

Michael **Fuchs** is an assistant professor of American studies at the University of Graz. He has coedited three books, including *ConFiguring America* (2013), and he has authored more than two dozen published and forthcoming essays on topics like horror and adult cinema, American television, video games, and science fiction.

About the Contributors

Benjamin **Halligan** is the director of the doctoral college of the University of Wolverhampton. His publications include the books *Michael Reeves* (2003) and *Desires for Reality* (2016) and coedited collections, including *The Music Documentary* (2013) and *The Arena Concert* (2015).

Liam **Hathaway** is an independent scholar. His research focuses on contemporary body-horror narratives as products of their cultural moment. While he is interested in all aspects of film, his key interest is in the cultural analysis of genre cinema, including horror, science fiction, the thriller, and the black comedy.

Daniel **Klug** is a postdoctoral research assistant at the Seminar for Media Studies at the University of Basel. His work focuses on reality television and media realities, popular culture, and media sociology. He has published several articles on reality television and edited books on popular music and video clips.

Elizabeth **Lowry** is a lecturer at Arizona State University. Her work has been published in *The Rhetoric Review* and in edited collections. She also studies and writes about nineteenth-century spirit medium autobiographies.

Craig Ian **Mann** is an associate lecturer in film studies at Sheffield Hallam University. His specialty is in the cultural analysis of popular cinema; he has a particular interest in countercultural and anti-capitalist narratives. He is writing a cultural history of the werewolf film.

Donna **Mitchell** is a post-doctoral teaching fellow at Mary Immaculate College, University of Limerick. She is a book reviewer for the University of Stirling's "The Gothic Imagination" website and coeditor of *Fantastika Journal*. She is working on an examination of female identity through the figure of the doll in Gothic narratives.

Katarzyna **Nowak-McNeice** is a Conex–Marie Curie Research Fellow at Universidad de Carlos III Madrid, Spain. She is the author of *Melancholic Travelers* (2007) and coeditor of *Interiors* (2010). She has published on American literature and postcolonial literature as well as translations of essays and poetry.

Tomas **Pollard** is the coordinator of the American studies minor at the University of Applied Sciences Utrecht (Hogeschool Utrecht), where he teaches courses on literature, American culture, and writing. He has published essays on Willa Cather, Henry James and Joseph Heller.

Kathleen M. **Vandenberg** is a senior lecturer in rhetoric and composition at Boston University. Her main areas of interest are the rhetoric of Joan Didion and quantitative research on the efficacy of imitation pedagogies. Other scholarly interests include style, the essay, and the rhetoric of the urban environment.

Agata **Zarzycka** is an assistant professor at the Institute of English Studies, University of Wrocław, Poland. Her publications deal with role-playing games, video games, speculative fiction, and participatory culture. Her research interests include Gothic influences on popular culture, game studies, transmediality, and subcultures.

Index

Absence see Kölsch, Kevin, and Widmyer, David
abuse 89, 103, 147, 164, 185, 187; domestic 84; environmental 134, 144; sexual 34, 53, 136; substance 73, 105, 177, 181
activism 71, 169–171, 173
The Addiction see Ferrara, Abel
"The Adventures of Rain Dance Maggie" *see* Red Hot Chili Peppers
advertising/commercials 56–7, 102, 162, 165, 167
Afghanistan 125
African Americans 53, 70, 72, 100, 145
"Afterbirth" (episode) 93–4; *see also* American Horror Story
AIDS 105–6, 113–4
Alderaan 179; *see also* Star Wars
alienation 2, 11, 12, 50, 52–3, 58–9, 69, 130, 137, 153–4, 167, 184
Alighieri, Dante *see* Dante
Almereyda, Michael 121, 125; *Nadja* 123
the American Dream 77, 118, 132, 135, 137, 174–6, 179; *see also* Californian Dream
American Horror Story 6, 11, 127; *Freak Show* 88, 95; *Hotel* 88, 90, 92–99; *Murder House* 88, 90–91, 93–99
American Indians *see* Native Americans
American Mary (2012) 106; *see also* body-horror
An American Werewolf in London 76, 79–80
the American West 6, 14, 116, 122, 150, 188
Americana 153
Amirpour, Lily 115, 118–119, 122, 125; *see also* A Girl Walks Home Alone at Night
Anaheim, California 117, 189; *see also* Disneyland
Anderson, Paul Thomas 150; *Inherent Vice* (film) 151
Angel see Greenwalt, David
Anglos 147, 150
anthology series (genre) 88, 127, 193
anti-theatricalists 155

Antiviral (2012): body-horror 101, 104, 107, 112, 113; *see also* Cronenberg, Brandon
anxiety 19, 25, 36, 53, 108, 109, 112, 155, 166
apocalypse 12, 57, 59–61, 113, 153
Arcadia: *Inherent Vice* 148; *see also* Lemuria; myth
architecture 3, 13, 46, 140, 151
Arden, California 189
"Around the World" *see* Red Hot Chili Peppers
Associated Farmers 170
Asylum 88
Atlantis: *Inherent Vice* 148–9; *see also* Lemuria; myth
Attebery, Brian 5, 13
audience 16, 54–5, 58, 69–70, 102, 109, 112, 122, 155–161, 172, 188
Austin, Mary 3, 13
authenticity 11, 39, 158
Avalon: *Inherent Vice* 148; *see also* Lemuria; myth

Baez, Joan 20, 23
Bakersfield, California 118
Barlow, Toby 11, 75–87
Barton Fink 104
Baudrillard, Jean 2, 38–9, 42, 45, 47, 48, 55, 110, 111, 113, 115–7, 124–5, 184, 191
Bauman, Zygmunt 4–5, 13
Baywatch 179
beach 62, 76, 78, 82, 85, 142–3, 150–1, 168, 177
The Beach Boys 66, 159, 161, 176; *see also* Wilson, Dennis
The Beast Within see Mora, Philippe
beauty 18–9, 27–8, 31, 97, 101–2, 106, 132, 136, 175–6, 178–9, 184
the beauty myth *see* Wolf, Naomi
Bel Air 64, 66–7, 72n13
Benjamin, Walter 155, 161
Beverly Hills 46
Beverly Hills Cop 164
Beverly Hills, 90210 179

195

Biafra, Jello *see* Dead Kennedys
The Big Sleep see Chandler, Raymond
Big Sur 62
"BigTaters" 109–10
Birdsall, Derek 62
"Birth" (episode, *American Horror Story*) 93
the Black Dahlia 40–1, 43, 96, 98
Blackenstein 96
Blackstar 103; *see also* Bowie, David
Blacula (1972) 96, 117; *see also* Crain, William
Blade 118; *see also* Norrington, Stephen
Blade Trinity see Goyer, David S.
Blake, Amanda 106; *see also* AIDS
Blaxploitation movies 96
Bleeding Edge 139, 150n1, 152; *see also* Pynchon, Thomas
body 25, 30, 34, 41, 46, 48, 67–8, 71, 121, 123–4, 155; destruction of 22, 28, 40, 111; female 29, 98, 109, 156–9, 179; Grotesque 112; image 104–5, 107–8, 113
body-horror 12, 101, 104–7, 112–3, 194
Bogart, Humphrey 129
Bonaventure Hotel 116, 118; *see also* Los Angeles
Bosch, Hieronymus 89
Boss, Pete 105–6, 113; *see also* body-horror; Brophy, Phillip
Boston 89
Bourgeois 65, 159
Bowie, David 66, 72n7, 103, 179; *see also* Blackstar; Visconti, Tony
Braddock, Pennsylvania 118; *see also* Martin
Braidotti, Rosi 1, 9, 14
Breakfast at Tiffany's see Edwards, Blake
Brecht, Bertold, and Weill, Kurt 89
Brolin, Josh 150n3, 151
Brophy Phillip 105–6, 113; *see also* body-horror; Boss, Pete; *Screen*
Brown, Charles Brockden 130
Browning, Tod 118–9, 125; *Dracula* 126; *see also* Universal Studios
"Brudna Kalifornia" *see* Wale Grubo
Brynner, Yul 105
Buffy the Vampire Slayer (film) *see* Kuzui, Fran Rubel
Buffy the Vampire Slayer (TV series) *see* Whedon, Joss
Bunker Hill *see Inherent Vice*; Los Angeles
Butler, Judith 186, 191
"By the Way" *see* Red Hot Chili Peppers

California: California Oregon Trail 185; northern 140, 147, 149; southern 3, 14, 40, 115, 119, 131–133, 136, 140, 143, 153, 174–176, 181
California Camp 189; *see also* Mielno
"California Dreamin" *see* The Mamas and the Papas
"California Love" 65–6, 176; *see also* Dr. Dre; Troutman, Roger; 2Pac
"California Mon Amour" 189, 191; *see also* 2+1
"California Über Alles" 189; *see also* Dead Kennedys
Californian Dream 140, 147, 149; *see also* the American Dream
The Californian Ideology 11, 62–4, 66–7, 71, 73
Californication (music album) 175; *see also* Red Hot Chili Peppers
"Californication" (music video) 13, 174–6, 178–82; *see also* Red Hot Chili Peppers
"Californication" (song) *see* Red Hot Chili Peppers
Californios 185
camera 45, 50–1, 55–6, 94, 119, 153, 155–6, 158–60
Cameron, Skyla Dawn 83
cannibalism 106–7, 186
Canterbury Tales 89; *see also* Chaucer
capitalism 2, 52–3, 55, 57, 59, 60n6, 67, 115, 125, 128; *see also* commodity; consumerism
car culture 4, 32, 40–1, 46, 47n4, 56, 62, 120, 123
Cara, Irene 105; *see also Flashdance*
Carpenter, John 105, 117
Carson, California 132; *see also True Detective*
Carter, Angela 10–11, 25–9, 31, 33–6
Cawelti, John 5, 14, 131, 138
celebrity (culture) 12–13, 20–1, 88, 95, 101–7, 109, 112–4, 153–4, 156–60, 166
Central Park 15
Chandler, Raymond138 173
"Channel View Estates" 144–7; *see also Inherent Vice*
Charles Manson Superstar see Schreck, Nikolas
"Charlie" *see* Red Hot Chili Peppers
Chaucer 89; *see also Canterbury Tales*
Chavez Ravine *see Inherent Vice*; Los Angeles
"Checking In" (episode, *American Horror Story*) 95–6
Chicanos 4, 147
Chinatown 47n7
The Chinese (nationality) 4, 185
ChiPs (TV series) 164, 169
Christine 117; *see also* Carpenter, John
cinema 27, 41–2, 44, 72n13, 73, 76, 92–3, 95–6, 100, 102, 117, 125–6, 128–9, 134, 137n1, 154–5, 157, 161, 173, 179, 183, 193
city 2, 8, 10–11, 24, 27, 37–43, 45–8, 52, 64–5, 75, 77–91, 97–9, 113, 118, 120–1, 124–5, 128, 131–3, 137–8, 141–4, 146–51, 174, 177–8, 180–2, 184; *see also* urban space
City of Angels (movie) 89
City of Quartz see Davis, Mike

civil rights 164
"Clair de Lune" *see* Debussy, Claude
Cobain, Kurt 179
Coetzee, John M. 71
Cohn, Henry 110; *see also* Columbia Pictures Corporation
Cold War 168
Collier, Jeremy 154
Colorado 98, 175
Columbia Pictures Corporation 110
Columbine High School massacre 93, 98
comedy 172, 194
commodity 55–6, 97, 112, 155, 167
commune 64, 67, 73–4, 136, 150
Communists 168
Constantine (movie) 89
consumerism 50, 115, 175; *see also* capitalism; commodity
Cooper, James Fenimore 17
Cop shows 13, 162–9, 172; *see also* police; television
counterculture 11, 63–4, 73–4, 159, 162
Coven (American Horror Story) 88
Cracow 189; *see also* Poland
Crain, William 117; *see also Blacula* (1972)
crime 34, 40–1, 43–5, 52, 58, 84, 88, 94, 96, 98–100, 129, 131–3, 137, 149, 172, 193; *see also* gangs
the Crips and the Bloods *see* crime; gangs
Cronenberg, Brandon 107; *Antiviral* 101, 104, 107, 112, 113
Cronenberg, David 104–5
The Crying of Lot 49 see Pynchon, Thomas
Cullen, Edward (character) 125*n*9
cyborg 1, 9, 41, 48; *see also* Haraway, Donna

Dahmer, Jeffrey 99
"Dani California" *see* Red Hot Chili Peppers
Dante 89
Davis, Mike 4, 37, 48, 117, 124–5, 133, 151*n*7, 184; *City of Quartz* 2, 14, 125, 151, 191
Day, Doris 159, 161
The Day of the Locust (film, 1975) 104
Dayton, Jonathan, and Faris, Valerie 177–8
Dead Kennedys 65; "California Über Alles" 189
Dean, James 103, 120, 153, 160
death 11, 20, 26, 39, 45–46, 56, 60*n*3, 64, 67, 88, 90, 93–99, 103–104, 106, 113, 117, 119–120, 122, 124–125, 130, 133, 154, 156–7, 160–1, 163–4, 171
Death Grips 11, 62–63, 65, 72–73; Hill, Zach 68, 72*n*9; MC Ride 66–71, 72*n*8, 72*n*9
De Beauvoir, Simone 27–8, 30, 32, 36
Debussy, Claude 159
The Deeds of Esplandian 6
"Deep Archer" 139; *see also* Bleeding Edge
"Deep Kick" *see* Red Hot Chili Peppers
Deep South 176
Deleuze, Gilles, and Félix Guattari 2, 14, 125, 190–191; *see also* nomadic subject; rhizome
Del Rey, Lana 159; "Freak" 158–160; "God Knows I Tried" 160; *Honeymoon* (music album) 12, 153–154, 157–158, 161; "Honeymoon" (song) 157–158, 160; "Swan Song" (song) 159–160
Deneuve, Catherine 125*n*7; *see also* The Hunger
Denver 82
Depp, Johnny 103
"Desecration Smile" *see* Red Hot Chili Peppers
desert 2–3, 10–11, 25–36, 58, 66–67, 117, 135, 146, 158, 178
desire 1, 21–22, 27–28, 34, 45, 52–54, 56–57, 59, 79, 85, 104, 107, 110, 112, 123, 136, 141–143, 157, 161, 167, 176
detective fiction 43, 129, 131, 138; *see also* formula
Detroit 82
devil 59, 66, 111, 160
"Devil's Night" (episode, *American Horror Story)* 99
Dezeran, Louis *see Starry Eyes*
Didion, Joan 3, 6–7, 10, 14–24, 186, 191, 194
disease 44, 50, 77, 82, 105, 107, 11, 144, 149, 155; *see also* sickness
Disney, Walt 50, 117, 175
Disneyland 115–117, 124*n*1; *see also* Anaheim, California
Divine Comedy see Dante
Dr. Dre 72*n*6; "Nuthin' but a G' Thang" 176; *see also* "California Love"
Dodger Stadium *see Inherent Vice*; Los Angeles
"The "Dollars Trilogy" *see* Leone, Sergio
Donner-Reed party 185–187
"Don't Die of Ignorance" (campaign) 106
The Doors *see* Morrison, Jim
Dracula see Browning, Tod; Universal Studios
Dracula, Count (character) 118–119, 121, 124
Dracula's Daughter see Hillier, Lambert
Dragnet 169
drugs/narcotics 21, 34–35, 51, 54, 56, 70–71, 75, 95, 120–121, 123, 125*n*6, 136, 164–165, 168–169, 177, 181; *see also* DEA
Dumbo (character) 166
Duncan, Glen 78
Dunn, Nora 53
Dunne, John Gregory 20–21
Dust Bowl 185
dystopia 1, 2, 5, 10, 12, 13, 25–27, 29, 35, 37, 47, 52, 65, 66, 72, 89, 107, 118, 141, 143, 147–8, 150, 174, 176, 181, 185–7, 189; *see also* utopia

The Eagles 160, 176
earthquake 23, 75, 178, 180
Eastwood, Clint 122–123, 125*n*8, 164

Easy Rider 72n3
Eat 101, 105–106, 112–113
eating disorder 107
ecology 144, 151n6; *see also* environment
Eden 14, 18, 48n7, 148
Edwards, Blake 120
El Dorado 1, 148; *see also Inherent Vice*; Lemuria; myth
El Salvador 15
Elfman, Richard 117, 125; *Modern Vampires (Revenant)* 118, 123, 125
Eliot, T.S. 51, 58
Ellroy, James 41
the Elysian Fields 148; *see also Inherent Vice*; Lemuria; myth
"Emit Remmus" *see* Red Hot Chili Peppers
entertainment 6, 10, 53, 65–66, 72n14, 102, 115–116, 118, 123–124, 169, 179, 181
environment 3, 12, 26, 30, 32, 38, 41–42, 53, 81, 121–122, 135, 140, 147–150, 159, 190, 194; degradation of 51, 65, 132, 134, 137, 143–4, 146
Eraserhead see Lynch, David
Ericson, Leif *see The Saga of Erik the Red*
eroticism 27–28, 65, 68, 154, 158, 167
escapism 176
Essoe, Alex *see Starry Eyes*
Europe 7, 13, 21, 60n6, 82, 122, 125, 151n9, 184, 191, 193; Eastern 119
evil 44, 48, 50, 59, 89, 98, 129–131, 154–155, 167, 184; *see also* devil
exceptionalism 3, 149
Excess Flesh 101, 105–106, 112–113
Excision 106
Ext. Life see Kölsch, Kevin, and Widmyer, David

Facebook 103, 114
The Faerie Queene see Spenser, Edmund
fame 11–12, 15, 18, 26, 36, 39, 66, 70, 88, 92, 95–6, 101–104, 107, 110–111, 113–114, 154, 158, 160, 178, 180
family 22, 32, 47n5, 50, 66, 67, 77–78, 88, 92, 94, 98, 134, 156, 159, 162–163, 165, 167–170, 172–173
fandom 154
fantasy 5, 13, 27–28, 31, 55, 75–76, 86, 154, 158, 161, 164, 166, 167, 169
Fantasy Island 164; *see also* sitcom
Farewell, My Lovely see Chandler, Raymond
Fargo 127
Faris, Valerie *see* Dayton, Jonathan
Farris, John 75–7
Faustian narrative 154
FBI 73, 146
fear 1, 32–33, 47–48, 55, 60–61, 67, 85, 93, 106, 108, 130–131, 141, 144, 156, 163, 184, 187, 191; *see also* terror
feminism 10, 14, 25–27, 29–30, 33, 35, 193

femme fatale 128
Ferrara, Abel 121
film 12, 15, 27, 37, 42, 45, 50–51, 54, 58, 67, 72n3, 73n17, 75–76, 79–83, 86, 90, 96–97, 99–101, 104–109, 111–126, 128–130, 132, 138, 144, 153–158, 160–161, 163–166, 168–170, 173, 175, 177, 179, 193–194; *see also* noir
film noir *see* noir
Fincher, David 96
First Blood 164
A Fistful of Dollars see Leone, Sergio
fitness 105, 112
Flashdance 105; *see also* Clara, Irene
"Flashdance ... What a Feeling" *see* Clara, Irene; *Flashdance*
Flea 180; *see also* Red Hot Chili Peppers
"Flicker" (episode, *American Horror Story*) 96–7
Florida 88, 99
The Fly see Cronenberg, David
Footloose 105
For a Few Dollars More see Leone, Sergio
Fordism 143
formula 5–6, 14, 26, 131, 138
Forsyth, Derek 62
France 15; critics 38, 128
"Freak" *see* Del Rey, Lana
Freak Show see American Horror Story
freedom 17, 19, 22–23, 33, 62–65, 135, 162–164, 188–189
Freud, Sigmund 26, 36, 80, 87
Fright Night see Holland, Tom
frontier 6–7, 13, 17–18, 125–126, 136–138, 179, 191
Frusciante, John 178; *see also* Red Hot Chili Peppers
Fuller, Richard Buckminster 146–7, 151
fuzzy set 5

Gacy, John Wayne 99
Galenorn, Yasmin 82
gangs 47n3, 65, 72n7, 76–8, 82–7, 131, 176; the Crips and the Bloods 75, 85
Gangster Squad 41, 47n7, 48
The Garden of Eden 148; *see also Inherent Vice*; Lemuria; myth
Geneva 154
German expressionism 177
ghosts 8, 14, 29, 92–94, 96–97, 99–100, 126, 136, 140, 146, 171, 191
A Girl Walks Home Alone at Night 115–116, 118–119, 121–122, 124–125; *see also* Amirpour, Lily
girlhood 19, 27–28, 31–32, 96, 98, 119–125, 166–167, 176, 180; *see also* teenager
Glee 88
God 56, 97, 99, 109, 112, 142, 161
"God Knows I Tried" *see* Del Rey, Lana
Gold rush, Californian 125n3
Golden Age (of cinema) 96, 109

Index

The Good, the Bad, and the Ugly see Leone, Sergio
Gordita Beach see *Inherent Vice*; Los Angeles
Gordon, Stuart 105
the Gothic 5, 11–13, 36, 76, 96–97, 99, 112, 114, 118–119, 126, 128–131, 133–134, 185–187, 191, 193–194; see also Hollywood; horror; terror
Goyer, David S. 115; *Blade Trinity* 118
Grand Theft Auto 47n4
Grant, Cary 103
Grauer, Ben 40
Greenwalt, David 117, 125; *Angel* 118, 123
Griffith, D.W. 44
grotesque 70, 75, 112
Guattari, Félix see Deleuze, Gilles
Guns N' Roses 176
Gutierrez, Sebastian 118

"Halloween, Part 1 and 2" (episode, *American Horror Story*) 93–4, 98
Hammet, Dashiell 129, 138
"Happiness Loves Company" see Red Hot Chili Peppers
Haraway, Donna 9, 87; see also cyborg
hard-boiled fiction 128–134, 137–8; see also noir
Harris, Wood 53
Harry Potter see Rowling, J.K.
Hartal 189, 191
Hawaii 165
Hawaii Five-0 165
Hawthorne, Nathaniel 17
HBO 127, 131, 138
Healy, Pat see *Starry Eyes*
Hell Town 118–119, 124–125; see also Los Angeles
Hepburn, Audrey 120
heritage 20, 185
Herlihy, Ed 40
heterotopia 144
High Bloods see Farris, John
Hill, Zach see Death Grips
Hillier, Lambert 121; *Dracula's Daughter* 123, 125
hippie movement 23, 54, 60n7, 67, 141, 147, 169
history 3, 7, 10, 14, 18–19, 20, 22–23, 44, 48, 60n2, 63, 76, 80–81, 87, 92–93, 98–99, 113, 116, 125, 132, 134, 139, 145, 148, 151–152, 157–159, 163, 168, 177, 182, 185–191, 193–194; oral 12, 162, 169–170, 172
Holland, Tom 117
Hollywood 4, 12–13, 15, 40, 45–46, 64, 75, 80, 96, 98–104, 106–113, 116, 119–122, 124, 128–129, 138, 153–155, 158–161, 164–165, 168–170, 173–181, 193–194; "Hollywood Gothic" 118, 126; Hollywood Hills 108, 112; and Vine 153; Walk of Fame 178; see also satire

"Hollywood" (song) see Madonna
Hollywoodland 41, 48
Holmes, H.H. 85; "Murder Castle" 98
hologram 4, 7
"Home Invasion" (episode, *American Horror Story*) 98
The Homebrew Computer Club 63
Honeymoon (music album) see Del Rey, Lana
"Honeymoon" (song) see Del Rey, Lana
Hong Kong 124n1
horror 5–6, 11–12, 76, 86–88, 90, 92, 95, 98–99, 101, 104–107, 109, 112–113, 126–127, 146, 154, 157, 186–187, 193–194
Hotel see *American Horror Story*
"Hotel California" see The Eagles
Hudson, Rock 106; see also AIDS
Humboldt County, California 140
The Hunger see Scott, Tony
Hunt Jackson, Helen 6
Hurricane Katrina 88, 127
Hurt, John 106
hybridity 7, 9, 12, 107, 127, 139, 141
hyperrealism 38
hyperreality 2, 10–12, 37–39, 42, 115, 117

Ice-T 66, 176; *The Iceberg (Freedom of Speech... Just Watch What You Say)* 65
The Iceberg (Freedom of Speech ... Just Watch What You Say) see Ice-T
iconography 72n9, 96, 99, 103, 120, 122, 125n6, 128, 132, 140, 153, 164, 166, 177–178, 180, 184–'85, 187–190
Identical Dead Sisters see Kölsch, Kevin, and Widmeyer, David
identity 1, 3, 5–6, 9–10, 13, 25–35, 43, 79–81, 84, 103, 109, 116, 123–124, 130, 153–154, 156, 164, 166, 188, 190, 194
idol 96, 102, 107, 109–113, 153, 161; see also celebrity; stardom
Illinois 99
illness 103, 106
The Illuminatus! Trilogy see Shea, Robert, and Wilson, Anton
imaginary 12, 15, 17, 42, 72n11, 75, 115, 117, 124n2, 140, 142, 148, 154
Independence, Missouri 185; see also Donner-Reed party
industrialization 131–133
industry 53, 64, 75, 81, 96, 102, 104, 108, 110, 112–113, 115–118, 123–124, 144, 168, 175, 178–181
Inherent Vice (film) see Anderson, Paul Thomas; Pynchon, Thomas
Inherent Vice (novel) see Pynchon, Thomas
"Into the Great Wide Open" see Tom Petty and the Heartbreakers
Intolerance see Griffith, D.W.
Iran 115, 118, 120–123, 125n6, 126

Index

Irigaray, Luce 34, 36
Italy 116, 122, 125

The Jack Benny Program 40
Japan 39–40, 171
Johnson, Mark, and Lakoff, George 5, 14
Jones, Brian Thomas 105
journalism 20, 64, 72n8, 102, 150n5, 188

"Kalifornia" *see* Hartal
Kasten, Jeremy 117
Katrina *see* Hurricane Katrina
Keeping Up with the Kardashians 102
Kelljan, Bob 117
Kelly, Grace 103
Kelly, Richard 11, 50, 58–60; *see also* Southland Tales
Kickstarter 104
Kiedis, Anthony 177–179, 182n3, 182n4, 182; *see also* Red Hot Chili Peppers
the Killers 54
King, Rodney *see* Los Angeles
King, Stephen 95, 97
kitsch 156
Kitty Norville see Vaughn, Carrie
Kölsch, Kevin, and Widmyer, David 101, 107, 114; *Absence* 101, 104; *Ext. Life* 104; *Identical Dead Sisters* 104
KPIX 106
Kuzui, Fran Rubel 117
La Brea Tar Pits 44

L.A. County Museum of Art 44
L.A. Noire 6, 11, 37–49
L.A. Quartet novels *see* Ellroy, James
Lacan, Jacques 11, 54, 57, 60n8, 60, 154
lack 11, 23, 43, 63, 92, 123, 136, 186; void 11, 52, 54–55, 57, 59, 91, 161, 167
Lady Gaga 94, 96
Lakoff, George *see* Johnson, Mark
land 2–3, 6–7, 10, 13–14, 17–19, 21, 23–24, 32, 37, 75–76, 83, 85, 112, 118–119, 134–137, 140, 144–145, 147–149, 151n9, 151–152, 175, 180, 185–186, 191
The Land of Milk and Honey 1, 132, 148; *see also Inherent Vice*; Lemuria; myth
The Land of Prester John 148; *see also Inherent Vice*; Lemuria; myth
landscape 3–4, 6–7, 11–12, 14, 18, 21, 23–24, 43, 132, 141, 148, 153, 178, 186; industrial 118, 135; of terror 12, 127–131, 133–135, 137; urban 43, 46, 144
Lange, Jessica 92, 95
L.A.P.D. (Los Angeles Police Department) 146
Las Vegas 82, 146
The Last Werewolf see Duncan, Glen
Leberecht, Scott 118
Lemuria 141, 147–149, 152; *see also* Atlantis; *Inherent Vice*; myth

Leonardo da Vinci 179
Leone, Sergio 125–126; The "Dollars Trilogy" 125n8; *A Fistful of Dollars* 125n8; *For a Few Dollars More* 125n8; *The Good, the Bad, and the Ugly* 94
Let Me In see Reeves, Matt
Letters from the Journeys in America see Sienkiewicz, Henryk
Levinas, Emmanuel 186, 191
Liberace 106; *see also* AIDS
Locus amoenus 151n6
Lolita 153
London 82, 103
Long Beach 85
Los Angeles 2–3, 7–8, 10–14, 19, 21, 37–52, 47n4, 54, 58–59, 75–76, 79–80, 83, 86–92, 95–101, 104, 107–108, 113–114, 125n3, 125n4, 125–126, 141, 150n4, 150n5, 151, 169, 173–176, 181–182, 184, 191, 193; Bunker Hill 145, 151n7; Chavez Ravine 145, 151n7; Dodger Stadium 145, 151n7; Downtown 43, 94, 98, 131, 143, 177–179, 180; Gordita Beach 142–5, 147, 149–150; Palos Verdes 144; Rodney King riots 185; Rolling Hills 145; unmappability of 116–117; Venice Beach 51, 177; Watts riots 145, 150n5, 152
Los Angeles County 150n4
The Lost Boys see Schumacher, Joel
Louisiana 127
Lugosi, Bela 119, 121
lycanthropy *see* werewolves
Lynch, David 132
Lynn, Kirk 75–77
lyrics 67–69, 71, 72n11, 72n12, 169, 174–181, 182n1, 182n2, 182n3, 182n4

Mad Max 176
madness 54, 66, 104, 159
Madonna (singer) 176
Madonna and Child 35
the male gaze 27–28, 31, 34; *see also* Mulvey, Laura
Malibu 15, 19
The Mamas and the Papas 176
Manhattan Beach, California 150n4
Manicheism 129
Manifest Destiny 47n6
Manson, Charles 20–21, 64, 66–67, 72n9, 98, 141, 143, 158; Melcher, Terry 159, 161; *see also Charles Manson Superstar*; Wilson, Dennis
Maps to the Stars see Cronenberg, David
Marlowe, Philip (character) 129, 131
Martin see Romero, George
Marx, Karl 52, 56–57, 60n4, 60n6, 60
Mason & Dixon 139, 150n1, 151n9, 151–152; *see also* Pynchon, Thomas
Mayer, Louis B. 110
MC Ride *see* Death Grips
McWilliams, Carey 3–4, 14

Index

Mecca 91, 148; *see also Inherent Vice*; Lemuria; myth
media 37, 41, 47*n*2, 48–49, 63, 73, 116, 169, 174, 183, 190, 193–194; mass media 6, 13, 21, 28, 89, 102, 108, 111–114, 166–168, 170, 180
Melcher, Terry *see* Day, Doris; Manson, Charles;
melodrama 27, 131, 157, 160
Melville, Herman 71
memento mori 156
memory 3, 9, 18, 23, 33, 120, 125, 193
Memphis 89
metamorphosis 29, 36, 92, 105, 110–111, 147
Mexico 20, 75, 135–136, 145, 150
Meyer, Stephenie 78, 84; *Twilight* series 81, 100, 125*n*9
MGM Studios (Metro-Goldwyn-Mayer) *see* Mayer, Louis B.
Miami 15
Middle East 60, 119
Midnight Son see Leberecht, Scott
Mielno *see* Poland
Milton, John 89
Milwaukee 99
misery literature 103
misogyny 33
MOB City (TV show) 41, 47*n*3, 49
Modern Vampires see Elfman, Richard
modernity 4, 8, 13, 37, 48, 67, 81–83, 90–91, 97, 99–101, 105–106, 108, 112, 118, 120–121, 125, 129, 131, 137, 139, 151*n*10, 155, 184
Modjeska Canyon 188
Modrzejewska, Helena 188, 191; *see also* Modjeska Canyon
"Moja Kalifornia" *see* Vixen
Mojave Desert 26, 31–32, 35, 67
"Mommy" (episode, *American Horror Story*) 96
Monroe, Marilyn 54–55, 103, 154
monstrosity 30–31, 48, 75, 77, 79–80, 87, 96, 99, 105, 124, 193
Montalbán, Ricardo 164
Mora, Philippe 105
Morrison, Jim 73*n*16, 73, 153; The Doors 20, 69
Mortenson, Norma Jeane *see* Monroe, Marilyn
motherhood 10, 23, 25, 29–35, 94, 96, 120, 164, 166–167, 169–171
MotionScan 37–38
Mount Shasta 149
MTV 106
Muir, John 3, 14
Mulholland Drive 104
Mulvey, Laura 27–28, 30–31, 36; *see also* the male gaze
"Murder Castle" *see* Holmes, H.H.
Murder House see American Horror Story
"Murder House" (episode, *American Horror Story*) 92

Murnau, F.W. 97; *Nosferatu* 96
music 11–12, 54, 64–66, 68, 70–71, 72*n*2, 72*n*5, 72*n*8, 72*n*9, 72*n*14, 73–74, 81, 105, 119–120, 123, 141, 145, 153–154, 159, 161 168–169, 174–177, 179–182, 189, 191, 194; punk rock 65, 72*n*8, 72*n*9, 72*n*13, 176, 189; rock 7, 142; video 13, 105, 158, 174–178, 180–183, 194
myth 2, 7, 12–13, 16–18, 23, 39, 41, 49, 64, 96, 98, 113, 128, 136–138, 141, 144, 147–150, 151*n*9, 152, 154, 160–161, 170, 184–186; *see also* beauty myth

Nadja see Almereyda, Michael
Native Americans 78, 145, 148, 185, 188
nature 14, 18, 28, 80–84, 86, 134–135, 148, 180, 188; *see also* environment
Neo-Marxism 11, 50, 52–53, 56–57
neo-noir 12, 127, 129, 132, 138; *see also* noir
The Neon Demon 101
New Age 142, 149
New Jerusalem 148; *see also Inherent Vice*; Lemuria; myth
New Orleans 82, 88
New York 27, 72*n*13, 139
New York Times 24, 132, 138, 152, 172–173
Newton-John, Olivia 105
"Night Finds You" 133, 138; *see also True Detective* (TV series)
9/11 attacks 71, 139, 187
1984 see Orwell, George
Nip/Tuck 88
Nixon, Richard 40
noir 5, 43, 131–132, 140, 151, 162, 187, 193; film noir 37, 128–130, 132, 138; *see also* hard-boiled fiction; neo-noir
nomadic subject 1, 5–6, 9–14, 184–185, 190
Norrington, Stephen 117
Norse (expedition) *see* myth; Vinland
Nosferatu see Murnau, F.W.
nostalgia 45, 48, 54–55, 143, 153, 153, 172
"Nuthin' but a G' Thang" *see* Dr. Dre; Snoop Doggy Dogg

occultism 66–67, 69, 110, 148
the Okies 185
The Omega Man see Sagal, Boris
Once Bitten see Storm, Howard
Oregon 175, 185
Orwell, George 165
The Osbournes 102
Oteri, Cheri 53
the Other 2, 17, 28, 34, 54–57, 60*n*8, 85–86, 169, 184
"Other Lives" 135–136, 138; *see also True Detective* (TV series)
"Otherside" *see* Red Hot Chili Peppers
Otherworld see Galenorn, Yasmin

202 Index

Our Worst Fears: The AIDS Epidemic see KPIX
"Out in L.A." *see* Red Hot Chili Peppers

Pabst Blue Ribbon 153
Pacific Ocean 7, 14, 21, 39, 75, 148–149, 152, 182
Pacific Palisades 19
Palahniuk, Chuck 104
Palimpsest 10, 16, 120
Palos Verdes Estates *see Inherent Vice*; Los Angeles
paparazzi 103
Paradise Lost see Milton, John
paradox 3, 6, 11, 13, 17–18, 22, 31, 39, 45–46, 49n6, 60n3, 65, 112, 147, 175, 186, 190–191
"Parallel Universe" *see* Red Hot Chili Peppers
Paris 124n1; 1968 uprisings 142
parody 112, 129; *see also* pastiche; satire
pastiche 129, 153; *see also* parody; satire
patriarchy 108
Patriot Act 50
Peccinotti, Harri 62
The People vs. O.J. Simpson: American Crime Story 88; *see also* Simpson, O.J.
Pepsi 153
performativity 28, 156, 159
Pershing Square 44
Persian (language) 119
Petty, Tom *see* Tom Petty and the Heartbreakers
Philadelphia 89
Phoenix, Joaquin 150n3, 151
Photography 118, 161
"Physical" *see* Newton-John, Olivia
"Piggy Piggy" (episode, *American Horror Story*) 98
Pinkerton 170
Pirandello, Luigi 155, 161
Pirelli 62, 71n1, 74
Pizzolatto, Nic (Nicholas Austin) 129, 138; *see also True Detective* (TV series)
The Player 104
Poe, Edgar Allan 130
Poehler, Amy 53
Poland 13, 187–191, 193–194; Cracow 189; Mielno 189; Polish culture 187–188; Upper Silesia 189
Polanski, Roman 20
police 11, 38–39, 42–44, 48, 75, 77, 83, 125, 133, 162–165, 169, 172; *see also* cop shows
politics 2, 4, 8–10, 12–13, 16, 18, 20, 22, 25, 29, 35, 51, 54, 63, 66, 71, 73, 108, 125, 131–132, 141–142, 161–162, 168–173, 180, 185, 187
popular culture 5–9, 13–16, 21–23, 76, 78–79, 81, 83, 85–86, 96–97, 103, 112, 114, 138, 140, 162–166, 168–170, 172, 175, 179, 181–182, 189, 194
pornography 50–51, 53, 60, 154, 167, 175, 179

Postcards from the Future 104
posthumanism 9
postmodernism/postmodernity 4, 6, 67, 125
Prairie (character) 140, 147–148, 165–171; *see also Vineland*
Presley, Elvis 103, 153
producer 45, 53, 103, 110–111, 159
The Promised Land 148, 185; *see also Inherent Vice*; Lemuria; myth
Proposition 8 185
prostitution 120, 122, 136, 167
punk rock *see* music
purgatory 11, 88–91, 93–94, 97, 99–100; *see also* Roman Christians
"Purple Stain" *see* Red Hot Chili Peppers
Pynchon, Thomas 6, 12, 139–141, 143–149, 150n1, 150n2, 150n4, 150n5, 151n6, 151n8, 151n9, 151n10, 151–152, 162, 165–166, 168–169, 172, 172n1, 173; *The Crying of Lot 49* 139–140, 148, 150n1, 152, 162, 172; *Inherent Vice* 12, 139–143, 148, 150–152, 162, 172; *Vineland* 13, 150n1, 139–140, 148, 150, 150n4, 151, 151n8, 152, 162, 169–170, 172–173

quality TV 127, 138; *see also* television

radio 40, 47n4, 78, 102, 180, 182
Ramirez, Richard 98–99
Ramona see Hunt Jackson, Helen
Reagan, Ronald 63, 73, 113, 150, 168, 172n1, 173
the real 11–12, 38, 42, 50, 58, 100, 115, 117, 119, 121, 124
realism 38, 45, 131, 138, 141
reality television 102, 194; *see also* television
Red Hot Chili Peppers 174–178, 181, 182, 182n1, 182n2; "The Adventures of Rain Dance Maggie" 177; "Around the World" 175; "By the Way" 177; "Californication" 13, 174–176, 178–179, 181–182, 182n1, 182n4; "Charlie" 177; "Dani California" 176, 180, 182n2; "Deep Kick" 174; "Desecration Smile" 177; "Emit Remmus" 175; "Happiness Loves Company" 174; "Otherside" 177; "Out in L.A." 174; "Parallel Universe" 175; "Purple Stain" 175; "Road Trippin" 177; "Suck My Kiss" 177; "Tell Me Baby" 177; "Under the Bridge" 177, 182n3
Reeves, Matt 125n5
Reisz, Kristopher 82
Revenant see Modern Vampires
revolution 54, 56, 66, 77, 100, 139–140, 151n6, 151, 163, 168–169, 171–172
rhizome 2, 13, 190
Rice, Anne 78
Rise Blood Hunter see Gutierrez, Sebastian
River see Cameron, Skyla Dawn
"Road Trippin" *see* Red Hot Chili Peppers
roads 48, 60n2, 104, 134–135, 140, 153, 170, 177, 193; *see also* car culture

Index

rock *see* music
Rodriguez, Richard 7, 14
Rodriguez Cabrillo, Juan 90
Rolling Hills 145; *see also Inherent Vice*; Los Angeles
Roman Christians 154
Romance 5–6, 14, 24, 81, 128, 130, 138, 157–158, 176
Romanticism 16, 23, 129–130, 132, 137–138, 158–160, 169, 172
Romero, George 118
Rose, W. Axl *see* Guns N' Roses
Rousseau, Jean-Jacques 154, 161
Rowling, J.K. 76
Rules for Werewolves see Lynn, Kirk
Run's House 102

"Sachem" *see* Sienkiewicz, Henryk
Sacramento 15, 17–19, 65
The Saga of Erik the Red 148, 152; *see also* Ericson, Leif
Sagal, Boris 115
San Francisco 22, 178
San Pedro 85
Santa Ana (winds) 21
Santa Monica 54, 150, 151n10
satire 89, 105, 112, 172; Hollywood 104, 107, 109–112
Schreck, Nikolas 158
Schumacher, Joel 117
science-fiction 36, 64, 127, 179, 193–194
Scotch, Cher 80, 82
Scott, Tony 121, 125n7
Scream Blacula Scream see Kelljan, Bob
Scream Queens 88
Screen Actors Guild 168
"The Second Coming" *see* Yeats, William Butler
segregation 147, 150, 150n5
the self 9, 16, 21, 23, 28, 31, 51, 79–81, 87, 103, 113, 124, 154–155, 169, 182; veridical 103, 112
self-destruction 12, 71, 104–105, 112, 159–160, 163; *see also* self-harm; self-mutilation
self-harm 108
self-mutilation 106
Seven see Fincher, David; Spacey Kevin
The Seven Deadly Sins see Brecht, Bertold, and Weill, Kurt
sexuality 26–28, 35, 129, 135, 159, 193
Shakur, Tupac *see* 2Pac
Shanghai 124n1
Sharp Teeth see Barlow, Toby
Shea, Robert, and Wilson, Anton 60
Shoot! see Pirandello, Luigi
sickness 113; *see also* disease; health
Sienkiewicz, Henryk 189, 191; *Letters from the Journeys in America* 187–188; "Sachem" 188, 191
Sierra Nevada 178, 185–186
signified 119; *see also* signifier

signifier 116–117, 122; signified 119
Simpson, O.J. 21, 88; *see also The People vs. O.J. Simpson*
simulacrum 4, 48, 55, 115–118, 120–125
sitcom 13, 162–167, 172; *see also* television
the Sixties 16, 19–20, 22–24, 54, 62–64, 67, 69, 73–74, 139–141, 143, 149, 150n4, 159, 168–171, 176; Summer of Love 63–64, 66–67, 176
Slaughterhouse-Five see Vonnegut, Kurt
Snoop Doggy Dogg 176
Snyder, Gary 3, 14
social justice 12, 139, 141–142, 144, 150n5, 152, 185
social media 64, 72n2, 102
Soja, Edward 3, 12, 14, 116–117, 125n4, 120, 124, 126, 142–144, 147, 150n5, 152
Solanas, Valerie 156
Southland 140–141, 145; *see also* California, southern
Southland Tales 11, 50, 52–54, 56, 59–60, 60n2; *see also* Kelly, Richard
Spacey, Kevin 96
spaghetti western 116, 118, 121–122, 124–125
Spain 6, 90, 116, 122, 146
Spenser, Edmund 89
"Spooky Little Girl" (episode, *American Horror Story*) 98
Stadium Arcadium 176, 182, 182n2; *see also* Red Hot Chili Peppers
Star Trek: The Original Series 179
Star Wars 179, 182
stardom 12, 15, 24, 28–29, 51, 66, 73n14, 75, 92, 96–97, 101–104, 106–107, 109, 111–113, 153–161, 164–165, 174, 177–178, 182; *see also* celebrity
Starry Eyes 12, 101, 104, 106, 108, 111–114; Dezeran, Louis 110; Essoe, Alex 107; Healy, Pat 109
Staszewski, Kazik 189; KNŻ (Kazik Na Żywo) 191
Station to Station 179; *see also* Bowie, David
Statue of Liberty 166
Stegner, Wallace 3–4, 10, 14
Steinbeck, John 17
Stiefvater, Maggie 78
Storm, Howard 117
storytelling 127–128, 138
suburbs 10, 76–77, 82, 88, 92, 115, 117, 119, 121, 124, 142, 146, 148
"Suck My Kiss" *see* Red Hot Chili Peppers
suicide 45, 71, 92, 135–136, 159, 165
Summer of Love *see* the Sixties
Sunset Boulevard 104
the supernatural 2, 58, 84, 99, 122, 130, 156
"Swan Song" *see* Del Rey, Lana
Sweden 178

tabloids 21, 102
teenager 82, 85, 166, 167, 169; *see also* girl

Index

Tehran 125n6, 126; *see also* Iran
television 72n9, 99, 102, 106, 119, 125, 127, 138, 146, 161–165, 167, 169–173, 176, 179–180, 182, 193, 194; *see also* cop shows; quality TV; reality TV; sitcoms
"Tell Me Baby" *see* Red Hot Chili Peppers
telos 156
Tennessee 89
The Terrestrial Paradise 148; *see also Inherent Vice*; Lemuria; myth
terror 34, 95, 99, 131, 130, 133–134, 187; *see also* the Gothic
Tertullian (Tertullianus, Quintus Septimus Florens) 154
theater 69, 73, 154–155, 157, 161, 193; English 154
The Thing see Carpenter, John
The Thirst see Kasten, Jeremy
Thompson, Jim 129
The Three Stooges 166
Tinseltown 37, 102; *see also* Hollywood
Tokyo 124n1
Tom Petty and the Heartbreakers 176
trade unions 163, 168, 170
tragedy 1, 18, 45, 154, 160–161, 186; in theater 157
Tralfamadorians *see* Vonnegut, Kurt
transmediality 7, 194
Transylvania 118; *see also* Dracula
trauma 34, 59, 71, 101, 112, 114, 125, 136, 151n9, 186, 193
Treasure Island 148; *see also Inherent Vice*; Lemuria; myth
trichotillomania 108
Troutman, Roger 72n6, 176; *see also* "California Love"
True Detective (magazine) 129
True Detective (TV series) 6, 127–134, 136–138, 137n1; Pizzolatto, Nic (Nicholas Austin) 129, 138; Vernon 131–132, 138
Twilight series *see* Meyer, Stephenie
The Twilight Zone 127
2+1 (band) 189
2Pac 72n6; "California Love" 65–66, 176

UK 106
the uncanny 5, 86, 92, 126, 156, 187
"Under the Bridge" *see* Red Hot Chili Peppers
Universal City, California 118
Universal Studios 118, 125; *see also* Browning, Tod; *Dracula*
Unleashed see Reisz, Kristopher
Upper Silesia *see* Poland
urban space 11, 37, 42, 121, 142–143, 150; renewal 145–146; *see also* city
urbanization 79–80, 116, 120, 124, 137
ustopia *see* utopia
utopia 1–2, 12, 14, 19, 24, 29–30, 36–37, 39, 45–47, 62–3, 65, 89, 124, 140–142, 146–148, 151n9, 150, 185, 188–189; ustopia 25; *see also* dystopia

Vamp see Wenk, Richard
vampire 12, 82, 93–94, 96–100, 115, 117–126, 125n5, 125n7, 125n9, 193
Vanity Fair 21, 132, 138
Vaughn, Carrie 78, 82
Vaye Watkins, Claire 10–11, 25, 36
Venice Beach *see* Los Angeles
Vernon, California *see True Detective* (TV series)
veteran 44, 51, 71, 144, 164
video games 6, 11, 37–39, 41–42, 45–46, 48–49, 164, 178–181, 193–194
Vietnam 14, 23–24; War 67, 144, 171
Vineland see Pynchon, Thomas
Vinland/Vineland 140, 151n8, 147–149, 151n9, 164, 171, 173; *see also* myth; *Vineland*
violence 45, 54, 57, 59, 64, 75, 77–81, 84, 100, 125, 130–132, 137, 155, 157, 160, 169–170, 172, 176, 191
virtuality 8, 11, 38–42, 46, 47n4, 63–64, 67, 71n2, 73–74, 129, 139
Visconti, Tony 103, 114; *see also* Bowie, David
Vixen 189, 191
void *see* lack
Vollmann, William T. 6, 10, 16–17, 22–24, 193
Vonnegut, Kurt 171
voyeurism 155–156, 158

Wagner the Werewolf 78
Wale Grubo 189, 191
Walk of Fame 178; *see also* Hollywood
War on Drugs 165, 168
Warhol, Andy 55, 153, 156
Warner Bros. Entertainment, Inc. 110, 151, 182
Washington 15, 168
wasteland 26, 28–29, 31, 128–129, 131–135, 137
water politics 4, 19, 29, 145
Watts riots *see* Los Angeles
Weill, Kurt *see* Brecht, Bertold
"Welcome to the Jungle" *see* Guns N' Roses
Wenk, Richard 115
The Werewolf's Kiss 80, 82; *see also* Scotch, Cheri
werewolves 11, 75–87, 193–194
Western 45, 116, 122, 137
"The Western Book of the Dead" 135, 138; *see also True Detective* (TV series)
Whedon, Joss 117
Wheeler, Zoyd (character) 140, 147; *see also Vineland*
Whitman, Walt 3, 14, 22
Widmyer, David *see* Kölsch, Kevin
The Wild West 65, 122, 138, 182; *see also* American West

wilderness 2, 17, 36, 76–77, 80–83, 86, 130, 139; *see also* desert; landscape
Wilson, Anton *see* Shea, Robert
Wilson, Dennis 159, 161; *see also* The Beach Boys; Manson, Charles
Wilson, Owen 150*n*3, 151
Wolf 82–83
Wolf, Naomi 30, 111; beauty myth 28, 36, 108, 114
The Wolf-Man 76, 79–80
Wolfen 82
Wolves of Mercy Falls 78; *see also* Stiefvater, Maggie
The Wolves of Midwinter 78; *see also* Rice, Anne

womanhood 25–31, 34–35
Woodstock 74, 163
World War II 37–42, 44, 48, 164, 170
Wuornos, Aileen 99

Yeats, William Butler 21, 24
Yosemite 17; National Park 178, 180
You Must Remember This 158, 161
Yurok tribe *see* Native Americans
Yuzna, Brian 105

Zanuck, Darryl F. 110; *see also* Warner Bros. Entertainment, Inc.
Žižek, Slavoj 52, 54, 57, 59–61
the Zodiac Killer 99

www.ingramcontent.com/pod-product-compliance
Lightning Source LLC
Chambersburg PA
CBHW032057300426
44116CB00007B/774